C000242967

Praise for *The Gamifica and Instruction I*

"A wonderfully useful hands-on, step-by-step guide to the creation of games, gamification and simulation experiences. This book is a must read and conveys clear and precise instructions for designing and developing learning that will creatively engage members of the current and future workforce. If you are in the field of learning and development and want to create meaningful instruction, this book is for you!"

—**Jeanne Meister**, founding partner,
Future Workplace and coauthor of *The 2020 Workplace*

"It's refreshing when an author turns a 'what' book into a 'how' book. For anyone who is trying to work their way through creating meaningful and effective learning games, this book is a godsend. The questions help you focus, the examples help you visualize, and the worksheets help you succeed."

—**Dawn Adams Miller**, Learning & Development
Solutions Group, Cisco

"Bridging the digital media landscape between the worlds of learning and games, gamification and simulations, this is the perfect guide book both for instructional designers and game developers. Whether you're looking for ways to bring gaming elements to training, or if you're seeking solid instructional principles for games, this book by Kapp, Blair, and Mesch is an essential companion in your journey."

—**Rick Raymer**, game designer

"A long overdue book that gives corporate trainers and managers lots of facts and inspirations for how games and gamification can not only make training more engaging, but the content so much more sticky than traditional approaches."

—**Mario Herger**, CEO of Enterprise-Gamification.com

FREE Premium Content

▼

This book includes premium content that can be accessed from our Web site when you register at **www.wiley.com/go/kappfieldbook** using the password ***professional***.

The Gamification of Learning and Instruction Fieldbook

Ideas into Practice

Karl M. Kapp
Lucas Blair
Rich Mesch

WILEY

Cover design by Jeff Puda

Cover images: (creatures) © beaubelle/Veer; (game designer) © R1/Veer

Published by Wiley
One Montgomery Street, Suite 1200, San Francisco, CA 94104-4594
www.wiley.com

For additional copies/bulk purchases of this book in the U.S. please contact 800–274–4434.

Wiley books and products are available through most bookstores. To contact Wiley directly call our
Customer Care Department within the U.S. at 800-274-4434, outside the U.S. at 317-572-3985, fax
317-572-4002, or visit www.wiley.com

Wiley publishes in a variety of print and electronic formats and by print-on-demand. Some material
included with standard print versions of this book may not be included in e-books or in print-on-
demand. If this book refers to media such as a CD or DVD that is not included in the version you
purchased, you may download this material at http://booksupport.wiley.com. For more information
about Wiley products, visit www.wiley.com.

Library of Congress Cataloging-in-Publication Data

CIP data is available on file at the Library of Congress.

9781118674437 (pbk),
9781118677247 (ebk),
9781118677803 (ebk)

Printed in the United States of America

PB Printing   10   9   8   7   6   5   4   3   2   1

Karl Kapp
To my wife Nancy and my two wonderful sons—Nathan and Nick.

Lucas Blair
To my wife Danielle, for tolerating my obsession with making and playing games, and to my parents Donald and Cheryl, for always letting me play "just five more minutes."

Rich Mesch
To my friend Eve, for her unwavering support and constant encouragement to think big.

Contents

SECTION I: Getting Started

SECTION V: Case Studies

Website Contents

The following materials are available for download from
www.wiley.com/go/kappfieldbook
password: professional

Chapter Two

Case Study: Deloitte Leadership Academy

Getting Started Worksheet

Chapter Three

Games and Blooms Taxonomy

Games and Type of Knowledge

Games and the Affective Domain

Games and Psychomotor Skills

Chapter Four

Critical Questions

Chapter Six

Story Design Worksheet

Chapter Eight

Game Building Model

Sample Game Design Template

Chapter Ten

Best Practices

Pitfalls to Avoid

Pro-Social Gaming

Chapter Eleven

PepBoys Case Study

Figures, Tables, and Exhibits

Figures

Tables

Exhibits

Foreword

SERIOUS GAMES HAVE NEVER enjoyed the limelight that simulations seem to garner. The immediate legitimacy and the perceived value of simulations have allowed training and learning organizations to leverage them as powerful tools that have made a difference. But not their red headed step-cousin. Not games. Games were for home. For nights and weekends and the occasional elicit break time diversion. Today I announce that this dark era has finally reached the beginning of the end. Games are no longer a dirty word at the office. We can shout the word "GAME" from the rooftop and we won't be ostracized by our colleagues. (We might be stared at, we might be deemed a little nuts, but we won't be ostracized.) People are starting to get it. We are starting to get it. And it's about time.

When people ask me what I do, I've always struggled to find the answer. I don't fancy myself a game designer, although I have designed games. I don't consider myself an instructional designer, although that is a role I certainly play on occasion. I don't know how to code, draw, or animate. I am an unlikely success in the games industry.

Since you've asked, what I do is probably not all that different from what you do. I try to find ways to make learning better through the use of games. Now, when I say better, I don't mean faster, or cheaper, or funner (yes, I realize that's not really a word, which makes using it more fun). I mean making the process of learning better—by including games. You and I probably agree that this is a worthwhile investment of our time, but getting started can present unique challenges that even a lifetime of experiences has never really prepared us for.

You are lucky. When I started working in the serious games industry fifteen or so years ago, there wasn't a lot of information about how to tackle a games project for learning. The entertainment industry can offer us lots of useful information, but they have a very different measure of success. If their game isn't good, it won't sell. They will go out of business. I've never seen multiple games being developed with the intention of seeing which was more popular in a learning program. Our games are often one-offs. Therefore, this book was written for the rest of us, the rogue learning game believers who just want to make learning better.

I have had the honor of spending the last six years of my career as the "Games Czar" to the Defense Acquisition University, a DoD corporate university that understood early on that the future of the organization would include games and simulations. In my tenure here, I have delivered more than forty games for use in online courses, classrooms, continuous learning, and yes, even casual play. Many lessons have been learned, some the hard way. One resounding truth has always remained: if we don't make our learning memorable, then . . . well . . . people won't remember what we were trying to teach them.

Karl Kapp and I are very similar in that we share a passion for games in learning, and we are both collectors. We collect stories about how people use games. In this book, Karl and his co-authors Rich and Lucas have curated the best of those stories and the best of the best practices to provide you with a foundation for success in your game, gamification, and simulation learning endeavors. What you do with this book is largely dependent on your current need and your ability to be inspired by the perspectives presented. Karl,

Lucas, and Rich have created a book that will help you get smarter about how, when, and why you could use games; now it's up to you to make it happen.

This book was written to help anyone interested in learning games, gamification, or simulations in a variety of ways. First, it provides some nice definitions that will help you both decide what you are hoping to do and then effectively communicate your ideas. There are lots of misconceptions about games, simulations, and gamification that can derail your project pretty early if you aren't able to distinguish what you want. Second, I think that the authors have done a great job at laying out a process for an organizational approach to game, gamification, and simulation development. They give you the information needed to make decisions informed by their experiences and the research that has been reviewed. Maybe you just want to get smart enough on games and game development to hire the right person to do this for you. Maybe you want to try some things out within your own teams. Maybe you need to create a simulation for a new piece of equipment. This book will help you decide how to proceed with the highest probability of success.

In my time as Games Czar, I have stood strongly opposed to the use of learning games for gratuitous entertainment and fun. If I wanted my students to have fun, I would have piñatas installed in every classroom and/or online course. I want them to learn. If they have fun doing it, then great, we try to make our games and simulations enjoyable, but fun is never at the forefront of our design process. What we strive for is relevance. Students have to know why the information they are being presented with is important to them. They have to be motivated to learn it because the content is important to them, even if they don't know why yet. Students have to understand how and when and where they may apply this information, and how to transfer it into the wide variety of situations in which they might need it. The content must be important to your students, otherwise you wouldn't be teaching it, right?

One of the most frequent questions I am asked is "What's your favorite game?" I love being asked this question, because my answer changes often. And, let's be honest, there is a direct difference between what I like to play and what I'm good at. I am always going to love first-person shooter games. I am not very good at them, but I love them. After that, the games I like are highly dependent on the medium. Without specifically endorsing any one, the point is: I play. I play everything. I learn from every game I interact with, and I find new ways to represent game play dynamics in the learning games I create. It is essential that you play, too. Sometimes I find myself in game stores just reading instructions on game boxes to see whether there is anything different in the play dynamic that I can use in learning. I wouldn't talk about texting if I didn't own a phone. You can't talk about games if you never play them.

Interestingly enough, I have never become addicted to playing a learning game. I've never stayed up all night trying to beat one. I've never crammed the fridge with Hot Pockets and Mountain Dew in anticipation of the release of one. The reality is that creating great games, for any purpose, is hard. Serious games often don't get a lot of attention in the mainstream, and a fair share of projects fail because their designs don't center on their learning objectives or they don't have the right people to make the project successful.

So how do great game designers do it? They do it by understanding a lot about how people learn, and how people play. Sid Meier once told me that his team really didn't do anything to make Civilization a learning game, but his games are used in classrooms around the world. Will Wright, who designed SimCity, created a simulation of . . . life, and people loved it. His philosophy? Humans can turn even mundane tasks into play. They both keynoted Defense Acquisition University (DAU)–sponsored e-learning conferences because they both understand and appreciate the power of games within learning. The most successful game designers are a lot like us, but they are also artists. They just use a different medium for their art. I think designers are born, not necessarily created. But it's okay. Because there are people out there who can and do make amazing games. We just need to know enough to be dangerous.

Once you have read this book, I beg you to keep going. Our industry is far too small and with too few people to have great conversations with. Keep reading. Look at the research yourself, make some games and play everything you can get your hands on!

Dr. Alicia Sanchez
Games Czar, Defense Acquisition University
Ft. Belvoir, Virginia

About the Authors

Karl M. Kapp, Ed.D., CFPIM, CIRM, is a scholar, writer, and expert on the convergence of learning, technology, and business operations. Karl is a professor of instructional technology at Bloomsburg University in Bloomsburg, Pennsylvania, and serves as the assistant director of Bloomsburg's Institute for Interactive Technologies. Karl teaches graduate level courses, including "Instructional Game Design," teaching students to leverage technology and interactive design to promote learning. He is a co-principle investigator on two National Science Foundation (NSF) grants. One is titled "Simulation and Modeling in Technology Education (SMTE)." The goal of the grant is to develop a 3D interactive video game teaching middle school students math, science, and engineering concepts. Karl's team is responsible for combining game play and pedagogy. The other project is titled "Virtual Online Tensile Strength Testing Simulation," and Karl's team is heading up the design and development of the simulation.

He also consultants with many organizations, including Pearson, where Karl's role was to help guide the addition of game elements to high-stakes test preparation in a project called Zeos Academy. Since that time, the product has been highly successful creating engaged and motivated learners as they prepare for high-stakes testing. Karl has consulted with organizations such as Black & Decker, Genentech, L'Oreal, Kellogg's, and most major pharmaceutical companies. He is a participant in the National Security Agency Advisory Board (NSAAB) Emerging Technologies Panel, sits on several National Science Foundation visiting committees, and is a board member of several startup companies.

Karl has written five books, including *Learning in 3D* and *Gadgets, Games, and Gizmos for Learning*. His latest book is called *The Gamification of Learning and Instruction*. In the book, Karl explores the research and theoretical foundations behind effective game-based learning. He examines everything from variable reward schedules to the use of avatars to the gamification of pro-social behaviors. He is currently working on his sixth book, a field book to accompany *The Gamification of Learning and Instruction*.

Karl has been interviewed for and published articles in *Training*, ASTD's *T&D, Software Strategies, Knowledge Management, Distance Learning*, and *PharmaVoice, Training Quarterly, Forbes Online, Mashable*, and by general television and radio programs concerning his work with learning, technology, and game-based design. He appeared in the March 2013, Long View feature of *Training* magazine. Karl is quoted in several volumes of Jeannie Novak's "Game Development Essentials" series. He blogs at the popular "Kapp Notes" website and is a frequent international keynote speaker, workshop leader, moderator, and panelist at national and international conferences as well as events for private corporations and universities.

Karl is committed to helping organizations develop a strategic, enterprise-wide approach to organizational learning using interactive techniques from the field of game-design. He believes that effective education and training are the keys to increased productivity and profitability. He can be reached at www.karlkapp.com.

Lucas Blair, Ph.D., is the founder of Little Bird Games, a serious game development company, which specializes in educational and therapeutic games. He has also taught instructional game development at Bloomsburg University and developing games and simulations at Harrisburg University of Science and Technology. He received his Ph.D. in modeling and simulation from the University of Central Florida in 2011 after completing his doctoral research on the use of video game achievements to enhance player performance, self-efficacy, and motivation. This research enabled Lucas to take an active role in the digital badges for education movement, including being a finalist in the Badges for Lifelong Learning competition with a badge creation platform called Badge Forge. While at UCF Lucas was a game designer at RETRO Lab, a group that researches and develops serious games. During his time at RETRO the lab created award-winning courseware and serious games for over a dozen clients, as well as several published research papers. Awards for games created at RETRO during Lucas's time included the Bronze Medal winner 2011 International Serious Play Awards: Devil's Advocate, Finalist 2011 Serious Games Showcase and Challenge: Devil's Advocate, Gold Medal 2011 winner Serious Games Showcase and Challenge: Garden Defense, and Finalist 2010 Serious Games Showcase and Challenge: (CPI) Trainer. Prior to becoming a game designer Lucas was an instructional systems designer for defense training systems and simulators. Lucas was a graduate of Bloomsburg University's Instructional Technology Master's program in 2006.

Rich Mesch is the senior director of customer engagement at Performance Development Group of Malvern, Pennsylvania. He has been working in the field of experiential and contextualized learning for more than twenty-five years. He has worked with dozens of top global organizations to help them achieve their business goals through behavior change and performance improvement.

He joined the learning and performance space in 1985, temporarily abandoning his first love, playwriting. He found that his skill for storytelling translated well into learning applications, and he helped develop the structures and technologies used in scenario-based learning. His early work was primarily in the field of leadership learning, where storytelling resonated well. Given that leadership content was often easy to understand but difficult to implement, Rich found that simulation was particularly useful in developing effective leaders.

In addition to simulation, Rich is fascinated by emerging learning technologies, having done extensive work with mobile learning and immersive learning environments.

Rich's learning designs have won many industry awards, including three Brandon Hall Excellence Awards, the New Media Invision Award for Simulation, the New York Festival's Silver Medal, and the HR Executive Top 10.

Rich presents frequently at conferences and events, including the American Society for Training and Development (ASTD), Society for Human Resource Management (SHRM), eLearning Guild Learning Solutions, Learning 3.0, Society for Applied Learning Technology, and Linkages Leadership Conference.

He has published multiple articles in major journals, including *Training*, *Focus*, and *Technology for Learning* newsletter. His feature, Spinning Yarns: Seven Tips for Using Stories to Enhance Simulations and Learning explored the best ways to capture learner attention using storytelling techniques. He is the author of the recent white paper The Mobile Learning rEvolution: How the use of mobile devices is slowly changing the way we learn.

Rich draws a great deal of inspiration for his designs from his work as a playwright. His plays "Temporary Arrangements" and "Figment" have both been produced professionally. He was recognized as outstanding playwright by the Pittsburgh New Works Festival, and "Temporary Arrangements" was awarded outstanding production. He is also an avid musician and musical instrument collector, and plays guitar in the band Blues Society.

Rich is the editor and a frequent contributor to the learning industry blog Performance, Punctuated (http://blog.performdev.com), which explores experiential learning, performance support, and new learning technologies.

About the Contributors

Bryan Austin, throughout his twenty-five-year career with leading organizations like SkillSoft and Kaplan, has dedicated himself to helping organizations develop high performing employees through innovative learning solutions. His initial exposure to corporate learning and development came when his first employer, a systems software company, asked him to develop a technical training program for new systems engineers. He and his team rented a small college campus in northern California, set up a mainframe computer lab, and taught classroom sessions during the day and computer labs all night. Seeing the positive impact of the program first-hand ignited Bryan's passion for the power of learning. From there, Bryan went on to work for, and lead, companies that provide cutting-edge, technology-delivered learning solutions to medium, large, and global companies. For Bryan, it has been fascinating to be a part of the evolution of corporate learning and development. He has seen multi-media training evolve from audio/videotape/

workbook packages, to PC and LAN-delivered training, to the sophisticated e-learning solutions of today.

Robert Bell is Enspire Studios' minister of games, the creative lead in the company's custom game and simulation group. He has worked at Enspire since 2008 and has a decade's worth of experience in education and instructional design. Robert is a graduate of the University of Texas at Austin and Brooklyn College, where he received an M.S. in education. In his time at Enspire, he has worked on serious game and simulation projects for a variety of organizations, including ConAgra Foods, International Disaster Assistance and Relief Training (IDART), Doorways to Dreams (D2D), and the Federal Reserve Bank of New York. Robert has presented sessions on the subject of serious games and simulations at ASTD: TechKnowledge, *Training* magazine's Conference and Expo, and Serious Play Conference, among others.

Kristin Bittner is a designer through and through. She is inspired by great design, whether it is a wallet, a website, or a wine label, and believes great design transforms ordinary everyday objects into beautiful works of art. Kristin works as an instructional designer for Penn State Harrisburg and Penn State World Campus. She specialized in online course design and supports programs in criminal justice and Homeland Security. Kristin has a master's degree in science in instructional technology from Bloomsburg University. Prior to joining Penn State, she was an instructional designer for Lockheed Martin and designed aircrew training for the U.S. Air Force. She has more than twelve years of military service and is currently serving as a Force Support Officer in the Pennsylvania Air National Guard.

Sharon Boller is president of Bottom-Line Performance, Inc. (BLP), a learning solutions firm she founded in 1995. Sharon has grown BLP from a single-woman sole proprietorship that employed one to a $2M company employing twenty team members. Sharon is also the creator of the Knowledge Guru™ brand affiliated with BLP that focuses on game-based learning. She is the lead game designer for its inaugural product, known as Guru Classic, and she is leading the development of a second, more robust offering known as Guru Game Builder that will allow users to create multi-level learning games. Sharon frequently speaks on game-based learning and learning design topics at the local and international level. Organizations where Sharon has been featured include the International Society for Performance Improvement (ISPI), Society for Applied Learning Technologies (SALT), the Central Indiana, Cincinnati, and Western Ohio chapters of the American Society for Training and Development (ASTD), as well at various eLearning Guild conferences and *Training* magazine conferences. BLP and/or Sharon have won several awards for their efforts. Client awards include quality awards from both Eli Lilly and Roche Diagnostics. Industry awards have been received from eLearning Guild and the Central Indiana Chapter of ASTD. In 2005, ASTD Press published Sharon's book, *Teamwork Training*, which reflects her love of experiential approaches to developing teamwork skills as well as her own experience growing and developing the virtual team that is.

Helmut Doll, Ph.D., is a professor in Bloomsburg University's Department of Instructional Technology. He teaches the authoring and technical courses in the department's graduate program in instructional technology. For the last fifteen years he has followed the technical currents in the field so that the graduating students know the software and have the technical skills that are most relevant at the moment and for the near future. He has been active in mobile development for several years and teaches instructional game development courses for the graduate students in the program. As a big supporter of these technologies, he has given numerous talks at conferences on mobile technologies and on game development and frequently works on grants and projects with academic and corporate partners.

Mohit Garg, MBA, has a diverse work experience spanning across fourteen years and four continents. Prior to co-founding MindTickle, he was a director in PwC's management consulting practice at New York and has been a senior member of product teams. He was awarded "Entrepreneur of the Year" by Startup Leadership Program (SLP) in 2012. Mohit holds an MBA degree from ISB and an MSEE from Stanford University. At MindTickle, Mohit has been focused on sales and marketing efforts of MindTickle's employee learning and engagement SaaS products. Mohit leads the BD, sales, distribution, and marketing efforts for MindTickle along with business development, partner strategy, and sales. Mohit also co-led the effort of fundraising and successfully raised funding for MindTickle from top-tier VCs and angels. Mohit is passionate about the education sector and transforming the way humans engage and learn from digital content. He enjoys running and travel, and regularly blogs on www.mindtickle.com.

Robert Gadd is president and co-founder of OnPoint Digital and is responsible for OnPoint's vision and strategy. OnPoint's online and mobile-enabled offerings support more than one million workers and include innovative methods for content authoring, conversion, and delivery extended with social interactions, gamification, and enterprise-grade security for workers on virtually any device. Prior to OnPoint, Robert spent ten years as CTO of Datatec Systems and president of eDeploy.com. He is a frequent speaker on learning solutions, including mobile, informal, and gamification at international conferences. He is also co-host of "This Week in mLearning," a podcast exploring all aspects of mLearning.

Kevin Glover, M.Ed., M.S., is the corporate vice president of clinical education and sales training at B. Braun Medical, the fourteenth largest medical device manufacturer in the world. He is responsible for sales training, sales leadership development, internal clinician education, and all external customer education for the therapeutic markets that B. Braun Medical serves. Kevin received his master's in education in 2004 from Temple University and his master's in science in instructional technology in 2010 from Lehigh University, where he is now an adjunct professor in the College of Education. He currently serves as vice president on the board of directors for The Society of Pharmaceutical and Biotech Trainers and vice president on the board of directors for the Southeastern Pennsylvania Air Force Academy Parents Association. Kevin is a staunch advocate of EFFORT and passionately believes that elite performance in any profession requires deliberate, increasingly difficult, repetitive practice, undertaken over a long period of time, with corrective feedback for the elimination of error.

Anders Gronstedt, Ph.D. (anders@gronstedtgroup.com) is the president of Colorado-based Gronstedt Group, which helps global companies like GE Healthcare, Eli Lilly, United Healthcare, Deloitte, Dell, Avaya, American Eagle Outfitters, Microsoft, Kimberly-Clark, Jamba Juice, and government clients like the City of New York improve performance with innovative learning approaches, including next-generation digital simulations, gaming and immersive 3D virtual worlds; teaching people the skills they need in a context that's immersive and energizing. His articles have appeared in the *Harvard Business Review* and he is the host of the popular weekly virtual world speaking series "Train for Success" (www.facebook.com/TrainForSuccess).

Andrew Hughes founded Designing Digitally, Inc., which specializes in e-learning, training simulations, serious games, and virtual immersive learning. Andrew has extensive experience in education as a professor at both the University of Cincinnati and at the Art Institute of Ohio–Cincinnati. Currently, Andrew is the president of Designing Digitally, Inc., a professor at the University of Cincinnati, and a curriculum evaluator for ACICS, the private college accreditation board. The majority of Andrew's experience has been in the development of enterprise learning solutions for government and for corporate clients. Andrew also was a consultant for the Ohio Board of Regents and the U.S. Department of Education for the Office of Innovation, where he helped to develop groundbreaking learning spaces for the K–12 sector. Having successfully taken on responsibilities in instructional design, project management, sales, and leading his own team, Andrew has propelled Designing Digitally, Inc., to be an award-winning serious game and e-learning company.

Jim Kiggens is the CEO of Course Games, a serious game publisher of games for education and training. A studio business owner since 1988, Jim is a certified Scrum Master, Softimage Trainer, Adobe Trainer, Virtools and Unity game developer who has been specializing in the production and development of serious games since 1996. In parallel with his production career, Jim also has more than twenty years of experience in instructional design, program development, and teaching digital animation and game development at the college and university levels. Jim has a master of science degree in education with an option in online teaching and learning from California State University, East Bay, and a bachelor's degree in technical education from National University.

Kevin Thorn is a self-taught designer and developer with a passion for the art of visual communications and an award-winning e-learning designer. He earned a B.S. degree in information technology management from Christian Brothers University after retiring from the Army, followed by a fifteen-year career in the corporate workforce. He is a frequent speaker at training industry events and created an interactive comic-book style learning piece for the Centers for Disease Control.

How to Read and Use This Fieldbook

Introduction

This is not a book designed to be read once and then put on a bookshelf. This book should be dog eared, underlined, scribbled on, marked up, with doodles in the margins and a broken spine. This is meant to be a book for you to use while designing, developing, and creating interactive learning experiences like simulations, games, and gamification experiences. This book brings together experts from a variety of backgrounds and experiences creating games, gamifying learning experiences, and designing and implementing simulations. The book is designed to provide first-hand accounts of the creation of engaging learning experiences. It is a follow-up to *The Gamification of Learning and Instruction*—it is a fieldbook that can be used for implementing the ideas from *The Gamification of Learning and Instruction*.

The goal is to provide insights into the work these experts have done, the battles they have fought, and the results they have achieved from creating engaging instruction. Use these insights, lessons learned, and creative ideas to craft your own engaging, interactive learning experiences. There is an entire section of case studies so you can gain insights into what others have done and apply some of their lessons learned to your situation.

Key Definition

Before we examine the content of the book and how to use it to create great games, gamification, and simulations, the first order of business is to coin a term we can use to continually discuss games, gamification, and simulation. As shorthand to make it easier to read the words "games, gamification, and simulations," we are going to lump all three of these items together in a term called "interactive learning event" or ILE. The term will be used to discuss games, gamification, and simulation.

Why This Book?

This book is needed because ILEs are becoming commonplace. Learning and development (L&D) professionals need to have the skills and knowledge to intelligently create effective games, gamification, and simulations. The time for wondering whether ILEs are appropriate for learning has passed; the time to implement these solutions is now. These experiences are occurring everywhere and L&D professionals need to use these tools in our toolkits to help our fellow employees, customers, and students learn.

It's not hard to see that games, gamification, and simulations are everywhere. From the game you play at the grocery store to win free food to fast-food games to children playing games in school to corporate and military leadership games. Games, gamification, and simulations abound. There are many reasons for this influx into common culture, and the workplace and halls of education are not immune. It is not unreasonable to believe that within a short amount of time, the idea of games and gamification will be common throughout all workplaces and educational institutions and an acceptable practice.

Not convinced? Here is an analogy that might help. About twenty years ago, just the thought of wearing a pair of khakis and a polo shirt to a meeting with a potential client would get you fired. If you didn't wear a suit, you were not serious about business. The workplace has evolved and continues to change at a rapid pace. For example, it used to be that the only acceptable business phone was a BlackBerry. Any other phone wasn't for serious business. Today, all sorts of smart phones are used within a business context and the BlackBerry has lost its grip on mobile corporate communications.

There are several reasons why games, gamification, and simulations are becoming more common:

- Games are easier to build than ever before. There are software programs that make building a simple game easy and quick.

- The average age of a person who plays video games is getting older. As these older people obtain positions of power within organizations, the stigma of games in corporations, the government, academic environments, and in non-profits is waning.

- More colleges and universities are graduating people who have created games in game development programs, and not all of these folks are finding jobs in the game industry so they are working for software development firms and bringing game sensibilities with them into business software design.

- Games are available on smart phones. Now that many people carry a smart phone, they are also carrying games with them. This allows them to play games anywhere and has helped to fuel interest in games, especially games that can be played across distances on a smart phone such as "Words with Friends."

So the thought that games will eventually become an integrated part of work and everyday activities is not crazy. Things are changing; games, gamification, and game-like computer interfaces are becoming common.

While it may be easy to accept the idea that games are everywhere, there is still reluctance to the concept of gamification, but it, too, is expanding into our everyday lives. The reduction in the cost of making sensors and the ability to miniaturize them are making it possible to track all kinds of activities that were previously difficult to track. This tracking of almost everything means that scores or values can be placed on everyday activities.

One such example is the Nike+ FuelBand.[1] The FuelBand is a watch worn on a person's wrist capable of tracking movement through a built-in accelerometer. The accelerometer allows the watch to track daily activities, including running, walking, basketball, and dancing. It tracks each step taken and calories burned. You can set goals, known as NikeFuel goals. Then, as you move throughout the day, you can check your progress against your goal.

At the end of the day, you can synchronize your data with an app and then view your activity history, track your progress, and even connect with friends. This allows you to see your activity patterns and perhaps modify your behaviors. As you progress, you receive achievements and rewards. You can get on a streak, exceed your goal, and hit milestones all on the way to your personal fitness objectives.

Another example in the health field is the creation of a gamified inhaler called the T-Haler.[2] The T-Haler is an inhaler that is fitted with WiFi connectivity and a number of sensors. The device senses how it's being used and gives real-time feedback on a computer screen to the person using the inhaler. The feedback is related to three elements of using an inhaler: shaking, actuation (pumping the inhaler), and inhalation. These steps need to be done properly to ensure the right amount of medicine is provided to the user each time he or she uses the inhaler.

During the process, the user of the inhaler watches a ball roll across what looks like a tic-tac-toe board filled with different failure points on the computer screen. The virtual ball rolls down a hole in the middle if done correctly and to one of the failure points if done incorrectly. The makers of the T-Haler indicate that the proper use of the inhaler can go from 20 to 60 percent by using the T-Haler and playing the computer game to get it right.[3] The feedback provided by the interactions is what the learner is focusing on.

Another example on the horizon is a product called Google Glass or, more commonly, Google Glasses.[4] The idea is simple. A heads-up display (HUD) like the ones seen in video games is projected onto a person's glasses. The HUD places a layer of data and information overtop of reality—as you look through your glasses, information is displayed in front of you. The layer can be data about a particular location, directions guiding you through a foreign city, or information about the buildings you are passing as you walk down the street. At the airport the status of your flight could be displayed as you walk to your gate or the weather in your destination city can be provided right in front of your eyes as you deplane.

This is not unlike the heads-up display now available on different cars where the turn-by-turn directions are projected onto the windshield to guide you on your way. Cars are incorporating other features that make them more gamified. Several brands of hybrid vehicles provide graphical feedback on how efficient the driver is being during trips. This graphical feedback provides information to the driver, who can then modify her driving habits in response to the feedback.

The concept of adding game elements on top of reality in such items as Google Glasses as well as the Nike+ FuelBand are part of a growing collection of consumer products that are becoming commonplace. These items will drive the need to add gamification elements to learning environments. Imagine a repairman being able to see the overlay of the insides of a gas stove as he begins to look for leaks or repair a malfunction. Or a person on the manufacturing floor receiving instant information about the location of a needed, but late, piece of raw material. Or a salesperson pulling up information about a product as she describes the features and functionality to a potential client.

What's Coming in This Book

To help you create instruction in this changing environment, this book is divided into five sections. The first section is "Getting Started." In this section, we outline why it's so important to focus on creating engaging, interactive instruction. We highlight the similarities among games, simulations, and gamification. We also provide an overview of the entire process for building an interactive learning event. This is to make it easier to read and less redundant. There are many similarities among the three common approaches of games, simulations, and gamification.

Therefore, we decided to write in general about the topic for most of the book and then highlight the differences specific to each type of ILE in the design section. Most of the differences, we discovered, were in the design of the ILE. The other areas such as audience analysis, identification of learning objectives, technological considerations, brainstorming, and implementation were all closely aligned. Throughout the book, you will see special callouts or information specific to one of the three types of ILEs when appropriate.

The second section of the book, provides a variety of content we call "Basic Elements." These topics cut across all ILEs and are critically important to developing your own ILE. The topics include such items as identifying what you are trying to teach and managing the data you collect from learners interfacing with the ILE.

This section contains information on the basic elements shared by all three ILEs and the importance of the narrative context or story. Regardless of what type of learning you are developing, a clear understanding of how to wrap instruction around compelling narrative is of critical importance. It is the context of the learning. Also important is learning how to make a case for a game, gamification, or simulation.

Finally, this section finishes with a discussion on how to manage a large scale game development project. While the case study given is focused on game development, the same process can be used to create a large scale gamification or simulation project.

The third section of the book is focused on "Design Considerations" required to create an ILE. In fact, the design aspect of creating an ILE is the most critical aspect of the creation. The technological obstacles are usually secondary to the need for a good, effective design. The section starts with some ideas for brainstorming. How does one brainstorm for a game or a simulation? What elements should be considered when thinking about a gamification solution? These types of questions are addressed in this section.

The bulk of this section is the division of the chapters. One chapter each describes how to design a gamification experience, a simulation, and an instructional game. In this section, you'll learn from experts who have designed these types of learning experiences. You will learn what they consider when designing each type of ILE and how they design them to help people learn.

The fourth section covers the "Development" of ILEs. The section begins with a discussion of the various tools that are used for creating ILEs and helps to define a method for choosing which tools are best for which type of development, ranging from templates all the way to programming the ILE from scratch.

Storyboarding is another subject covered in this section. A process is provided that outlines the methods of storyboarding, with illustrations and examples. A quick discussion of the virtues of storyboarding to obtain the proper flow of an ILE is also provided.

"Case Studies" is the final section of this book. We have included a variety of case studies from a number of different fields to show creation and implementation can be done in almost any industry with a variety of content. We've included live face-to-face classroom simulations, a full scale online game to teach negotiation skills, a mobile learning gamification example, and even a board game. The idea is to provide you with a range of examples of how to apply the concepts and ideas from the book. Others have done this; the pioneering days are almost over, and now is the time to implement proven techniques. The final section of the book shows what others have done.

The Best Way to Read This Book

In the spirit of learning by doing and from experience, this book is focused on providing worksheets, examples, samples, tables, and instructions for creating your own ILE. This book can be used as a primer or introductory text to introduce the topic of designing instructional games, gamification, and simulation, but it is primarily designed as a practical fieldbook to help teams in the midst of creating games, gamification, and simulation projects. It is the companion to the bestselling book *The Gamification of Learning and Instruction: Game-Based Methods and Strategies for Training and Education*.

If you are reading this book as a primer, it makes most sense to read the chapters in chronological order. Pause after each part to ensure you understand the key arguments, research findings, and suggestions of each chapter and then move on to the next part. Understand there will be overlap in content and some ideas that don't always 100 percent agree with each other. The reason is because several experts teamed to write this book and purposefully crafted it so that different perspectives and ideas were presented. The book is not going to read like a novel; instead, it will be more like a reference guide to help you with the process of creating your own ILE.

If you are reading this book as part of a class, a good idea would be to actually design and, if capabilities exist, create an ILE following the worksheets and suggestions of the book. You will learn a great deal creating even a small ILE.

Another approach to consider might be to cover the contents of the book as a team or group, as shown in Figure 1.1. Divide your team, department, or faculty into reading clubs and read a chapter each week. If you are geographically dispersed, do it as a virtual book club using Twitter or Facebook. Then, once a week, the group should get together and discuss the salient and thought-provoking points. How can we help the organization design meaningful games for learning? What guidelines should we establish for the gamification of learning in our organization? How can we put this data about the effectiveness of these game elements in the hands of upper management? How do we implement these ideas? Is a simulation needed in our environment?

This group approach will spark discussion, provide insightful solutions, and guide you to develop your own methods of applying the ideas and concepts to your own organization or classroom. It will also begin discussions about the future of learning within your organization that may not have occurred otherwise. These conversations, even when slightly off-topic, will be valuable in strengthening your organization in terms of maximizing the knowledge needed for the design, development, and delivery of games, gamification, and simulations for learning with the organization.

If you are in the midst of designing a project, we encourage you to become intimately familiar with the key takeaways at the end of every chapter and the worksheets and models provided to move the process forward. Work with your peers on the design team to ensure that you understand each of these takeaways and what they mean to the creation of games, gamification, and simulations for learning and instruction.

Graduate and undergraduate students will particularly find this book of interest as a foundation to building dissertations, creating games, gamification, and simulations, and pursing lines of research, especially as a generation that has grown up playing video games.

Figure 1.1 Reading the Book as a Team to Generate Discussions and New Ideas

Image reprinted with permission of the artist, Kristin Bittner.

Continuing the Discussion

A topic like this does not remain static; it is always moving as technology and our understanding of games, gamification, and simulations to foster learning and collaboration continues to grow. In an effort to continue the dialogue in real-time and to make real progress in helping others we have created a Facebook page for easy collaboration, posting of games, gamification, and simulations, and interactions among readers. The page is https://www.facebook.com/gamificationLI.

Enjoy the book; we hope you have as much fun reading it as we did writing it.

Getting Started

2

Why Games, Gamification, and Simulations for Learning?

CHAPTER QUESTIONS

- What are the wrong reasons for implementing an ILE into an organization?
- Why does it matter if an ILE is for the wrong reason?
- What are the right reasons for implementing an ILE into an organization?
- What are the potential positive outcomes of implementing for the right reasons?

Introduction

Alexander Pope, in his work "An Essay on Criticism," famously observed "fools rush in where angels fear to tread."[1] Unfortunately, the same is often said of efforts involving games, gamification, and simulations. It is not uncommon for an interactive learning initiative to be undertaken for the wrong reasons and subsequently fail miserably. The game doesn't teach the content, the gamification effort quickly wanes, or the simulation doesn't provide the desired behavior change.

Typically, the reaction is to blame the delivery vehicle—games don't teach or gamification is just a gimmick—neglecting that the biggest single contributor to failure is undertaking the initiative for the wrong reasons. In second place are poorly or hastily designed games, gamification, and simulations. The problems are not with the delivery mechanism. The problems are with the expectations, reasons driving the initiative, and with the ultimate design of the solution.

Avoiding costly mistakes and investments in games, gamification, and simulations is an important element in this growing field. Too many misguided attempts and the idea of using these methods for learning quickly becomes discredited and falls out of favor and, on a more immediate level, jobs can be lost and careers stymied when poor choices are made. And worse, the employees who really need to learn the content contained in the interactive learning experience end up not learning.

The solution is to choose to undertake the development of games, gamification, and simulations for the right reasons. Avoid requests to engage in these types of solutions from well-meaning individuals who have an incorrect expectation of what interactive learning experiences can do for the learners or the organization.

This chapter explores five reasons given for the creation of games, gamification, and simulations that are not valid business drivers for undertaking the expensive and time-consuming task of creating an interactive learning experience. The chapter then explores valid reasons to undertake the development of a game, gamification, or simulation.

Wrong Reasons

It is important to keep in mind that often the person making the request for a game, gamification, or simulation is not purposely asking for the wrong reason; it's because he doesn't know. Most people's experiences with games is through their smart phones or game consoles and they have unrealistic expectations of what a learning game can accomplish, what it costs, or even how others will react. They see gamification elements in consumer products and think those types of elements can easily be added to the toolkit of the Learning and Development Department of their organization. While costs are dropping and tools for creating interactive learning experiences are becoming less expensive, any initiative in this area is still expensive and time-consuming. The most common wrong reasons for wanting a game, gamification, or simulation include:

- They are cool/awesome/fun/neat.
- Everyone is doing it.
- The learning will be effortless (stealth learning).
- Everyone "loves" games, gamification, and simulations.
- It's easy to design them.

ILEs Are Cool/Awesome/Fun/Neat

This argument is more often an undertone than a full, head-on reason. The person leading the effort or requesting the intervention loves to play games or loves the concept of gamification and thinks that the way to increase learning is through these types of interventions.

First, games, gamification, and simulations are cool, awesome, fun, and neat. However, so is paid time off, skipping work, and getting to stay home because of a snow day. Yet, none of these elements contributes to employee learning or development. Just because something is fun or entertaining doesn't mean that it naturally is the right thing to do or that it even leads to learning.

Be on the lookout for this sentiment when you are having initial discussions with stakeholders or clients who think that the fun factor is the driving force behind the development of an interactive learning experience. The element of "fun" can be present in the final solution but should not drive the solution.

In a study of studies, called a meta-analysis, it was found that simulation/games do not have to be labeled as "fun" by the learners to be educational. In other words, learning can happen from a game, gamification, or simulation even when the participants indicate that the experience wasn't that fun. What this means is that if the focus is just on fun and not on learning, the learners might have fun but might not learn anything or, worse, learn the wrong thing. This can be a colossal waste of time and effort. But a learner who did not have "fun" can still learn the required information.

If you are getting an indication that the only reason a person is asking for an interactive learning experience is that he thinks it will be fun or neat. Don't walk away from that person, run. Or better yet, ask some questions from the worksheet in Chapter 4 to focus the person making the request on the business and learning reasons why interactivity might be the solution. Don't undertake a development project in a work environment to create something fun; instead, create something that contributes to the growth and development of both the employees and the company. Create something focused on learning, not on fun, cool, neat, or awesome. Those elements should be integrated into the solution, but should not drive development. The desired learning outcome must drive the development.

Everyone's Doing It

It does seem that every time you turn around, there is an article or press release about another company or college implementing games, gamification, or simulations. In fact, this book is filled with case studies of those types of implementations. While the trend is growing, jumping on the bandwagon simply because you don't want to be left behind is a poor excuse for a strategy.

To be truly competitive and nimble, organizations need to focus on their own goals and objectives and not continually look outside for solutions. It might be that games work well in your competitor's organization but would not work well within your organization. It could be that gamification does drive behavior in some types of organizations but drives away consumers in others.

An effort related to developing games, gamification, or simulations must be driven by internal needs and not a perception of what everyone else is doing. In fact, more companies are not implementing games, gamification, or simulations than are actively engaged in these activities. The trade publications and vendors tend to expose the use of innovative technologies and new methodologies, both to sell publications and to sell the products of the vendors. From an unexamined viewpoint, it does appear that everyone is engaging in the practice of developing interactive learning experiences, but in reality that is not the case.

Games, gamification, and simulations are not growing in popularity because everyone else is implementing them. They are growing in popularity because they are effective in meeting particular learning needs in particular situations. Organizations that match the learning needs to the right learning design achieve the most success.

Lessons can be learned from others' implementation of games, gamification, and simulation but don't predicate your entire strategy of implementing these tools on the fact that you don't want to be left behind or because everyone else is implementing these types of solutions. Instead, focus on what these solutions can do for your organization. Don't jump on the bandwagon just to be on the bandwagon. Ultimately, that is an unsustainable position in terms of defending the costs and efforts required to create meaningful games, gamification, and simulations.

The Learning Will Be Effortless (Stealth Learning)

The argument is that we'll create a game, gamification, or simulation for learning and the people involved will never know they are learning. It will be stealth learning. The reality is that it won't be stealth learning; people are pretty smart. They'll know they are learning and, in fact, you want them to know they are learning.

The research is pretty clear on games and simulations for learning. The best levels of retention, content acquisition, and learning transfer come when the playing of the game or simulation is couched between pre-work and post-work. The learners need to know what they should be focusing on when they play the game or simulation, and they need to be debriefed afterward to make sure the lessons intended to be conveyed during the game or simulation were actually conveyed.

The idea is not to hide the learning; the idea is to highlight the lessons learned and to anchor the learner's experience with the game or simulation to tasks and responsibilities he will be asked to do on the job. Make the learning explicit. Tell the learners what they will be learning and then ask them what they learned. Use the game or simulation as a catalyst to discuss the key learning points. Don't make the learners figure out those points themselves.

Some people may think that giving away the learning points or "setting up the game beforehand" spoils the experience or makes the game play less meaningful. That is not the case. The playing of the simulation or game can actually help to solidify the knowledge told to the learners before they begin playing the game or simulation. The pre-work or pre-learning serves as an advanced organizer to help the learners frame their experiences correctly for the future.

An analogy is when you tell a small child not to touch a stove because it's hot. The scenario usually works like this. You tell the child, "Don't touch that stove. It's hot and you could be burned." The child then decides to have the experience on her own and touches the stove. Of course, the child gets burned and upset (we hope only a minor burn). Then the parent reminds the child, "I told you not to touch the stove, I told you it was hot and you'd get burned." The child internalizes the experience and the lesson and decides that touching a hot stove is a bad idea. Then, when they are in the kitchen again and the child reaches for a pan that was just taken off the stove, the parent says, "Don't touch that pan; it's hot. Remember what happened when you touched the stove?" The child puts her hand down, remembering the experience of being burned.

The game or simulation works in the same fashion. You tell the learners what they are going to learn and then you allow them to have the experience with the game or simulation. They may be successful or they may be unsuccessful. Then provide a debriefing to the learner so he or she can internalize the lessons and transfer those lessons to other experiences. The debriefing provides the chance for generalization of the learning.[2] Without the generalization, the learning is confined only to that one experience. In other words, experience without reflection is just experience.

Everyone "Loves" Games, Gamification, and Simulations

To those who love games, gamification, and simulations, the thought that someone might not like these experiences is almost unthinkable. Who doesn't want to earn points? Everyone wants points. What kind of curmudgeon doesn't play games? It turns out, a lot of people don't play games and don't like earning points or badges or even being on a leaderboard.

This doesn't mean that the concept of using games, gamification, or simulations for learning should be abandoned because it turns out that not everyone likes classroom instruction, e-learning, or even social media. In any organization of almost any size, there will be a subset of people who do not like your chosen delivery method. This doesn't mean the delivery method should be abandoned or switched for something else, but it also doesn't mean that one method or another will be universally accepted.

Two mistakes related to the concept that everyone loves interactive learning experiences are common. The first is that an overly enthusiastic individual or team assumes everyone likes these experiences and begins to "sell" the experience as a great game, gamification, or simulation and then becomes bitterly disappointed when people retort "I don't play games" or "I have serious work to do." Take a look at the organization and make a decision as to whether or not it might be better to sell the concept as an "interactive exercise" or an "application-focused e-learning" or an "interactive role-play experience." Consider renaming the launch of the interactive learning experience to more closely match the culture of the organization. If the organization is all about games, then by all means call it a game or gamification. If the organization is not so cutting-edge, back off the terminology.

The second mistake is that as soon as the enthusiastic team or individual hears that someone doesn't like games or gamification, he feel that he's done something wrong and begins to back away from the idea. At this point it is important to remember that the reason the interactive learning event was created was because it was tied to business and learning outcomes (see Chapter 4). If this is the case, stand by the delivery methodology. Not everyone is going to like it, but not everyone likes Disney World or even going to the beach. Different people like different delivery methods for learning, but almost all must suffer through classroom lectures or online learning so they can "suffer" through the game or gamification. Don't abandon because of the overly vocal.

For some reason people are not so vocal about disliking classroom lectures or disliking online learning, even though a percentage don't like it. I think that is because they can do other things while the lesson is progressing without them. With a game or gamification, if the person is not providing his full attention, he loses the game or doesn't earn points and everyone knows he is not paying attention.

The point here is that making an argument to create a game, gamification, or simulation because everyone will love it is not an effective argument. It would be far better to make an argument related to the effectiveness of the learning and the increase in performance or the opportunity for hands-on application of knowledge then trying to sell it because "everyone will love it." They won't all love it.

It's Easy to Design

It's not. Creating a game, gamification, or simulation is a time-consuming, difficult process. You must continually weigh the need for meeting instructional objectives against the dynamics of scoring points, creating interactions, and keeping the learner motivated.

Development efforts for interactive learning experiences require long hours, multiple interactions of the learning experience, and a careful attention to detail. Not to mention the need for quality graphics and a careful melding of content and game play. The typical instructional designer has no experience with game development or gamification, and it is rarely taught in schools.

Storyboards need to be created, flow charts developed, code programmed, all within a typical short and tight timeline. Too often people equate a simple, easy-to-play game with a simple easy-to-create design and development process, whereas the two are inversely related. When a game is easy to play and intuitive, the process to ensure those features is usually involved and complex.

So when beginning the process of developing a game, gamification, or simulation for learning, don't hesitate to remind others that the process is more complicated and complex than designing a linear lecture or a static online learning module.

Right Reasons

With all those negative reasons, it almost seems that developing any type of game, gamification, or simulation is more trouble than it's worth. However, there are many "right" reasons to implement an interactive learning experience.. Here are some of those reasons:

- Creating interactivity in learning delivery
- Overcoming disengagement
- Providing opportunities for deep thought and reflection
- Positively change behavior
- Authentic practice

Creating Interactivity in Learning Delivery

Almost everyone in the learning and development field has had an experience with a rather boring, mind-numbing online course. We are all familiar with the design strategy—page of text followed by page of text, followed by a page of text and then a multiple-choice question thrown in for good measure. Repeat.

In fact, a number of us have probably created such courses. But it doesn't have to be limited to online courses; plenty of lectures and training programs are equally as mind numbing due primarily to the lack of interactivity between the person delivering the content and the learners sitting in the room. Not to mention the lack of visible application and the nagging uncertainty that, without some type of practice, the knowledge being provided will be forgotten and unreachable at the exact time it is needed the most.

Research shows that the level of interactivity within a learning environment is what drives learning. The more the learner interacts with other learners, the content, and the instructor, the more likely it is that learning will actually occur.

The typical lack of engagement, interactivity, or any "learning by doing" is fueling the desire among chief learning officers (CLOs) and college faculty members to create learning events that are interactive and engaging. Many organizations are seeking the opportunity to create instruction that transcends mere lectures, moving into active participation by the learners. Ironically, many of us start our educational endeavors in highly active school settings known as pre-school or Kindergarten, where we do projects and move from station to station—interacting with manipulatives and the content we are learning, even going on field trips to experience the environment in which learning is applied. However, as we grow older and move up in the schooling system, the opportunities for "learn by doing" become less and less—when just the opposite is needed.

The superficial learning that occurs with slide-based online modules or ineffective lectures is inadequate. We are not going to train future employees, managers, and leaders with slide after slide of text or images. What is needed is a new perspective on employee and student training. What is needed is a focus on game-based learning, gamification, and the use of simulations.

There appears to be a growing backlash against the linear design of instruction by both the designers of the instruction and the consumers of the instruction. People are beginning to realize that just because a person sits in front of a computer screen or sits staring straight ahead at an instructor and answers every question, it doesn't mean he or she is actually learning. To learn, a person needs to be engaged. The traditional page turning online learning and classroom lecture styles are proving to be less and less effective for deep and meaningful learning.

Overcoming Disengagement

Not only do the courses lack engagement, but gaining employee attention is difficult because the employees themselves are less engaged at work than ever before. Every year, the Gallup organization conducts research to measure the level of engagement of employees within organizations. They use the terms "actively disengaged," "not engaged," and "engaged" to describe the state of the employees.[3]

An actively disengaged employee is a person who is not only unhappy at work but actually acts out that unhappiness. These employees close themselves out of any solutions to organizational problems; they thwart efforts for improvement. They tend to exude negativity and aren't interested in learning or development or in anything related to the company. They are truly putting in time until retirement or something better comes along. These aren't necessarily people who are negative toward everything, they are just people who have become negative about their work situations and who have stopped trying to be actively involved within their working community. This isn't a single event; it's a consistent negative attitude toward the organization for which they are employed.

Employees who are merely "not engaged" aren't necessarily negative or positive about the organization. They simply hang back and wait to see what happens during a certain initiative or effort to see how they might be impacted and whether or not the initiative will actually work.

Engaged employees are those who are positive and perform at consistently high levels. They leverage their talents fully to create new initiatives, products, and services. They are the drivers of organizational change and champion the causes of the organization.

Unfortunately, according to a meta-analysis of data compiled by Gallup, the average company has as many as 18 percent of its employees actively disengaged and 49 percent of employees not engaged. Lack of engagement can lead to less productivity, higher accident rates, lower rates of quality, and higher employee turnover.[4]

Why the lack of engagement? The causes are numerous and include not having the right equipment or procedures to do the job, lack of communication with upper management, dismissal of a person's opinions by others, and a lack of growth and learning opportunities. While learning and development folks cannot solve all of these problems independently, they can have an impact on a person's opportunities for learning and growth. But for that to happen, the learning and development professional must understand how to create learning that is engaging, motivational, and positively impacts an employee's ability to perform his or her job.

Creating instruction that is meaningful to employees and, in the case of academia, meaningful to students is becoming increasingly difficult. Nevertheless, the imperative to create meaningful instruction is stronger than ever, and games, gamification, and simulations can drive that engagement.

One of the reasons gamification is becoming so popular is because it has been shown to engage employees. Here is one example from the Deloitte Leadership Academy (DLA).[5] Deloitte is a "brand" under which tens of thousands of dedicated professionals in independent firms throughout the world collaborative to provide audit, consulting, financial advisory, risk management, and tax services to selected clients.

Deloitte Leadership Academy is an innovative digital executive training program for more than fifty thousand executives at more than 150 companies worldwide. DLA delivers lessons and insights from business schools and global leaders such as Harvard Business Publishing, Stanford, and the International Institute for Management Development (IMD). They enable executives to develop their management and leadership skills while also connecting them within a community of business leaders.

With extensive online offerings, including certification from top business schools, blog entries, webinars, and interviews by industry leaders, DLA utilizes a variety of content types and development options to accommodate for different learning preferences. However, Deloitte faced an obvious challenge. How do they persuade executives to take valuable time of out of their busy schedules to actually sit down and fully engage with Deloitte's content?

Deloitte looked to gamification. They decided to employ the Behavior Platform by a company called Badgeville to embed game mechanics throughout the DLA website to drive desired user behavior and to increase engagement. They knew they needed an innovative alternative to the traditional methods of delivering education and learning management if they were going to keep executives engaged. Figure 2.1 shows the leadership academy profile screen from the leadership gamification experience.

Deloitte leveraged three game mechanics to help measure, surface, and reward engagement by the executives. The first was rank and rewards. As executives interacted with DLA content and preformed high-value behaviors, they earned points and achievements to showcase on their profiles. The next game mechanic was the use of missions. DLA designed missions as sets of achievements and challenges to keep executives on track to complete their courses and monthly learning goals. The third element was leaderboards. Based on their level of engagement in DLA's twelve development areas, executives could compete to become experts on different topics. The results speak for themselves.

Figure 2.1 Deloitte Leadership Academy Profile Screen

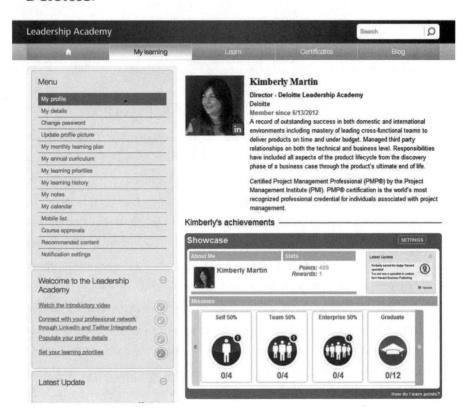

- Increased user retention across the program:
  - More than 46.6 percent of users returned daily.
  - More than 36.3 percent of users returned weekly.
- Active user engagement and adoptions
  - Average of three achievements unlocked per active user.
  - Top users have earned as many as thirty achievements.
  - Within six months, a user unlocked the Leadership Academy Graduate achievement, a milestone that was expected to take twelve months for the average user.

Users have also commented that the experience has become "addictive," inspiring friendly competition between peers and spurring more people to complete their learning plans.[6]

This example clearly shows how using gamification elements can drive engagement. The game mechanics employed in the leadership development program were enough to drive the executives to work to complete the program in spite of all the other demands for their time.

Providing Opportunities for Deep Thought and Reflection

In today's fast-paced world, there are few opportunities for deep thought and reflection. This can be problematic when working on big issues such as organizational strategy or the interdependencies within an organization among different groups such as research and development, sales, and operations. Seeing relationships, correlations, and cause and effect often requires a stepping back from everyday actions and interactions to attempt to visualize the big picture. It also requires a "slowing down" and a reflection upon experiences and reactions to those experiences.

Not all ILE provide a chance to look at interdependencies and encourage strategic thinking, but a surprising number provide such opportunities. Specifically, a game or simulation can release a learner from the confines of everyday stress and strain and provide a time and place for examining what might otherwise remain unexamined.

The primary reason games are good for allowing a learner time for deep thought and reflection is that the games are an abstraction of reality allowing for a narrow focus. As explained in *The Gamification of Learning and Instruction*, abstracted reality has a number of advantages over actual reality:

- It helps the player manage the conceptual space being experienced.
- Cause and effect can be clearly identified.
- Extraneous factors are removed.
- Time required to grasp concepts is reduced.

Combined, these factors contribute to the opportunity to reflect. Instructionally, games and simulations are most effective when they are embedded into a larger curriculum structure that includes a post-game debriefing or, in military terms, an after-action review (AAR), an opportunity to reflect on and analyze the outcome of the game or simulation, look at what happened, why it happened, and how it can be done more effectively in the future. Implementing an AAR into a game, gamification, or simulation experience can have the result of forcing a person to step back and reflect. It also provides an opportunity to think deeply about cause-and-effect relationships and about problem solving.

This attribute isn't available in every ILE, but it can play a significant role in many experiences. Leveraging the ILE to give people a break from the daily grind can be a liberating and thought-provoking experience.

As an example, one time some insurance executives were playing a board game together as part of a merger activity. One of the players was on a lucky streak and grabbed a number of "growth" cards as he grew his business to win the game. After obtaining a number of cards and thinking about his next move, he suddenly had an epiphany. The only growth he was able to achieve was through acquisition and mergers; he was not growing the business through new customers. He used this insight to later develop a strategy focused on growing the actual business through new customers rather than just by acquisition, as his predecessor had done.

Learning and development and business professionals are recognizing that, when it is positioned correctly, reflection and deep thought can be the result of pausing from the daily grind and participating in a learning activity. Those types of activities are always valuable, as they provide thinking time not ordinarily placed into the flow of a work day.

Positively Changing Behavior

For years, scientists have been researching the ability of positive video games and video game environments to influence a person's behavior. The studies indicate that a person can be positively influenced through actions taken as an avatar within a virtual space and by playing pro-social video games.

In one example, researchers discovered that when research participants fly around a virtual world as a superhero those subjects are subsequently nicer in the physical world. The study was conducted by Stanford University's

Virtual Human Interaction Lab with thirty male and thirty female participants. The participants were immersed in a virtual world and assigned either to play a superhero character who could fly or to become a passenger in a helicopter.

The subjects were then directed to either join a tour of the city or to save a lost diabetic child in dire need of insulin. After the game was over, participants were asked to wait. While waiting, a researcher "accidentally" spilled a cup of pencils a few feet away and waited to see whether the participant would help pick up the pencils. The question was "Would the participant be helpful toward the researcher?"

The results were interesting. Of the participants who did not help pick up the pencils, every one of them had been a passenger in the helicopter in the virtual world.. Every former superhero helped pick up the spilled pencils. People who played superheroes took an average of just two seconds to respond and help, while those in the helicopter scenario took between six and seven seconds to help. The "former" superheroes were both more likely and quicker to help.[7]

This is interesting by itself, but when you combine it with the results of other similar studies, it becomes clear that pro-social games can and do influence behavior positively.

In a study led by Douglas A. Gentile from Iowa State University with researchers from around the world, the findings indicated that video games in which game characters help and support each other in nonviolent ways increase both short-term and long-term pro-social behaviors.[8] The research team reported on three studies conducted in three countries with three age groups.

In a correlational study, Singaporean middle-school students who played more pro-social games behaved more pro-socially. In two longitudinal samples of Japanese children and adolescents, pro-social game play predicted later increases in pro-social behavior. In an experimental study, U.S. undergraduates randomly assigned to play pro-social games behaved more pro-socially toward another student. These results across different methodologies, ages, and cultures provide robust evidence that pro-social games can positively impact pro-social behavior.

In another study, researchers wanted to see whether a person's empathic reactions to social issues could be influenced by playing an interactive digital game. The study focused on a game called "Darfur Is Dying." It is a narrative-based game where the player, from the perspective of a displaced refuge, negotiates forces that threaten the survival of his or her refugee camp. It is meant to highlight the plight of people who have been displaced by the fighting in the Sudan region of Africa. Two experiments were conducted.

The first experiment demonstrated that playing the "Darfur Is Dying" game resulted in greater willingness to help the Darfurian people than reading a text conveying the same information.[9]

The second experiment added a game-watching condition, and results showed that game playing resulted in greater role taking and willingness to help than game watching and text reading. The study provides empirical evidence that interactive digital games are more effective than non-interactive presentation modes in influencing people's empathic reactions to social issues.[10]

These demonstrated positive effects of pro-social games is driving the idea that placing learners into a positive game environment can help them to achieve goals and objectives through positive reinforcement of activities undertaken during game play.

Authentic Practice

Simulations provide a rich opportunity to give learners a chance to practice in an environment as close to the actual situation as possible. Games provide a more abstracted version of the environment, but can still be helpful for allowing authentic practice.

Research indicates that the ability of simulations to teach skills that transfer to real-life, on-the-job situations is abundantly positive. In a study by ADL, it was found that computer-based simulations—assessed as an alternative to other means of training, as a supplement to other means of training, as a device to combat skill decay in experienced trainees, and as a means of improving performance levels as they stand prior to training—show positive results for transfer a majority of the time.[11]

It is helpful to look to life-and-death situations to determine the effectiveness of simulations for learning. In the Johns Hopkins Medicine

Simulation Center, the simulations use medical mannequins to train future nurses, among others. The nurses are given the opportunity to run a "code" with a life-sized simulation dummy. The computer-controlled patient (the dummy) is given a heart attack and a team then goes through the process of trying to save the patient–complete with injections and CPR. It is as realistic as it can be. The actions are then recorded and measured against standards and the nurses have an opportunity to practice again until the actions become second-nature.

In a nuclear power plant in Pennsylvania, there is an exact replica of the operations room that is used for training. The training room even has the same ambient sounds.

When lives are on the line, the learning process is studied, calculated, and formalized to a degree of realism as close to 100 percent as possible. In these life-and-death training situations, the actions of the individuals involved in the training are timed and measured against objective standards. If you don't administer oxygen within the prescribed time frame in the simulation, you know about it as you watch a recorded version of your actions as an instructor provides feedback. The fidelity between the environment in which the performance is required and the environment in which it is trained and practiced is extremely high.

We like to think knowledge workers spend all day "problem solving," but in reality they spend all day finding out what procedure should be followed in what situation. Salespeople have procedures for overcoming objections, managers have procedures for dealing with a crisis or an upset customer, insurance agents have procedures for handling claims, and instructional designers have procedures for creating role plays or teaching concepts versus facts.

Formal feedback loops, reflective learning opportunities, established standards, and prescribed activities are all critical to the success of the learner in nuclear power plants, in hospitals, and while flying planes. All of these environments use simulations to train the people who will be and who are immersed in these jobs. Expected behaviors are not left to chance, actions are parsed, best practices studied, conclusions drawn from data and the experience of experts. This is because the difference between a radioactive disaster and successfully creating electricity is authentic practice.

So if you want a highly trained individual capable of performing his or her job to the highest standard, you need a simulation conducted in an authentic learning environment. Anything less is not as effective and the performance will not be guaranteed.

Extending this concept then, do we expect college students in an economics class to understand entrepreneurship without ever having run a business? Do we expect managers or leaders to effectively operate in a crisis situation when they've only read about the five steps needed to operate in a crisis or discussed it in a chat room?

In any type of work environment, learning and development professionals need to take a page from high-risk industries and decide that, if an organization really wants effective, mistake-free results, only simulation in an environment as authentic as possible can provide the desired level of performance and outcomes.

Questions to Ponder

When taking into account the appropriate and inappropriate reasons to develop a game, gamification, or simulation, it is helpful to answer a few questions to make sure everyone is on the same page and the intent is clear. Table 2.1 provides a list of questions to ask stakeholders to ensure everyone has the same expectations and to ensure the game, gamification, or simulation is being built for the right reasons.

How the questions in Table 2.1 are answered will guide you in determining whether the stakeholders for this project are behind the project for the right reasons. Consider alternatives or a different approach if you find the questions do not provide the answers needed for the project to be successful.

Ensuring Success

To ensure that the learning goals of a game, gamification, or simulation are met, the first priority is to design the game to focus on learning objectives from the beginning and not as an afterthought. One cannot bolt game elements onto traditional learning after it has been developed and expect it to

Table 2.1 Important Questions to Ponder Before Beginning Development

1. What are the top three reasons driving this game, gamification, or simulation?
2. Does an alternative exist? Why is the alternative not chosen?
3. Does the emphasis seem to be too much on the fun aspects of the game and not enough on the learning?
4. Do people expect the game, gamification, or simulation to stand alone with no other supporting educational materials?
5. Is this being created because "everyone loves games"?
6. Are the design and development elements framed within the proper expectations?
7. Is a high level of interactivity one of the goals of the ILE?
8. Can the design overcome disengagement? Does it provide an opportunity for engagement?
9. Does the game play include an opportunity for after-action review of the learning?
10. Are you trying to change learner behavior? What kind of behavior are you trying to change?
11. Do you need to provide authentic practice to the learners?

be effective, interesting, or even instructional. Instead, you need to design the interactions, storyline, feedback, and levels in a manner that reflects the goal of the game, gamification, or simulation from the beginning.

The first step to achieving the goal is to co-design instructional elements along with gameplay elements. Designing the elements together means that the fun and non-entertainment goals "grow up" together and are in harmony as opposed to fighting one another for dominance. Too many interactive learning experiences error on one side or the other and fall short of their goals.

Second, research strongly indicates that what makes an interactive learning experience effective for learning is the level of activity of the players as they participate in the activity. If learners are engaged, they learn more and retain the knowledge longer. If the ILE has a large number of passive elements and the learner is forced to observe for much of the ILE, the learning is limited. Design with interactivity in mind. Create opportunities for the players to be interactive with the content of the ILE and with each other. The higher the level of interactivity, the more engaged the learner and the more likely one will achieve the desired non-entertainment outcomes.

Third, create a compelling story within the ILE that is tied directly to the desired learning outcome or message. For an ILE to be successful in changing attitudes or behavior or helping someone learn, it needs to engage the learner within the story of the game.

The activities within the story need to be linked to the goals of the game, gamification, and simulation and that link should be made explicit to the learners. The learner takes action within the story to help others, to further a cause, or to learn a proper behavior.

And finally, test and retest. Make sure that the ILE is engaging the learners, don't take it for granted. Conduct evaluations and "talk alouds" to determine what learners are thinking as they experience the ILE. Don't take anything for granted, test assumptions, pre- and post-test attitudes, or level of knowledge, observe what players do, and modify the game based on input from live players. The best games, gamification, and simulations are not created by accident. Study how learners react to the ILE you created and modify accordingly.

Key Takeaways

The key takeaways from this chapter are

- There are many reasons why games, gamification, and simulation projects are started. Some of the reasons are valid from a business and learning perspective, and some of the reasons are not valid.

- Focus the effort on engaging the learner through interactivity.

- Define the elements that will make the game, gamification, or simulation a success.

- Create a simulation when the situation calls for authentic practice.

- ILEs can provide a time for learners to reflect. Build reflection and pre-work into any use of an ILE within an organization.

- Games can help positively change behavior. Be conscious of this ability and design specific elements into your game, gamification, or simulation to elicit the desired behavior change.

Game, Gamification, or Simulation: Which Is Best, When, Why?

Introduction

No one learning solution fits every learning need. This is certainly true in the area of games, gamification, and simulations. In some ways these interactive learning events are similar. When well designed, they all engage the learner, encourage thoughtful consideration of content, and provide meaningful impact to the individual and the organization.

Yet, each one is different in purpose, results, and design. Knowing the differences among the three can help you to match each one to its specific purpose. This chapter explores the three types of interactive learning events and when to use each design approach. The chapter will help you choose the right ILE for your needs—it will help you chose the right door, as shown in Figure 3.1.

Figure 3.1 Determining Which ILE to Use Can Be Difficult

Image reprinted with permission of the artist, Kristin Bittner.

To understand when each design approach is appropriate, it's important to dig further into the definition of each term because the terms are broad. The term "game," for example, may represent a two-person challenge like tic-tac-toe but, to others, it might mean a multilayered, turn-based strategy game. If two people in the room discussing a game for learning have not defined what they are talking about, there can be misinterpretations, false starts, and frustration.

Even the emerging concept of gamification can be further dissected into two types. Simulations can be divided into several types. Knowledge of the types and application of the types helps a design team by providing a common vision and framework for the development of the ILE. Standard definitions keep everyone on the same page, and that means fewer design issues, development problems, and implementation roadblocks.

Games

"Game" can be defined as:

> A system in which players engage in an abstract challenge, defined by rules, interactivity, and feedback, that results in a quantifiable outcome often eliciting an emotional reaction.[1]

While this definition is helpful from a broad perspective, it provides no guidance into the various types of games that can be used to achieve learning goals. A more precise breakdown is needed. However, breaking down games is not a simple task. Games are varied and nuanced. Many games contain elements of other games. If you play a video game where you assume a role of a superhero, you may solve puzzles within the game, fight with bad guys, and search for a missing scientist or piece of alien spaceship. If you do those activities, you would cover several game types: puzzle games, fighting games, and exploration games. Additionally, there are different perspectives on games. One way to look at games is by content area, war games, puzzle games, or science fiction games; another way to look at games is by interface. Games can be side-scrolling games, platform games, first-person shooter games, or turn-based role-playing games.

For our purposes, we will look at games from a number of perspectives. The first will be the type of activities that take place within the game because one way to decide on a game or simulation or gamification is to examine the type of activities the learner needs to accomplish and match those activities to the right ILE. The second will be the type of content being taught within the game. Next, we will examine the concept of testing games versus teaching games. These various perspectives on games can help a design team better understand the game elements.

Types of Game Activities

Activities that take place within a game can help define the game and narrow your focus when designing and developing a learning game. The activities can lead to specific types of learning, especially when they are tied to a learning taxonomy.

Keep in mind that any breakdown of a game purely by activity is somewhat artificial. Few games can be boxed neatly and cleanly into just one activity. For example, Monopoly is a capture game in that a player wants to capture as much of the board as possible, but it's also a collection game because the player wants to collect as many of the same color cards as possible.

Matching

In a matching game, the player must match one item to another. The item can be within the game space, such as turning over one card and turning over another and matching the same items on the cards. Or the matching can be a process of matching something on the game space with an item not within the game space. An example of that is Hangman. In Hangman, all the letters are not visible on the game space. The player must recall letters from memory and enter them into the game space. Some of the letters correctly match and some do not.

A trivia game is a form of a matching game. In the trivia game, the player must match knowledge he or she processes with knowledge being requested by the game. In some cases the player is able to match the knowledge and in some cases the player is unable to because he never had the knowledge in the first place.

Collecting/Capturing

This is a game where the goal is to collect a certain number of objects. A classic example is Pac-Man, where the object was to collect a number of dots and the occasional fruit that popped up. You did not keep what you collected, as the entire purpose of the game was to go around and pick up items (or actually eat items).

Similar to collecting items is the activity of capturing items from others. For example, the card game "Go Fish" involves the ability of one player to capture another player's card by making a request for that card. The player who captures the most cards wins.

Allocating Resources

In SimCity you (playing the role of mayor) must balance many variables while growing your city. You must balance the need to build infrastructure in terms of basic utilities with the need to have education, health, parks, and leisure. You must balance the need to collect garbage with the need to keep government expenses low. As mayor, if you allocate all your resources to education, then the health of your citizens will suffer.

Balance is the key to success throughout the game—attempt to generate revenue through extreme taxation and citizens will not be happy. In resource allocation games, the player is responsible for a variety of resources and must allocate those resources appropriately. These games focus on the interrelationship among variables. Too much emphasis by the player on one or two variables will adversely impact other variables and outcomes of the game. Resource allocation requires an examination of the various variables and careful consideration of how one variable impacts another.

Strategizing

In a strategy game a player is allocating resources and determining what moves to make in a manner similar to a resource allocation game; the difference is that in a strategy game the player is competing against another person for resources such as land, cultural influence, or other items of value. An example is the game of Chess. In Chess, you use a strategy against another person and move your pieces and adapt your strategy based on the actions of the other person.

A massively multiplayer online strategy game, such as EVE Online, is a game where players can come together and form alliances called "corporations." One corporation can wage war on another corporation to obtain desired items and territory.

Building

In building games, players try to create an object out of given materials. A low-tech version of a building game is Jenga, where you attempt to build on top of the moves of other players while avoiding knocking down the tower.

A more technical version of a building game is Minecraft. According to the Minecraft website, the "game is about breaking and placing blocks. At first, people build structures to protect against nocturnal monsters, but as the game grew players worked together to create wonderful, imaginative things."[2]

Puzzle Solving

In these types of games, the players are trying to figure something out. They may need clues to solve the puzzle or they may have all the pieces in front of them while they attempt to figure out what they need to do or how one item relates to another. The game play does not need to literally be "solving a puzzle." A good example is Clue. The puzzle is "Who did it?" and the pieces are scattered around the board and the player figures out "Mr. Mustard did it in the Library with the Candlestick" as she goes around the board.

Exploring

In games with a focus on exploring, players interact within an environment looking for items of value. The items can be used to solve a puzzle or they can be collected and used to obtain points. The idea is that the player must explore the environment to learn what to do next, how to progress, and to achieve a winning state within the game. Figure 3.2 shows an exploring game.

The classic computer game Myst and its sister game Riven were examples of exploring games. The player was placed into a strange, mysterious world and had to walk through the world exploring the various elements in an attempt to solve a puzzle and achieve victory.

Helping

The helping activity involves one player assisting another player or a non-player character to accomplish a task or even saving another character from imminent doom. One example is a 1991 game called Lemmings. The objective of the game is to guide a group of humanoid lemmings through obstacles to a designated exit. The player had to save the required number of lemmings to win.

Another game where the player rescues others is a game called City Crisis, where the player is cast as a rescue helicopter pilot who must save citizens from fires that spring up around the city. The player can also put out fires using water dumped from the helicopter.

Role Playing

In role-playing games, the player assumes the role of another person, such as becoming Master Chief in Halo or Desmond Miles in the Assassin's Creed series. In other role-playing games, a player assumes a role that he doesn't

Figure 3.2 Exploring the Jungle by Swinging Through the Trees

Image reprinted with permission of the artist, Kristin Bittner.

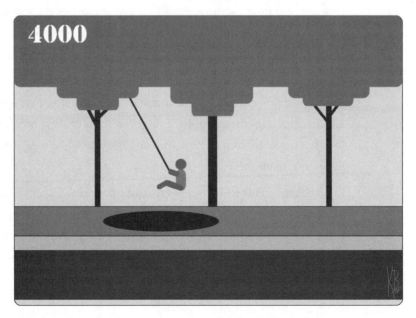

actually perform in real life, such as being a doctor in Operation. Role playing defines how a person plays the game and, in some cases, the activities that take place during the game.

A complicated role play is Assassin's Creed III, where you play the role of Desmond, who assumes the role of Ratohnhaké:ton, also known as Conner.[3] As Conner, you must battle the British; as Desmond you must match wits with the modern day bad guys Daniel Cross and Warren Vidic. You assume two roles within one game. I suggest that learning games not reach that level of complexity.

When to Use Games

One method of determining when to use a game is to match the game activities with a desired learning outcome. Matching in-game activities with an instructional taxonomy is one way of ensuring learning occurs. A taxonomy of educational objectives is a framework for classifying what is expected or intended of learners as a result of instruction.

Perhaps one of the best known educational taxonomies is Bloom's Taxonomy. It is used to classify types of learning into three domains:[4]

- *Cognitive*—This is thinking, what is traditionally taught in an educational or training setting. Cognitive knowledge revolves around understanding, comprehending, and synthesis of knowledge.

- *Affective*—This is the emotional domain. We don't often think of training initiatives being focused on the affective domain, but any time you try to influence the attitude of someone else, that is the affective domain, for example, trying to teach a positive attitude toward customers or a safety-conscious attitude while working in a dangerous environment.

- *Psychomotor*—This is the intersection of physical skills and cognitive knowledge when the combination of physical activity and thinking is necessary. A common type of psychomotor skills would be driving a commercial vehicle. The driver must control the braking with his foot but must know the correct braking distance and how to react when he suddenly has to stop.

Bloom's taxonomy was actually not developed by one person but was developed by a committee of individuals led by Benjamin S. Bloom, who was then the associate director of the board of examinations at the University of Chicago. Since that time, the hierarchy has served well in helping to create structured curriculum.

Approximately forty-five years later, a former student of Bloom's, Lorin Anderson, working with one of Bloom's partners in the original work on cognition, David Krathwohl, created a revised version of the taxonomy in the area of cognitive knowledge.[5]

Cognitive Domain

The new work refined the original cognitive taxonomy with several changes including the rewordings from nouns to verbs, the renaming of some of the components and the repositioning of the last two categories. The original and revised versions are shown in Table 3.1.

When thinking about what activities to incorporate into games, referencing Bloom can be helpful. Table 3.2 shows Bloom's revised taxonomy, the definition of each level of the taxonomy, verbs commonly associated with the taxonomy, matching game activities, and some example games.

Using this table can help you identify the type of activities to incorporate into a learning game based on the objectives to be met as a result of the instruction.

Table 3.1 Original and Revised Cognitive Taxonomy

Bloom's Taxonomy (1956)	Revised Version (2001)
Evaluation	Create
Synthesis	Evaluate
Analysis	Analyze
Application	Apply
Comprehension	Understand
Knowledge	Remember

Table 3.2 Bloom's Revised Taxonomy Matched with Game Activities

Revised Bloom's Taxonomy	Revised Definitions of Terms	Associated Verbs	Sample Game Activities	Example Game	Example from This Book
Creating	Putting elements together to form a coherent or functional whole; reorganizing elements into a new pattern or structure through generating, planning, or producing	Assemble, Construct, Create, Design, Develop, Formulate, Write, Generate, Plan, Produce	Building, building your own game	Minecraft	The entire process of creating a game, gamification, or simulation
Evaluating	Making judgments based on criteria and standards through checking and critiquing	Appraise, Argue, Defend, Judge, Select, Support, Value, Evaluate, Critiquing, Checking	Strategy	Chess, Stratego, Risk	
Analyzing	Breaking material into constituent parts, determining how the parts relate to one another and to an overall structure or purpose through differentiating, organizing, and attributing	Compare, Contrast, Differentiate, Discriminate, Distinguish, Examine, Experiment, Question, Organize, Attribute	Allocating Resources	Civilization V, Age of Empires, The Sims	

Applying	Carrying out or using a procedure through executing or implementing	Demonstrate, Dramatize, Employ, Illustrate, Operate, Schedule, Sketch, Solve, Use, Execute, Implement	Role Playing	Video-based sports games, Red Dead Redemption	Merchants
Understanding	Constructing meaning from oral, written, and graphic messages through interpreting, exemplifying, classifying, summarizing, inferring, comparing, and explaining	Classify, Identify, Locate, Recognize, Report, Select, Interpret, Exemplify, Summarize, Infer, Compare, Explain	Puzzle Solving, Exploring	Myst, Clue	
Remembering	Retrieving, recognizing, and recalling relevant knowledge from long-term memory	Define, Duplicate, List, Memorize, Recall, Repeat, Recognize	Matching, Collecting	Hangman, Trivial Pursuit	

Affective Domain

When thinking about the creation of games, it is also helpful to keep in mind the taxonomy of the affective domain. This taxonomy can be used to frame any emotional or attitudinal elements you want to elicit from learners. The affective domain categories, definitions, and associated verbs are shown in Table 3.3.

As indicated in Chapter 2, games can change behavior and even attitudes. If your instruction requires impacting a value, attitude, or belief, and you find yourself listing objectives using some of the verbs in Table 3.3, consider using a game to help change the attitude. A game is usually more effective for impacting attitudes, values, and beliefs than either gamification or a simulation.[6]

Psychomotor Domain

The psychomotor domain involves physical activity as well as cognitive activity, with the emphasis on physical activity. While Bloom's Taxonomy did not detail specifically the psychomotor domain, several researchers have since developed a taxonomy for the psychomotor domain. Table 3.4 is based on an adaptation from Elizabeth Simpson's work in the area.[7]

Table 3.4 does not identify game elements appropriate for the psychomotor domain because this domain is typically best served through the application of a simulation.

There are exceptions. When a computer mouse was first introduced on a large scale within organizations, computer manufacturers would ship the computers with a game of Solitaire or Minesweeper. The goal was to provide learners with practice using a mouse to click, double-click, and drag and drop items from one location to another, the same skills required when using a mouse for business applications.

Another exception is on the gamification side for a product called T-Haler, which is an inhaler with built-in sensors that provide game-like feedback on whether or not the person is properly using the inhaler. This is an example of using game elements and gamification to help someone learn a psychomotor skill.

Table 3.3 Affective Domain and Associated Definitions

Category	Definition	Associated Verbs	Sample Game Activities
Internalizing Values	Behavior is integrated consistently into a person's behavioral pattern. The value is recognized as part of a person's character.	Authenticate, Advocate, Characterize, Defend, Display	Strategizing, Helping
Organizing	Determination that a new value or behavior is important or a priority.	Adapt, Adjust, Alter, Change, Modify	Role Playing, Helping
Valuing	Willing to express a positive attitude toward a value or behavior	Accept, Adapt, Choose, Differentiate, Defend	Role Playing, Helping
Responding	Willing to participate at a basic level. Exhibits a reaction or change as a result learning the attitude, value or behavior but may not be permanent.	Behave, Comply, Cooperate, Discuss	Matching, Collecting, Helping
Receiving	Awareness, willingness to pay attention and notice a value or behavior. Will give attention but remains passive concerning a value or behavior.	Attend, Awareness, Observe, Recognize, Receive	Exploring, Helping

Table 3.4 Psychomotor Domain and Associated Definitions

Category	Definition	Associated Verb
Origination	Learner now creates his or her own physical activity and movement to accomplish a specific goal.	Arranges, Builds, Originates, Designs, Creates
Adaptation	Learner can now adapt the physical activity to meet exceptions to standard practice, make modification to adjust to different situations.	Adaptation, Adjustment, Recognize, Adjust
Complex Overt Response	Final step of learning a physical activity. Learner is proficient in the entire activity and performs without hesitation, thinking consciously about the steps or doubt about ability to perform the physical activity.	Effortlessly, Without Hesitation
Mechanism	Intermediate steps of learning a physical activity. This includes the activity becoming habitual and movements can be performed with basic proficiency to some standard. Some physical movements become subconscious and require less overt thinking. Less hesitation and doubt.	Imitation, Reenact, Copy
Guided Response	Early stages of learning a physical activity. Includes trial and error as well as imitation. Conscious thinking about every physical movement. A great deal of hesitation and doubt.	Attempt, Practice, Targeted Practice
Set	Readiness to perform the physical activity. A person's disposition toward doing the physical activity. This is sometimes called a mindset.	Volunteer, Express Interest, Recognition
Perception	The ability to use sensory cues to guide physical activity.	Identify, Observe, Select, Watch

Type of Knowledge

In addition to Bloom's Taxonomy, another method of looking at the elements of games or simulations or even adding gamified elements is to look at broad types of knowledge and match those broad categories with instructional strategies, game activities, and elements. Table 3.5 provides information matching the type of knowledge you are teaching with the activities, types of games, and/or simulations that are appropriate. This, along with using Boom's Taxonomy, can help you to think about the types of game or simulation you want from a learning perspective.

Teaching Games Versus Testing Games

There is an important difference between games that teach a learner how to do something and games that test what a learner already knows. Too often those two types of games are confused and an instructional designer places the wrong type of game into the curriculum.

Testing games are games to use when the learner needs to know the information to be successful. The focus of the game is not to apply knowledge but rather to recall knowledge. Good examples of testing games are Trivia games (where the person who knows the most usually wins) or games like Jeopardy!, matching games, games where the person is answering a multiple-choice question and something happens as a result. These can also be games where a person identifies items or parts of a piece of equipment. Players must know the parts before they identify the items.

If you want to use a testing game to teach, the key is to add repetition. Through getting an answer wrong, learning the right answer through feedback, and then repeating the process until all the answers are right, a learner can eventually learn through a "testing" format. It should be noted that the less previous knowledge the learner has, the longer it will take for her to learn all the information in this format.

Teaching games impart knowledge through a series of activities within the game that teaches the learner what he or she needs to do. For example,

Table 3.5 Matching Content to Game Type

Type of Knowledge	Definition	Instructional Strategies	Elements	Activities/Types of Game/ Simulations
Declarative Knowledge	An association between two or more objects. These are typically facts, jargon, and acronyms. Content that must be memorized.	Elaboration, Organizing, Association, Repetition	Stories/Narrative, Sorting, Matching, Replayability	Matching, Collecting
Conceptual Knowledge	A grouping of similar or related ideas, events, or objects that have a common attribute or a set of common attributes.	Metaphoric devices, Examples and non-examples, Attribute classification	Matching and sorting, Experiencing the concept	Matching games
Rules-Based Knowledge	A statement that expresses the relationships between concepts. Rules provide parameters dictating a preferred behavior with predictable results.	Provide examples, Role Play	Experience consequences	Board games, Simulated work tasks

Procedural Knowledge	A series of steps that must be followed in a particular order to reach a specific outcome. Step-by-step instructions for performing a task.	Start with the big picture, Teach "how" and "why"	Software challenges, Practice	Software scenarios, Equipment simulations
Soft Skills	Non-sequential guidelines for dealing with social interactions. This includes negation skills, leadership skills, and selling skills.	Analogies, Role playing	Social Simulator	Leadership simulation
Affective Knowledge	Knowledge about attitudes, interest, values, beliefs, and emotions.	Encourage participation, Believing success is possible, Celebrity endorsement	Immersion, Providing success, Encouragement from celebrity-type figures	Helping games
Psychomotor Domain	The intersection of physical skills and the cognitive knowledge.	Observe, Practice	Demonstration, Haptic Devices	Virtual Surgery, Simulator

in a game designed to teach negotiation skills, a player might first be given advice on how to negotiate and then given a small negotiation task. During the negotiation, the player could watch the reactions of the non-player character in the game to determine whether the negotiation is going well or not and then adjust input to make the non-player character happier with the negotiation.

A teaching game helps the players to adjust behavior or attitude based on the input they are receiving from the game environment and players in the game.

When creating a learning game, its important to match in-game activities with the skills you want to teach. The chart below illustrates an attempt to match gameplay, learning objectives, and assessment to determine the best combination.

Task to Be Learned/Objective	In-Game Activities/Game Play	Assessment
Three steps of qualifying a sales prospect.	Learner engages with four non-player characters from four different trading posts in a branching scenario format. Selecting questions to ask and items for follow-up in each discussion. Questions relate to the three steps of qualifying a prospect. At the end, the learner must go back to the proper trading post to make a sale.	Learner selects the proper trading post with which to trade the first attempt and within a minimal time frame.

It is not that one type of game (testing or teaching) is right and the other type is wrong; rather, it is a matter of when each game is appropriate. A designer must make a conscious choice as to which to use. It is important not to make a decision by default or through lack of understanding. Think about what type of game is needed and then work to include that game.

Fantasy in Games

There are several valid and research-based reasons for including fantasy as a key element in games to help people learn. In the 1980s Thomas Malone wanted to investigate why games are so much fun and motivational.[8] He conducted a study that looked at a number of games and dissected, as researchers do, the elements of fun. Through this process he developed a model for looking at motivation in games and came up with an idea of what made those games fun to play or "motivating." He identified three elements that make games intrinsically motivating: Challenge, Curiosity, and Fantasy. There are both cognitive and emotional reasons for evoking fantasy.

Cognitive

Cognitively, a fantasy can help learners apply old knowledge to understand new things. The learners can take what they know about a subject like negotiation and apply their skills in a new setting within a game to see how those skills work in different contexts. This allows for the safe testing of a skill and reinforcement of that skill. In most adult learning situations, we are not designing a game to teach something completely new; instead, we are typically trying to improve skills or have the learners apply skills at a higher level. So fantasy helps.

If the learners are applying the same cognitive schema within a fantasy-based game that they would within the actual work setting, the skills they are learning or reinforcing are transferred. The important thing is to create a fantasy setting in which the same cognitive schema and tasks are required in the game as are required in the actual work environment.

Again, when using fantasy in game design, it is not only the skills themselves that are important but also the underlying cognitive schemas the learners create that allow them to apply and adapt those skills. Focus the fantasy on helping the learners create the right schema.

Another cognitive advantage of fantasy is provoking vivid images related to the material being learned to improve memory of the material. This is related to the concept of "episodic memory," when a person is able to remember certain times and places because they have particular meaning, such as a major sports event, a reunion with lost relatives, or even a particularly compelling instructional event. Episodic memories are stored in such a way that each memory is identified by a personal "tag." Typically, such memories are recalled through association with a particular time or place and tend to be vivid as they are recalled. A fantasy-based game can help to evoke these types of memories.

Fantasy tends to evoke curiosity. If a game simply mimics the elements of real-life, on-the-job situations, a learner might know what is going to happen (at the end "a sale is made or lost"), but with fantasy, the element of unknown or surprise can evoke curiosity. Fantasy-based game environments can evoke a learner's curiosity by providing an optimal level of informational complexity and a novel and exciting game space.

Emotional

Emotionally, a fantasy-based game can allow players to connect with the learning experiences and not bring with it "real-world" concerns or fears. This means that they don't think to themselves "this is negotiation training with clients and I've never done well negotiating with clients." Instead, they consider the fantasy environment and work within that environment, and the instructions can help them transfer those skills to the real world.

Caution About Fantasy

One note of caution, however, is that you don't need to add fantasy to everything and at some point you need to allow the learners to rehearse the desired behavior in a real or realistic setting. Think of the fantasy learning game as one point on the continuum to total application of the learned skills, attitude, behavior, or knowledge.

Gamification

Closely related to games is the concept of gamification. Gamification can be thought of as using pieces of games to motivate learners. Here is an official definition:

> Gamification is using game-based mechanics, aesthetics, and game-thinking to engage people, motivate action, promote learning, and solve problems.[9]

Types of Gamification

Digging a little deeper into the concept of gamification, there are actually two types of gamification. The first type is structural gamification and the second is content gamification. It is important to note that the two types are not mutually exclusive; both can exist in the same course. In fact, taken together, they are most impactful.

Structural Gamification

Structural gamification is the application of game elements to propel a learner through content with no alteration or changes to the content. The content does not become game-like, but the structure around the content does. The primary focus for this type of gamification is to motivate learners to go through the content and to engage them in the process of learning through rewards.

An example would be a learner gaining points within a course for watching a video or completing an assignment when the assignment or video had no game elements associated with it other than the fact that the learner received points.

The most common elements in this type of gamification are points, badges, achievements, and levels. This type also typically has a leaderboard and methods of tracking learning progress as well as a social component where learners can share accomplishments with other learners and brag about what they have achieved. Although it is possible to add elements of story, characters, and other game elements to structural gamification, the content does not change to become game-like.

Content Gamification

Content gamification is the application of game elements and game thinking to alter content to make it more game-like. For example, adding story elements to a compliance course or starting a course with a challenge instead of a list of objectives are both methods of content gamification.

Adding these elements makes the content more game-like but doesn't turn the content into a game. It simply provides context or activities that are used within games and adds them to the content being taught.

How Gamification Is Different from a Game

A game is a self-contained unit. There is a defined "game-space" in which the players agree to engage in game activities. There is a clear beginning, middle, and end to a game. There is a defined winning state. The players know when they or someone else has completed the game. A game typically has multiple game elements. Games contain challenges, a mechanism for multiple attempts, some type of reward system, a clear goal that players work to achieve, and an ultimate end.

In gamification, while elements of games such as points, badges, freedom to fail, and challenge are used, the intent is not to create a self-contained unit—not to create a game. The intent is to use elements from games to encourage the learners to engage with the content and to progress toward a goal.

In gamification, it is possible to use just one element to engage a person, such as a badge. A person logs into a computer application ten times and receives a badge. Receiving a badge is an element of a game but in this case isn't related to other game activities such as moving to a new level, solving a puzzle, or matching two or more items. Another way to look at it is through word association.

Gamification is to Game as:

- Part is to Whole
- Piece is to Puzzle
- Slice is to Pie
- Steering Wheel is to Car

Gamification uses parts of games but is not a game.

When to Use Gamification

Gamification can be used to accomplish a number of goals related to learning. As with any learning intervention, gamification is not the answer to every learning situation and to gamify all content or learner experiences does not make sense. Gamification is especially effective when it is used to encourage learners to progress through content, motivate action, influence behavior, and drive innovation.

- *Encourage Learners:* Challenges, goals, and making progress are all traits that engage and encourage humans. Game elements can be added at the structural level of gamification through points and badges. This is adding a game layer on top of existing curriculum. Gamification can also be done at the content level, such as when a compliance online training module is turned into a "who-done-it" to find where the compliance violation took place.

- *Motivate Action:* The old saying "you get what you reward" holds true for structural gamification. If you want to motivate learners to move through instruction and to accomplish goals, gamification is a great solution. Chapter 2 provided the example of the Deloitte Leadership Academy, where one person was so motivated by the gamification that a twelve-month course of study was completed in six months.

- *Influence Behavior:* Game elements, when properly placed into a curriculum, or everyday employee activities can positively influence behavior. In Chapter 2, the description of people being nicer in the physical world because they were flying around as superheroes in the virtual worlds is a good example of how content gamification can influence behavior. Structural gamification works in a similar manner to influence learner behavior. The Deloitte example showed that when structural gamification was added, it increased learner retention across the leadership program.

- *Drive Innovation:* Gamification can drive innovative thinking and activities. One example is the game FoldIt![10] This game was developed to allow non-scientists to work on the incredibly difficult task of folding proteins into 3-D structures. Points are awarded for packing protein and other moves within the protein structure. Playing this game, the players are actually predicting protein sequences and players have designed new vaccines from the new and unique ways they've folded protein. Some organizations have created a gamified bug tracking system to provide points and rewards for reporting bugs within beta releases of software.

- *Skill Building:* If you want to learn how to use the Ruby on Rails, an open source web application framework for the Ruby programming language, you could sit down with a manual and plow through pages of text or you could program a website for zombie meet-ups. Rails for Zombies is a gamified approach to teaching someone how to gain the skills of using Ruby on Rails.[11] It builds programming skills as a person earns points and badges and completes a story about creating a product for zombies. Skills are built one level at a time as the learner discovers how to correctly write syntax.

- *Knowledge Acquisition:* The Knowledge Guru in Chapter 15 is an example of the gamification of knowledge. The Knowledge Guru provides an opportunity for the learners to obtain knowledge about cell phone service by engaging them to compete to climb the mountain to provide a scroll to the guru. The gamification elements include points, story, and levels and give learners a chance to practice through repetition.

Simulations

Simulations come in many shapes and sizes. While there are countless ways to define a simulation, here's the definition we'll be using for this book:

> Simulation is a realistic, controlled-risk environment where learners can practice behaviors and experience the impacts of decisions.

Let's break that down:

- *Realistic:* Simulations simulate reality. Some element of realism, even if it is not completely realistic, is a key component of simulation.

- *Controlled Risk:* The risk of flying an airplane without knowing what you're doing is very high. The risk of flying a flight simulator is comparatively very low!

- *Practice Behaviors:* A key element of simulation is the ability to practice and apply what you have learned elsewhere.

- *Experience the Impacts of Decisions:* What happens when I do it right? What happens when I do it wrong? What does "good" look like? These are all things we learn from simulations

While different types of simulations differ in their mechanics, the basic approach is the same. Effective simulation is always grounded in real-life *metrics*, or measures of performance. The metrics used in a simulation must match the same measures of performance that are used in real life. Metrics ultimately drive simulation design; participants have to see how new behaviors will drive success and improvement on the key items on which they are measured. If a behavior cannot be linked to a business metric, it raises a question as to why that behavior is important.

The links between behaviors and metrics are usually not direct; a behavior by itself may not change a metric. Usually, there are intervening variables, or *drivers*. The basic formula follows:

Inputs (individual decisions)→ Drivers (intervening variables)→ Metrics (measurable outcomes)

So an individual makes a decision; that decision impacts one or more drivers; and the change in the drivers in turn impacts the metrics.

For example, deciding to implement a new safety process in a manufacturing plant (input) would influence the overall safety profile of the plant (driver) and lead to cost savings on the P&L (metric).

Using this methodology, it is possible to build simulations that illustrate the links between individual behavior change and overall organizational success. In the simulation, individuals would receive reports on:

- Their own decision making
- How their decisions impacted key drivers
- How those drivers impacted key organizational metrics

Types of Simulations

There are many different types of simulations and I could fill this chapter and many more describing all of the possibilities. For the sake of parsimony, here are some high-level examples:

- *Branching Storyline:* This is one of the most common simulation types used for learning, and the type we will focus most of our discussion on. A branching storyline simulation tells a story through the use of text, graphics, video, or animation. The best simulations make the learner an active character in the story, not a passive observer. At various points in the simulation, the learner encounters a decision point. The learner makes a decision, and the simulation "branches"; that is, the rest of the story changes based on that decision. The learner could replay the simulation multiple times, having very different experiences, by making different decisions and experiencing different branches.

- *Systems Dynamics Simulation:* Systems dynamics simulations model how complex systems operate over time by using complex mathematical formulas to define how the system works. In simulating a business, for example, there would likely be hundreds or thousands of equations that define things such as how revenue is generated, how costs are incurred, or how product is brought to market. Even more important is defining the formulas for how those things interact. How will reducing price affect your revenue? Your market share? Your stock price? Each decision you make is passed through the formulas to create a "What if?" scenario that shows how the entire system responds when you change parts of it. When applied to modeling scientific systems, these are often called *process simulations*.

- *Equipment/Software Simulation:* An equipment/software simulation creates a representation of a mechanical or software system. Perhaps the most familiar type is the flight simulator. An equipment simulation, it accurately represents the operations of an airplane. In the software realm, often software simulations are used to teach a new software system such as a new enterprise resource planning (ERP) system. The demand for accuracy on equipment/software simulations is very high, as the simulations must operate exactly as the equipment or software does.

How a Simulation Is Different from a Game

Simulations have many similarities to games. They can be competitive and they often have scores of one kind or another. Both have an element of competition and achievement of goals (whether it is competition against another player, against the system itself, or just a competition with oneself to achieve).

Simulations and games have storytelling in common, although each may approach storytelling in a different way. Simulations are designed to be realistic representations of real-world environments and processes. While simulations do not have to be 100 percent accurate, they should be accurate enough to be recognizable. Games, on the other hand, may or may not reflect the reality of the situation; in fact, games are often quite fanciful. So the storytelling aspect of simulation probably has tighter boundaries.

Both simulations and games require a rethink of "traditional" instructional design methodology. For example, a good simulation design process is inherently a consulting engagement. Subject-matter experts tend to think of content as globs of knowledge, rather than as observable behavior. Traditional ID would let you chunk out the globs of knowledge into PowerPoint or an e-learning course. Behavior must be observable if you are to simulate it, so getting this information often requires different methods than the traditional ID method of "a binder dumped on you." Simulation designers have to determine what an organization needs to do in order to drive its success metrics—work the organization often hasn't done before the simulation designer arrives.

When to Use a Simulation

Simulations are wonderful tools, but they are not the answer to all learning challenges. Simulations are most effective as *application* of learning, rather than as primary learning. Ideally, a learner will acquire knowledge in another form of learning and have the ability to apply that knowledge and practice in a simulation. Simulations are great for taking knowledge that we comprehend in our heads (cognitive) and turning it into actions that we can actually execute (behavioral). Simulations help learners bridge the learn-do gap, turning knowledge into action.

Simulations work best with content that is

- *Behavioral:* Simulations are about doing. In order to design a simulation, you will have to be able to express all of your content behaviorally. What does your learner need to *do*?

- *Observable:* It's impossible to simulate something you cannot see, so simulation content is to be observable. What would we see someone doing if he were doing the job right? It's easy to tell a salesperson that he would be more successful if he were consultative, but what are the behaviors that comprise "consultative"? What would we see the person doing?

- *Has defined consequences and outcomes:* In a simulation, you need to be able to show the outcomes of actions. Therefore, these must be known and defined. This is actually one of the most difficult aspects of designing simulations, since often even subject-matter experts don't really know how things are likely to turn out.

- *Process- or System-Driven:* Simulation content doesn't have to be process- or system-driven, but process and system content make for great simulations. When you change one aspect of a system, it has potential ramifications for every other part of that system, and simulation is a very effective way of demonstrating that.

Applying Simulations to Learning Challenges

Simulations apply well to learning challenges that are process-oriented and behavioral in nature. As a result, there are scores of potential applications. Here are four categories of learning challenges that simulation is particularly well-suited to:

- *Future State:* In change scenarios, we often need to prepare learners to function in a world that doesn't exist yet. We often need to prepare people for emergency scenarios, corporate mergers, or new product lines before these events actually occur. Simulation can be used to create a "future state," so learners can work in a world that doesn't quite exist yet and be fully prepared when the change is put into place.

- *Leadership:* There are scores of great leadership books, and everyone has read at least one. The books are often inspiring and easy to understand. So why are there so few great leaders? Leadership concepts are relatively easy to understand, but incredibly difficult to implement. New leaders are often unprepared for the emotional complexity of their new roles, the inevitable conflicts of interest, and unexpected pushback from their teams. Simulation allows leaders to practice in a realistic environment so they can become more comfortable with new behaviors and become familiar with some of the inevitable challenges.

- *Skill Building:* Skill building is perhaps the most obvious application of simulation. Simulations provide a safe environment to apply and practice new skills and see what can go wrong (and what can go right).

- *Capstone:* New skills are often taught in a segmented way, as if that skill is the only thing we will do all day. In real life, challenges come flying at us and we need to use judgment to determine when to use these skills. Simulation works effectively as a capstone experience for a skill-based curriculum, allowing participants to synthesize everything they've learned into an application-based exercise.

Selecting the Right ILE

Selecting the right interactive learning event can be challenging. To help make that job a little easier, Table 3.6 matches the type of learning that might need to be accomplished with the appropriate ILE. Keep in mind that no matching scheme is perfect and you may want to creatively use another ILE to meet your specific needs.

Table 3.6 Matching the Learning Outcomes with the Right ILE

If you want to . . .	Then select a . . .
Build lead leadership skills	Simulation
Realistically prepare learners for a future state	Simulation
Provide a realistic capstone experience for learners at the end of a curriculum	Simulation
Test the learners' performance of specific procedures in a realistic format	Simulation
Train learners in the performance of specific procedures in a realistic format	Simulation
Provide a safe and realistic environment for learners to practice skills and to make mistakes	Simulation
Teach a learner psychomotor skills	Game, Simulation
Impact a learner's attitudes, beliefs, or values	Game (Fantasy, Strategizing, Helping, Role Playing, Matching, Exploring)
Test learners' knowledge of facts, concepts, and terms	Game (Testing, Matching, Puzzle Solving, Exploring)
Teach learners how to put elements together to form coherent or functional whole or reorganize elements into a new pattern or sequence	Build their own game, Game (Building)
Teach learners how to break material into constituent parts, determining how the parts relate to one another and to an overall structure or purpose through differentiating, organizing, and attributing	Game (Allocating)
Teach learners how to carry out or use a procedure through executing or implementing	Game (Role Playing), Simulation
Teach learners how to construct meaning from oral, written, and graphic messages through interpreting, exemplifying, classifying, summarizing, inferring, comparing, and explaining	Game (Puzzle Solving, Exploring)

Teach learners how to retrieve, recognize, and recall relevant knowledge from long-term memory	Game (Matching, Collecting)
Make judgments based on criteria and standards through checking and critiquing	Game (Strategy)
Avoid preconceived notions about a future state while preparing learners for that future state	Game (Fantasy)
Teach learners to generalize knowledge they already have to new situations	Game (Fantasy)
Motivate learners to move through a curriculum	Structural Gamification
Motivate learners through engaging content	Content Gamification
Encourage learners to return to a curriculum on a regular basis	Structural Gamification
Influence learner behavior within a course	Structural Gamification Game (Fantasy)
Drive learners to innovate	Content/Structural Gamification
Encourage learners to independently build skills or acquire knowledge	Content/Structural Gamification
Teach learners new content	Content Gamification

Key Takeaways

The key takeaways from this chapter include:

- Match in-game activities with the proper level on Bloom's Taxonomy for learning cognitive, affective, and psychomotor skills.

- It is the game activities that lead to learning, so choose the activities wisely to reflect the desired learning outcome.

- Use the fantasy elements of games when you don't want the learners to have preconceived notions about the application of the content and you want them to generalize their knowledge across content areas.

- Consciously make decisions related to games for teaching versus games for testing. Both can be of value, but do not confuse the two. Trivia games or question-and-answer games are typically designed for testing learning and not for teaching concepts.

- Gamification elements are appropriate when you want to propel learners through content and ensure they are engaged with the content that is being provided.

- Simulations are appropriate when a high level of fidelity is required to ensure the learner knows exactly what to do and how to do it given an unusual or unlikely situation.

- To build skills, either a simulation or gamification can be effective.

- Simulations can be an excellent way to provide a capstone experience for learners:

  - The future state of a process or approach

  - Building leadership skills

  - Building skills

  - Capstone experience

- Use a simulation when you want realistic and authentic practice of skills and application of knowledge.

4

Critical Questions for Creating an Interactive Learning Event

CHAPTER QUESTIONS

- What knowledge or information is needed before designing or developing an interactive learning event?

- What considerations must be weighed before developing an Interactive learning event?

- What questions should we ask as we begin to develop an interactive learning event such as a game, gamification, or simulation?

Introduction

Creating an interactive learning event requires asking and answering certain questions before actual development or programming begins. In the creation and development process, there are several types of questions you must ask before starting. These include:

- Foundational questions
- Practical questions
- Scoring and assessment questions
- Gameplay questions

A careful review of these types of questions helps ensure the project is successful. The mistake too many make is rushing headlong into the creation process of an interactive learning event and forgetting to consider critical elements like assessment and implementation. Answering these questions will help to ensure the design of the interactive learning event meets learning and business needs. It may not be possible to answer all the questions in one session and may take meeting with many people to ensure all the correct answers and information are obtained. Often, flowcharting a process helps to answer many of the questions as you explore the different possibilities for solutions, as shown in Figure 4.1.

Figure 4.1 Flowcharting Can Help Answer Some of the Questions a Team Might Have
Image reprinted with permission of the artist, Kristin Bittner.

Foundational Questions

Some questions should be asked for any type of training development, not just for games, gamification, or simulations, but it is more critical for these types of activities because they can be expensive and even controversial in their implementation. The best way to ensure that the interactive learning event is meeting its goals is to answer the following questions.

What Is the Real Problem?

The first question to ask is

- (Corporate) What is the business problem prompting the need for the ILE?

- (Academic) What is the educational need prompting the desire for the ILE?

This foundational question gets to the core of the reason to develop an interactive learning event. If you are not solving a tangible, visible problem, the likelihood of success or even completion of the ILE is diminished. Carefully discuss with the stakeholders, team members, and anyone else involved the need driving the desire for an interactive learning event. Needs can following various areas including:

- Lack of sales

- Lack of customer service

- Quality issues

- Time problems (processes taking too long, not enough time to complete customer orders, etc.)

- Safety issues

- Lack of performance

- Learners not understanding content

- Inability to apply knowledge after learning

- Need to connect emotionally with learners

Finding out the one or two needs underpinning the desire for more engagement makes the design, development, and deployment of the ILE easier, quicker, and more impactful. If you are in academia, you still want to consider these questions, but frame them from an educational perspective. You want to ask about what is driving the introduction of an ILE into the learning process. Consider the various reasons, such as:

- Deeper engagement of students

- Application of theory

- Increase motivation

- Better tracking of understanding

At this point, in academia or business, you should also consider two more questions:

- Is this actually a learning need?

- Is there an alternative solution that might be more cost-effective, efficient, or impactful?

This is the time to ask the tough questions and weigh the possibility that some other solution may solve the problem. First, if the problem is not learning based but, rather, due to a poor incentive program, badly designed business processes, poor teaching, vaguely articulated business objectives, or a poorly executed business policy, no ILE will make it better, no game will magically turn around the situation, and no gamification effort will lead students to the right level of understanding. So part of the process of identifying the business problem is to ensure that the problem can be solved by a learning intervention. If it can't be, then try an alternative solution.

Second, there might be a cheaper, faster, or easier solution than building an ILE. Consider this solution or solutions. It is better to consider the alternatives and carefully weigh the alternatives yourself, rather than have another person challenge your design with a "solution" or alternative you had not considered.

What Are the Learners Not Doing?

The next question to ask is: *What are the learners not doing now that they should be doing in terms of the identified problem?*

Now that the problem has been identified, the next question centers on what is lacking in the performance or knowledge of the learners. The answers to this question identify the major actions or activities expected from the ILE by identifying what is not being done currently by the learners. This is the gap between the desired behavior and the current behavior of the learners.

What Is the Desired Outcome?

The next question is: *What is the desired outcome of the ILE? What do you want the learner to be able to do or to know after interacting with the ILE?*

It is important to know what the desired outcome of the learning event before you begin to develop it. Gain agreement from the stakeholders on what the learners should be able to do once the ILE is complete. This should provide a laser-like focus for the design and development process; measure every decision against the desired outcome. Does this decision lead toward the desired outcome? Does the leaderboard support the desired outcome? Does the gameplay support what we want the players to be doing after they return to class or work?

What Is Needed to Achieve Success?

At this point, once you have defined the outcome of the ILE, the question to ask is: *What does the learner/player need to know to achieve the outcome of the ILE? What are the instructional objectives of the ILE?*

If the player could already achieve the desired outcome quickly and easily, an ILE would not be necessary. Therefore, focus on what needs to be done to help the player achieve the outcome you want. This should include what information has to be learned, what skills enable the final outcome, and what behaviors should be exhibited to create the outcome. This is a breakdown of the enabling objectives that support the final outcome or terminal objective of the ILE. This process can be done in the form of a mind map, a hierarchical flowchart, an affinity exercise with sticky notes on the wall, or some other form of diagramming process that identifies the relationships among the final objective/outcome and the enabling objectives relating to the necessary skills, knowledge, and behaviors.

What Are the Tasks of the ILE?

Next find out what the player does in the ILE: *What are the tasks that must be demonstrated to achieve the outcome?*

In an ILE, it is not enough to define the knowledge, skills, and behaviors that need to be exhibited by the learners; you must also define the tasks they need to perform to achieve the outcome, the outward signs they have mastered the knowledge or the tasks they will do on the way to mastering the knowledge. What actions are they going to be taking in the ILE that demonstrate they have learned the required information, skills, and behaviors? During the ILE do the learners need to do things like:

- Answer questions
- Apply content
- Drag items to the correct place
- Explore an area
- Identify information
- Apply values

Choose the actions and activities that define what the learner does. The tasks are the outward indication that learning is occurring.

A related question is: *What types of behaviors or actions will illustrate that the learners have learned?*

This is the end result. What do the learners do to indicate they have learned the content of the ILE, that they have achieved the desired learning outcome? Defining the end result drives design decisions and informs the creation of the ILE you are developing.

Table 4.1 Matching the Need to the Learning Outcome and Providing Evidence of the Result

Need	Skills/Knowledge/Attitude	
Gap	What needs to be learned to overcome the gap?	What evidence will indicate gap is overcome?
	Reduce time on calls with customers	Product knowledge
	Features of the new smart phone	Correctly identify and describe the features of the new smart phone

Summary of Foundational Questions

It's not enough to answer these question in isolation. The real benefit in answering the foundational questions is seeing the links among the various answers. Identifying the business need and linking it to the skills to be learned and evidence of learning establishes a clear relationship between the actions in the ILE, the business needs, the learning requirements, and the overall outcome. Use Table 4.1 as a guide for creating your own foundational questions before beginning the process of developing an ILE.

Practical Questions

The first set of questions dealt with the issue of what needs to be taught and the type of outcomes that can be expected from the ILE. These are highly strategic issues governing the overall design and development purely from a learning and business standpoint. The answers to these questions provide a vision of where you'd like to take the ILE.

The next set of questions is much more tactical. They deal with the basic issues of the audience, how they will engage with the ILE, and what technology is needed. Of course, the answers to these questions are as important as the answers to the strategic questions in the overall creation of a successful ILE.

Who Are the Learners?

The first question here defines the learners: *What is the skill level of learners/players?*

The goal is to obtain a clear picture of the types of individuals who will be interacting both with the ILE and with each other. The types of information you are seeking include:

- Technical knowledge

- Familiarity with games/simulations/gamification

- Reading level

- Knowledge level of subject matter

- Length of time in organization

Creating a learner profile or "persona" helps define the interactions within the ILE.

What Are the Logistics?

It is important to know the outcome of the ILE, the audience, and how the ILE is to be played and rolled out to an organization. To determine this type of information, ask logistics-related questions such as:

- When will the ILE be played?

- How often will the ILE be played?

- On what type of device will the ILE be played?

- What amount of time is available to play the ILE?

- When will the ILE be played?

- Where will the ILE be played?

These and similar questions help the organization think through logical issues and identify potential problems early in the process so that those problems can be overcome or mitigated during the implementation of the ILE.

What Are the Technical Issues?

Closely related to the logistical questions are technical questions, such as:

- What are the technical aspects of the ILE environment?
  - How will the ILE be delivered (HTML 5, Flash, on a mobile device, laptop)?
  - What information needs to go to the learning management system?
  - What type of artwork is required? Can it be 2-D or do you need 3-D or just simple badges?
  - Is a password needed?
  - How often can learners access the ILE?
  - What do we do if there is a technical problem? Who do we call? What hours is help available?
  - Is the ILE only played with Internet connectivity? Can it be downloaded and then the scores uploaded later?
  - Do we need to consider SCORM or Experience API?

Building an ILE to function within a specific technological infrastructure is key to making it work. Even the greatest ILE won't be of any use if a learner cannot access it. Involve the information technology folks in the ILE efforts early to understand the requirements, restrictions, and parameters under which you can develop.

Summary of Practical Questions

Once you have answered the practical questions, place your answers into a table to see all of the answers in a single location. This provides a quick look at the needs of the organization in terms of taking care of the learners and the technological needs for the ILE. Table 4.2 shows an example of a completed summary.

Scoring and Assessment Questions

These questions provide information to inform the development of scoring and assessment of the ILE. Ensuring that assessment and scoring are correct

Table 4.2 Identifying the Learners

Who are the learners?	What are their characteristics?	When are they going to learn?	On what devices are they going to learn?	What technology is needed?
Pharmaceutical sales representatives	Approximately 10 percent play games on a regular basis. Busy, motivated.	Between sales calls, while waiting to meet with physicians.	iPads just issued to the field three months ago.	Need WiFi connection, ability to upload content overnight.

is essential for focusing the learners and moving them toward the desired learning outcomes.

What Should the Measurement Criteria Be?

Determining how to measure the activities and actions within the ILE provides the framework for how the ILE will unfold for the learners. Make sure the measurement criteria are linked back to the outcomes of the ILE.

- What are the most important measurement criteria?
  - Time
  - Accuracy
  - Correctness
  - Knowledge of all the elements

It is worth noting that the ILE may have several measurement criteria. It might include a time requirement as well as an accuracy requirement. Typically, more than one is needed; otherwise, the learners may just focus on one element of the ILE and miss the learning opportunity because they are too myopic. Having multiple measurement criteria helps to broaden the focus of the learners because they can't just "game" the system.

What Drives the ILE?

The next question is: *Will the game be driven by points, levels, badges, or some other method?*

This question focuses on what drives the learner through the experience. Are they attempting to earn points, move to the next level, or correctly answer questions. The movement through the game does not need to be entirely driven by points or badges; it could be driven by solving a mystery or a puzzle. However, in most ILEs when an action takes place that is desired by the designer of the ILE, learners are somehow rewarded. This question focuses on the elements that move a player through the ILE.

What Is the Rationale Behind Scoring?

The next question is not so much a question as it is a task: *Describe the point and scoring system and rationale behind the system.*

The concept here is to write out what happens in various scoring scenarios. This is necessary because the developers of the ILE have to consider different scenarios that could occur during the ILE. Just because a developer thinks "A learner would never do that" doesn't mean a learner won't do that. Learners are surprisingly creative and resourceful; if there is a chance learners will do something that negatively or positively impacts the score, at some time, some learner will do that very thing. The design and development team must consider the possibility and decide the risk and consequences of the undesired activity. The first step in that process is to understand how scoring works and why.

Does the Scoring Match Learner Outcomes?

The final question in this section relates to matching the activities with the learner outcomes: *Do the ILE activities match learner outcomes?*

As a final check on the assessment and scoring created for the ILE, match the concepts being taught with the ILE activities. This ensures alignment within the game.

Summary of Scoring and Assessment Questions

To help ensure alignment, compare the concepts to be taught in the ILE with the activities of the ILE, the assessment, and the scoring. There should be clear alignment among these elements, as shown in Table 4.3.

Table 4.3 An Example of a Completed Table

Concept to Be Taught	ILE Activity	Assessment of Learning	Measurement Criteria	Scoring
Negotiation skills related to obtaining the best price in the shortest time for a given product.		Learners will be assessed based on starting bid, subsequent bids, and amount of time to acquire object.		
Bartering and purchasing supplies (for example, in a space game, jetpacks might be rare but extremely helpful within the game and, therefore, expensive and hard to obtain, while oxygen tanks might be abundant and easy to obtain).	Learners will be required to purchase a jetpack and oxygen tank within "the right price range" based on the scarcity of the item.	Accuracy of bids; correctness of bids; amount of time taken to obtain object.	5 points for correct price first time. 1 point deduction for each wrong guess (up to five). 1 bonus point for each second remaining on 30-second timer	

Game Play Questions

This section is designed to answer the question: *"What are the learners doing during the interactive learning event?"* Answers to this question describe the activities of the interaction. Earlier questions were about outcomes and what learners need to do to demonstrate they have learned; these questions are different in that they are focused on what actually happens during the ILE.

What Are the Learners Doing?

This seems like an easy question to answer, but it must be addressed and clearly understood by all of the individuals involved in the design and development process.

Are they moving a character around the screen? Are they collecting coins for correctly answering a multiple-choice question? Is it successfully inserting the IV into the arm of a simulation dummy? What is the game dynamic? Sample dynamics include:

- Allocating resources
- Building
- Chasing/being chased
- Collecting
- Discriminating
- Dodging
- Exploring
- Matching
- Problem solving
- Racing
- Role playing
- Stealing
- Strategizing
- Other (some other activity within the game, or multiple activities)

The answer is basically a description of the game play or activities that earn points. In addition to answering this question, it is usually a good idea to create a "walkthrough," a step-by-step description of what happens during the ILE. This helps everyone get on the same page in terms of vision.

How Do You Win or Lose?

The next question is fundamental for all ILEs: *What is the winning state of the ILE?*

In all learning activities, there is an end. The learning has occurred or it has not, but the instruction is over. An ILE is the same. Identification of what is a "win" is important to design toward and for clarification of what the learner goes through. It is not always simple to determine what a winning state is. For example, in a gamified course, is the person on top of the leaderboard the most often the winner? or Is the person who is on top of the leaderboard at the end of a designated time period the winner? Is the leaderboard reset each week or do players accumulate points over time? In a simulation, is it over if the player makes wrong choices or decisions throughout the entire game and is it over only upon successful completion of the simulation? Also consider whether there is more than one way to win and what learning might occur with each method of winning.

A closely related question is: *How many chances does the learner receive?*

If a learner is unsuccessful, he or she may not have learned anything. Therefore, it is in the best interest of the learner to experience the ILE again. How does the designer build in replayability? One method is to offer different chances to experience the ILE. For example, the concept of a weekly leaderboard might encourage learners to try every week instead of realizing at the end of the second week that they'll never win. Having three chances in a simulation might encourage the learners to go back into the simulation to try something different. Learners will look to see how many chances they receive and, sometimes, judge strategy and approach by the number of chances they receive. When you test the ILE, you can experiment with the number of chances, but framing the question now will encourage dialogue.

Table 4.4 Summary of the "Winning" and "Losing" Conditions

What is the winning condition?	How many chances does the learner receive?	What is the losing condition?	Does learning occur if the learner loses?
Collecting all ten badges	The learners will have three months to collect the badges	Collecting fewer than three badges requires supervisor remediation	If a learner does not complete the necessary badges, the learning will be incomplete and he or she will be required to receive alternative instruction

Next, explore what happens when a learner loses: *What is the losing condition? Does learning occur if the learner loses?*

Just as important as knowing the winning state is knowing the losing state. Is anything learned if the learner is unsuccessful at the ILE? Can learning be woven into conditions that lead to losing or is winning the only way to learn? In a gamification example, how many points or badges indicate that learning has occurred?

Summary of Game Play Questions

Once you have answered the game play questions, place your answers into a table like the one in Table 4.4. This provides a quick look at the game play.

Key Takeaways

Answering the questions in this chapter provides a strong foundation for developing an interactive learning event. The questions help to focus your thinking and provide the foundation for success. Table 4.5 contains the questions. Use this table as a guideline for running a meeting to determine the creation process of your ILE.

Table 4.5 Critical Questions for ILE Design

ILE Critical Questions

Answering these questions will help you design an ILE to meet your learners' needs. Write your answers in the space below each question. This template will take multiple iterations to complete. These basic questions must be answered before the design process can begin.

Foundational Questions

What business or academic problem prompted the need for the ILE?
    Lack of sales
    Lack of customer service
    Quality issues
    Time problems
    Safety issues
    Lack of performance
    Learners not understanding content
    Inability to apply knowledge after learning
    Need to connect emotionally with learners
    Deeper engagement of students
    Application of theory
    Increase motivation
    Better tracking of understanding

Is this actually a learning need?

Is there an alternative solution that might be more cost-effective, efficient, or impactful?

What are the learners not doing now that they should be doing?

What is the desired outcome of the ILE? What do you want the learners to be able to do or to know?

What does the learner/player need to know to achieve the outcome of the ILE? What are the instructional objectives of the ILE?

What are the tasks that must be demonstrated to achieve the outcome?
    Answer questions
    Apply content
    Drag items to the correct place
    Explore an area
    Identify information
    Apply values

What types of behaviors or actions will illustrate that the learners have learned?

Summary of Foundational Questions and Answers

Need	Skills/knowledge/attitude	
Gap	What must be learned to overcome the gap?	What evidence will indicate the gap has been overcome?

Practical Questions

What is the skill level of learners/players?
    Technical knowledgeable
    Familiarity with games/simulations/gamification
    Reading level
    Knowledge of subject matter
    Length of time in organization

What are the logistics?

When will the ILE be played?

How often will they play the ILE?

On what type of device will the ILE be played?

What amount of time is available to play the ILE?

When will the ILE be played?

Where will the ILE be played?

What are the technical aspects of the ILE environment?

How will the ILE be delivered (HTML 5, Flash, on a mobile device, laptop)?

What information needs to go to the learning management system?

What type of artwork is required? Can it be 2-D or do you need 3-D or just simple badges?

Is a password needed?

How often can learners access the ILE?

What do you do if there is a technical problem? Who should be called? What hours is help available?

Is the ILE only played with Internet connectivity? Can it be downloaded and then the scores uploaded later?

Do we need to consider SCORM or Experience API?

Summary of Practical Questions and Answers

Who are the learners?	What are their characteristics?	Where are they going to learn?	On what devices are they going to learn?	What technology is needed for them to learn?

Scoring and Assessment Questions

What are the most important measurement criteria? (Check those that apply.)
  Time
  Accuracy
  Correctness
  Knowledge of all the elements

Will the game be driven by points, levels, badges, or some other method?

Describe the point and scoring system and rationale behind the system.

Do the ILE activities match learner outcomes?

Summary of Scoring and Assessment Questions

Concept to be taught	ILE activity	Assessment of learning	Measurement criteria	Scoring

Gameplay Questions

What are the learners doing during the ILE? (Check those that apply.)
  Allocating resources
  Building
  Chasing/being chased
  Collecting
  Discriminating
  Dodging
  Exploring
  Matching
  Problem solving
  Racing
  Role playing
  Stealing
  Strategizing

What is the winning state of the ILE?
How many chances does the learner receive?

What is the losing condition? Does learning occur if the learner loses?

Summary of Scoring and Assessment Questions

What is the winning condition?	How many chances does the learner receive?	What is the losing condition?	Does learning occur if the learner loses?

Basic Elements

5

Foundational Elements

CHAPTER QUESTIONS

- What are the foundational elements of ILEs?
- How does feedback impact learning in ILEs?
- What constructs should I consider when creating an ILE?
- What should I consider when creating a story challenge for the ILE?

Introduction

In this chapter we will be discussing the elements that are the building blocks of simulations, games, and gamification.

A simulation is an interactive representation of an event, system, or action. If you add elements like feedback, constructs, artificial challenge, and exaggerated story to a simulation, at some point it becomes a game. The same "elements" you add to a simulation to make it a game can also be added to non-simulation environments to "gamify" them. The equation below describes this interaction:

$$\textbf{Simulation + Gamification = Game}$$

Feedback

We give feedback to players to create a feedback loop. In a feedback loop the system gives players information about their performance or the game state, and with this information the players can change their behavior. When creating feedback, we must account for the timing, tone, and delivery method.

Timing of Feedback

Whether you give your players immediate or delayed feedback depends on how you want them to use the information and the type of information you are giving. For actions taken by the player, like pushing a button or jumping, it is best practice to give them feedback immediately, unless you are simulating an action where that information would not be readily available. Immediate feedback is also important when players are receiving information about a changing game state that they must rapidly respond to. Examples of this could be a crackling sound of a fire or a player's health meter dropping to show he is being harmed.

For feedback that is based on the player's performance there are a few additional considerations. Sometimes immediate feedback, such as a "Good job!" message from the system, can encourage players. Other times delayed performance feedback, like an overview at the end of a round or level, is best. Consider how quickly you want players to respond to feedback, if the feedback would be distracting, and if you want the players to gauge their own performance. It is good to take into account the players' level of experience. Inexperienced players will benefit from immediate feedback more because they are unsure of their own performance and the state of the game environment. For more experienced players, it is beneficial to withhold feedback for a while so the players can evaluate their own performance and, ideally, change their tactics based on that evaluation.

Questions to ask when considering timing:

- Is the player new or experienced?
- Do you want the player to change behavior immediately or in the future?
- Do you want the player to self-correct?
- Do you want the player to see the consequences of a wrong move?
- Will immediate feedback be helpful or distracting?

Tone of Feedback

When developing your feedback system you have to account for positive, negative, and neutral tones. Most games and simulations have a combination of all three types of feedback tones.

Positive feedback tells the players they are doing well and to maintain their current strategy. Ideally this type of feedback should tell the player what they are doing well and why.

Examples of positive feedback include a note streak in a music game like "100 note streak!" or a kill streak in a first-person shooter like "Ultra Kill!"

Negative feedback tells the players that they are not doing well and must change their current strategy to be more successful. Ideally, you want to tell players what they are doing wrong and what they can change to be more successful.

Examples of negative feedback include the buzzer noise in the game Operation when you touch the side with your tweezers.

Neutral feedback does not address the players' performance. Instead, neutral feedback addresses their current situation or status and gives them information about their particular circumstance.

Examples of neutral feedback include tool tips when players roll over a button they have never seen or the tips that occur on loading screens between levels like: "This level is full of monsters made of fire; water spells will be effective against them."

The feedback tone you give players must be weighed against some kind of metric. The metric can be based on their performance, their performance relative to others, or an arbitrary measurement.

Questions to ask yourself when you begin to make your feedback system include:

- What constitutes a good or bad performance?

- How will you measure the players' performance?

- What information will players need to know how they are doing?

- What can the players do in response to a review of their performance?

- What situational information should you provide to players so they can understand the system better?

Designer Notes

- Playtesting to see how players utilize your feedback is important. It is difficult to anticipate some of the more complex interactions until you actually see someone doing it. The sooner the better.
- Feedback is critical to learning, so make sure it is targeted and provides a learning opportunity.
- Feedback is usually a time when you have the learners' undivided attention.

Feedback Delivery

Four delivery methods can be used to give the players feedback: visual, auditory, tactile, and movement. All four methods have the same purpose, to convey information. Using multiple delivery methods for different types of feedback can add realism to an experience, as well as spread information across multiple senses to avoid overwhelming players. Make sure your feedback delivery methods are consistent throughout the experience. Ideally, the feedback should also match standards already set by other popular game and simulation experiences. If every other game on the market places its mini map in the upper right-hand corner, you should consider doing the same unless there is a good reason not to.

A word of caution on using additional feedback in simulations meant to accurately reflect something in real life. Players can become dependent on a piece of feedback that will not be there when they attempt the real-life action. This could hurt their performance and would defeat the purpose of simulating an event.

Designer Notes

- What is too much information? Always playtest and remember that as a player advances in skill level, he will be able to handle more information.
- Consider different levels of feedback so that you are not just giving feedback on one dimension.

Visual Delivery Methods

The most used method for information delivery in games and simulations is visual elements. A subset of visual methods is the user interface, or UI, the on-screen menu(s) and graphics that overlay a game or simulation. Similar to a heads-up display, the players use the UI to gather information about the state of the game and to interact with the environment.

Score is one of the most fundamental feedback mechanisms on the user interface. Quantifying performance and giving players numbers that represent how they are doing is pretty straightforward and similar to how grading is done in schools. Always explain the scoring to the player.

Designer Notes

- Can you go beyond an arbitrary number score? Can performance be represented in a more meaningful way, such as a smile on a face in a simulation or counting the number of lives saved.
- Scores could also be related to time accuracy and other elements.
- Progress bars can be used for experience gain or player health.

Visual and Sound Effects

Visual effects can be things like explosions, pulses of light, or fireworks that are in the game environment behind the UI. These effects tell the players about the state of something that is happening in the world. They should be easily recognizable and easily distinguished from other types of feedback.

The *setting* that a simulation or game takes place in is also a visual effect that can be a type of feedback. If players step into a new place that looks dark and foreboding, their behavior will be different than if they are in a field of flowers. The setting can be used to reflect player performance and the current state of the game.

The second most used method for delivering information to players is sounds. Sound effects are caused by action. The action can be from the player, the system, or another source. Sound effects require acknowledgment or an immediate response from the player. Examples of sound effects relating to player performance are a ding or buzz for a correct or incorrect decision. An example of a sound that requires a response from the player is a hissing noise to ready the player for an impending explosion or so they are prompted to check to see if a tire is leaking

Ambient noises do not require immediate action from the player. They are secondary sounds that can reveal information about the setting or mood. An example of this could be crickets chirping or birds singing in a forest or the sound of a generator humming. If they stop suddenly, the player should question why.

Many games have music that helps to set the mood of a level. Music can also clue the player in to an event change. For example, if the music changes suddenly, in many games it means there is going to be a boss fight. Another example is music speeding up as the player needs to move faster to accomplish a task.

Designer Note

- Always allow users to mute extraneous sounds like music and ambient noises that are not essential to the feedback system.

Touch

Tactile stimulation is used in come controllers, particularly the controllers of consoles like the Xbox 360 and PlayStation 3. The vibrating controller often lets the player know he or she is being damaged or is used to accompany visuals like an earthquake or an explosion. In some arcade games and military simulations, compressed air is used to make guns and flight sticks react in a natural way by pushing back against the player.

Movement

The final and least used method for delivering information to players is moving the players in the real world to reflect actions. Flight simulators and some arcade games do this to enhance the experience. Driving on a bumpy road or turning in a jet will cause hydraulics in the platform to move the player in a manner that matches the simulated environment.

Designer Notes

- Rewards are an extension of feedback. However, a reward, unlike feedback, can be kept by players as a reminder or proof of their accomplishment.
- Don't make the rewards the reason they are playing, and for learning games don't make them more important than the knowledge being gained. Make the reward representative of the learning and the challenge that the player faced.
- Remember that in multiplayer games rewards can be used as credentials.

Constructs

A construct is a fabricated addition to a simulation that does not exist in the real world. Constructs are used to make the players' experience more interesting, give them better information, or enhance training effectiveness by accentuating certain aspects of an interaction. Constructs can also be used to limit or empower the players. Game mechanics such as the ability to slow or reverse time is an example of a construct. Things like points and levels are also a type of construct.

When creating a construct it is important that it have some kind of purpose. Never add things to a serious game or simulation because you think they are cool. Everything that you create will be competing for the players' limited attention. The challenge with educational games is to create constructs that are fun but also serve some value to the learning experience.

Constructs can take many forms. In this section we will discuss the use of game mechanics, allegory, laws, and rules.

Game Mechanics

The term "game mechanic" refers to a rule or set of rules that enable or restrict player action by creating a cause-and-effect relationship. Players know that when they perform an action or a certain game state occurs an expected consequence will ensue. Often when creating a game or simulation you will not come up with novel mechanics. You will instead repurpose, recombine, or modify them from other games that already exist. There are many different types of mechanics and the only way to be exposed to them is playing lots of games.

Examples of game mechanics and a justification for their use in a serious game or simulation include:

- *Stealth game mechanic*—Giving the players the ability to avoid being seen. This is typically accompanied by a penalty if they are seen. This type of mechanic can allow players in educational games or simulations to observe situations that they may not normally have access to. It is also a good way to see things from another person's perspective.

This type of mechanic was used successfully by RETRO Lab at the University of Central Florida in a game called Devil's Advocate—a game that dealt with post-traumatic stress disorder (PTSD) by using cognitive behavioral therapy techniques.

- *Time-slowing mechanic*—This type of mechanic allows the players to change the speed at which time passes to give them more time to react or outmaneuver enemies. This could be used to give players a closer look at the intricate details of a technique. By mastering something in slow-mo first, the transition to normal speeds might be smoother.

- *Resurrecting at a save point*—When players die in a game, they are allowed to restart at a place where they do not lose all of their progress. This allows players to experiment without fear of permanent consequences. An alternative to this is a game mode that is popular in RPGs called "Hardcore," which makes the player's character disappear after death.

Always explain the scoring methods to player so they can self-evaluate when the scoring is not available in real life.

- *Levels and experience*—These are built into many games as an indicator of progress and strength. Players often set goals around these values. These levels can be matched up with learning objectives to align players' game progression with knowledge.

- *Attributes like dexterity or motivation*—These are used in games to indicate what qualities the player exemplifies. They can be used in educational games to imply what qualities are most desired for a particular task.

Allegory

An allegory can be used when an analogous representation of an event or experience is more effective than the actual event in terms of training. Sometimes an allegory can be easier to apply an interesting story to or, in the case of therapeutic games, easier for the players to deal with issues indirectly. This is particularly effective when a process can be re-created using simple game mechanics.

Examples: Teaching how a lysosome cleans a cell by creating a game with mechanics similar to Pac-Man. In this game the players must respond to signals from within the cell and steer a lysosome around to eat garbage in a cell.

Do not become too abstract with your metaphors. Keep it simple and keep the mechanics as true to whatever you are representing as possible.

Laws and Rules

Laws and rules inside a game or simulation give players a framework to work within. Laws and rules are not the same thing. A *law* is something like gravity that is fundamental to the game or simulation world. A *rule* is something like speeding that we hold the player accountable to. Another example can be taken from a game children play where the floor is lava and you must navigate a room and not touch the floor. "Don't jump on the lava" is the rule that kids use in a game. How far they can jump is dictated by the laws of physics. You can break or bend a rule and the game can punish or reward you for that. Laws cannot be broken.

When creating the laws and rules in your game, think about how you want to limit the players. Are the laws you create similar to the real world or unrealistic? Are the rules guiding the player in a meaningful way? For example, the rule in the game Operation is not to touch the sides. That rule could be justified because when performing real surgery you wouldn't want to cut anywhere outside of the intended location.

Decide what is important to the learning experience and add rules based on that. Some questions to ask include:

- Is speed important? Add a timer.
- Is accuracy important? Add a metric for precision.
- Is it important to complete everything? Add a metric tracking progress.
- Is it important to instill a feeling of growth in the players? Add leveling and experience points.

Challenge

Challenge is a good thing in games, gamification, and simulations. Design challenge to scale with player experience to keep them engaged and motivated. Keeping players teetering on the fine line between boredom and stress is what makes players fall into a flow state.

We create challenge by doing several things:

- Having increasingly more difficult objectives (learning and game) and goals for players

- Chunking information in consumable clusters and distributing them evenly

- Sequencing information so it is relevant to players

- Scaffolding in assistance to players as they need it and taking it away at appropriate times so they can become more self-sufficient

- Shifting the rules to alter the players' current strategy and take them out of their comfort zones

In order to effectively accomplish the techniques listed above, it is essential that playtesting and tuning take place. It is impossible to predict how players will respond to your efforts to challenge them. If you go too far, they will be overwhelmed, and if you do not do enough, they will lose interest.

When playtesting you must observe players and assess their performance, stress level, enjoyment, and motivation.

Story

Using a story to complement a game, gamification, or simulation is a very common practice that has many benefits to players. One benefit is that it creates a setting similar to where the players would use skills or knowledge they acquire. The term used to describe learning in a setting similar to where the knowledge would be used is "situated learning." Having a story also helps players create a mental model of an entire process and in some cases stay motivated because they want to know what happens next. For more information on the importance of story, refer to Chapter 6 of this book.

Exaggerated Story

Exaggerated story is used in games to put the players in a situation when the typical experience will not keep them engaged or training for an extreme event will prepare them for all other possibilities. Events in the story can be used to give the players goals that might be outside of a normal operating environment for a task or to give new meaning to mundane duties. This almost always includes the element of "fantasy," which was discussed in Chapter 3.

Some examples include (1) aliens attacking earth so you must learn how to optimize performance in a factory using process improvement tools; (2) a day when everything goes unrealistically wrong; and (3) take whatever you are trying to teach and add the phrase "In spaaaaace" after it.

Designer Note

• When asking a subject-matter expert (SME) for a story to use for a simulated event, gamification, or game level, ask the person to create a story that he or she would tell to impress someone on a first date.

Key Takeaways

The key takeaways from this chapter are

- Simulation + Gamification = Game
- Carefully consider the tone, timing, and delivery of feedback.
- Game mechanics play a critical role in helping to move the learners through content.
- Consider the use of allegory to help the learners understand concepts and ideas.
- Laws and rules are important to how an ILE functions.
- Consider exaggerating a story to help the learners understand what you want them to learn.
- Have increasingly more difficult objectives (learning and game) and goals for players.

- Chunk information in consumable clusters and distribute them evenly.

- Sequence information so it is relevant to players.

- Scaffold in assistance to players as they need it and take it away at appropriate times so they can become self-sufficient.

- Shift the rules to alter the players' current strategy and take them out of their comfort zones.

6

The Importance of Narrative/ Context/Story

CHAPTER QUESTIONS

- What are the elements of storytelling?
- How can storytelling impact learning in ILE?
- What is the best way to architect a story for learning?
- What are the elements of storytelling?

Introduction

Here's the good news: you already know more than you think about storytelling. Every time you watch a movie or immerse yourself in a great novel, you're observing the structure of a story well told.

Virtually all learning design has an element of storytelling to it. So, too, does virtually all gaming and simulation design. Perhaps the only difference is that in game and simulation design, storytelling is moved to the forefront. But gamification is not left out either; applying story elements to both content gamification and structural gamification will help the learners progress through the content and provide the context for learning.

In this chapter, we'll look at the following aspects of storytelling:

- *Overview:* We'll look at why storytelling is an important part of many learning experiences.

- *Elements of Storytelling:* Some storytelling basics that remain true whether you're writing a novel or creating an ILE.

- *How Storytelling Is Different in ILEs:* Of course, games and simulations are not novels and have their own unique attributes. Even gamification has a sort of journey associated with it.

- *The Goal-Based Scenario:* Stories for learning need to have a purpose—what am I trying to accomplish—and why.

- *The Role of Reality:* Learning stories don't need to be just like real life, but leave out certain key details and you'll lose your learners fast.

- *The Predictable Unexpected:* One of the best ways to engage someone in a story is to offer a few twists and turns.

- *Architecting Your Story:* A tool for designing your story that incorporates everything in this chapter.

Overview of Storytelling

Storytelling is one of the most effective yet underused methods for enhancing adult learning. Have you ever heard someone yell at characters on a movie screen or talk back to the television? Ever stay up way too late one night because you had to read just one more chapter of a bestseller? Ever rearrange your schedule to make sure you're home for the conclusion of the cliffhanger episode of your favorite TV series?

Odds are good that you answered "yes" to at least one of these questions, and very possibly to all of them. It's not surprising. For many cultures, storytelling is one of the most pervasive methods of sharing information. A good story speaks to our minds, our hearts, and our deepest emotions. When we're truly wrapped up in a great story, we sometimes do things that are irrational; we speak to characters we know are fictional, we give up sleep that we desperately need; we laugh or cry or rejoice or despair over the lives of people we know are completely made up, completely fabricated. We're human beings; we are able to connect on many levels.

Learning can be irrationally emotional as well.

Every day, we can feel fear, anger, joy, despair, and elation. But for some reason, when we create learning interactions our approach too often becomes dry and bloodless. We engage the mind (if we're lucky), but not the heart. As a result, we reduce the likelihood that we will gain learner attention, that our message will be heard, let alone retained and applied.

Novels, movies, and TV may be more appropriate metaphors for adult learning than classrooms are. The key factor is immersion, an experience that takes you out of the here and now and fully involves you in another environment. When people care about how the story turns out, they will start making decisions based on their internal assumptions; they will be distracted from the textbook "right" way and start making decisions emotionally, as they do in real life. This creates an opportunity for not just learning, but real behavior change—by allowing them to examine what drives their behavior in the first place.

How do you apply some of the rules of storytelling to learning? The key is to focus on how the world works in real life. For example, there's a lot of good leadership content out there, and most of it is not hard to understand. So why is there such a shortage of good leaders? Because when someone actually tries to apply these ideas, he meets challenges, encounters resistance, and has to change the way processes and systems work. Although people may agree that this is the "right stuff," they don't do it because the risk and effort of doing it "right" outweigh the potential consequences of doing it "wrong."

Your story needs to address that. The same constraints and pressures that make your content difficult to implement in the real world need to exist in your learning solution. Otherwise, your learners will recognize it as a work of fiction, separate and divorced from the real world. No one can consider how to overcome the barriers to success until he comprehends what the barriers to success actually look like.

Elements of Storytelling

While storytelling is more art than science, here are a few points to keep in mind:

1. *Engage the heart as well as the mind.* Learning is emotional, so don't be afraid to get under people's skin. People should feel elated when they succeed, uncomfortable when they fail.

2. *Focus on what makes the new behavior challenging.* Is it the complexity of the product line? The demands of your boss? The intimidation factor of talking to people more experienced than yourself? Don't shy away from the tough stuff.

3. *Show, don't tell.* This is one of the oldest writer's rules. Instead of writing "he was nervous," show your character's behavior and let your learner conclude that he's nervous.

4. *Remember that there's more to storytelling than writing.* While a novelist employs narrative as her primary tool, ILE designers have many more tools available. Reading is best delivered in small doses. Tell your story with video, audio, graphics, and animation.

5. *Don't feel you have to cover everything in the story; not every aspect of learning works well with storytelling.* Learning stories work best when they are focused on those parts of the learning that are complex or difficult. In designing a sales simulation for a large pharmaceutical company, we determined that reps did well at explaining product benefits, but had opportunities for improvement in opening and closing sales calls. We designed a simulation that incorporated the entire call, but focused decisions specifically on openings and closings.

6. *Good stories demonstrate actions and consequences.* Your learners will be more engaged if you create a sense of anticipation, a driving desire to know what happens next. Watch the way an audience leans forward in their seats during an exciting movie, and determine what will make your learners lean forward in anticipation.

7. *Don't lose sight of the basics.* Good stories have a beginning, middle, and end. They chart a logical progression of conflict, resolution, and conclusion. That's part of what makes the process of reading a book or watching a movie so satisfying—the feeling that you've shared a journey with the characters. Make sure your story develops throughout your game or simulation and reaches a satisfying conclusion (or potentially several satisfying conclusions!) at the end.

How Is Storytelling Different in ILEs?

Novelists, playwrights, and screenwriters have it easy. They have complete control over their worlds. They can fully form the story in their heads and play it out exactly the way they want to.

Game designers have partners: the players. In order for a game to work well, the designer has to cede some control to the player. The more control the player feels he has, the more satisfying the game experience. But that creates a challenge for the designer; since the player determines how the story turns out, the designer does not have complete control. And that means the designer has to envision multiple possible outcomes. You cannot just take words on a page and coax them into a coherent story, as seems to happen in Figure 6.1.

In simulation design, we often talk about "the illusion of complexity." In a well-designed simulation, players often perceive that there is a greater degree of complexity than there really is. For example, in a branching storyline simulation, you may give your players four choices on how to proceed. If it was true branching, each of those four choices would have four choices, and so on. You can see how the geometric progression would quickly lead to

Figure 6.1 Converting a Written Story into an ILE Is Not as Easy as It Would Seem

Image reprinted with permission of the artist, Kristin Bittner.

thousands of possible outcomes. Realistically, we would design that scenario with a certain number of dead ends and causal loops to limit the number of events. However, that is often not visible to the player, who feels anything could happen.

In simplest terms, when designing a story for a game, you have to envision multiple outcomes and determine what you will allow the players to control and what you, the designer, will control.

Storytelling can't be left out of gamification either. In gamification, the concept, talked about by Amy Jo Kim and others, is the "player's journey." It is the idea that as a person experiences gamification, he or she progresses from being a passive observer to becoming a novice to a regular and then to a leader and then an elder. A player's journey equals lifecycle plus progression. This sense of progression and moving from Point A to Point B is well encapsulated in a story.[1] It provides the contents in which gamification can occur.

The Goal-Based Scenario

So what's the goal of this story?

Okay, there's a question you don't often hear when discussing novels or plays. What's the goal? Well, the goal is to reach the last page of the book or the curtain call at the end of the play. But when you're writing stories for learning, the goal is different. Not only are you telling a great story, but you're supposed to be helping your learner improve his or her performance.

Great learning stories include goal-based scenarios. In simplest terms, the story includes a goal or a set of goals that need to be achieved; the point of going through the story is to achieve the goal. That sounds simple enough, but here's the key: the nature of the goal impacts the way you perceive the story. Confused? Let's break it down.

- First and foremost, the goal of learning is not just to make you smarter; the goal is to help you build the ability to do something. A goal-based scenario begins to answer the eternal question of performance improvement: What am I going to be able to do as a result of this effort? Why is it important that I'm able to do this?

- In life, almost everything we do has a goal. Why should learning be any different? Ask yourself: What kinds of problems can I solve with this knowledge?

- Ultimately, storytelling for learning works best when it presents real-life conflicts. It can be pretty easy to regurgitate the "right" way to handle a problem, but can you really do it under pressure? You need to re-create that pressure for the learning to have emotional impact—and goal-based scenarios do that. Rather than applying learning in a vacuum, you're attempting to solve a real business problem—and actually having to apply what you've learned.

How can you create a goal-based scenario? You need to understand the subtleties of the job and challenges your learners face in achieving success. For example, if I'm learning selling skills, my ultimate goal is probably to close a sale. But what are the subtleties of effectively closing? Is my customer more likely to buy if I take one path over another? Will I sell more if I'm able to meet my customer's boss, who has more buying authority? Will I sell more long-term if I'm able to build a good relationship? Am I afraid to talk too much for fear my customer will realize I don't know as much as I claim?

The Role of Reality

Is there such a thing as too much reality?

The great thing about writing novels or screenplays is that you can make everything up. You're not bound by the reality of what's possible. But in a learning story, there must be some grounding in reality, however tenuous. In my simulation work, we often get hung up on reality. Does the simulation environment need to be a carbon copy of the real world? Arguably, the answer is no. One of the reasons we don't always learn effectively is because our environments are full of distracters; your learning story can focus people on what's important. But aren't those distracters part of the learning experience? If you give me a nice clean environment to learn in, won't I just have difficulty applying it in real life?

So how real do you need to be? The answer is, "It depends," and not in a philosophical way. The real question: "What are the variables that need to be considered to tell the story effectively?"

The most important word here is *relevance*. How relevant is the story to the learning goals? Some very effective learning games take you out of the here and now and put you into fantasy worlds. However, they work because they establish relevance to the actual behavior that is being learned. I once experienced a fantastic live-action role-play game where I and my team members acted as the crew of a spaceship. The tasks we engaged in included plotting courses, acquiring supplies and resources, negotiating with aliens, and reacting to unexpected emergencies. What we were learning was leadership, delegation, team building, and crisis management. The story of the game made it intriguing and fun; the relevance of the game made it easy to debrief and generalize the game play to the real challenges we had every day.

The most recognizable kind of simulation is probably the flight simulator. The failure to fly a plane properly will likely lead to mechanical failure, damage, and death. There are so many factors that can lead to failure (gauges, mechanics, alertness, weather, etc.) that flight simulators must be completely realistic. The adherence to reality in a flight simulator is remarkable.

But in many environments, we want learners to focus on specific items, where, in fact, presenting the whole reality of the job might actually be confusing. So it's generally okay to leave stuff out or consolidate things. How do you that? Well, there are no hard-and-fast rules, but here are some guidelines:

- Make sure the things you leave out won't distract the learner.

For example, if the learners work on a team where all of the members are in different cities, they might be distracted by a story that involves a scenario where everybody is co-located; however, they might be fine with a story in which some team members are co-located and some are distributed.

I worked on a customer service simulation design with a company that made many different types of paper and packaging products. The client was very concerned that no one scenario (food packaging, office paper, print stock, etc.) would resonate with every member of the audience. Ultimately, we made the decision that the company in the simulation made bottles instead of paper. This way, the manufacturing and customer service environment was very recognizable to learners, but they weren't distracted by the fact that the company didn't make their exact paper product.

- Make sure you leave in the things that makes the job challenging.

If we go all the way back to the beginning of this series, we established that one of the powers of storytelling in learning is that you can focus on those areas that make a job challenging. Is it a demanding boss? An industry that's consolidating? Technology that changes rapidly? Clients who don't know what they want? The power of storytelling is incorporating these elements in a way that affects people emotionally.

- Focus on the element of time.

For example, some businesses are seasonal; in retail, fall is all about planning for the holiday season, summer is all about planning for back to school. If you leave this out, your story won't have resonance. Also true is the impact of time; some decisions look different if you play them out over time. Make sure your learners can see the short-term and long-term impact.

The Predictable Unexpected

Stories are compelling when you think you know what's going to happen next and then the story throws in a twist. You can do the same thing in your learning stories; the only issue is that you need some grounding in reality.

Movies frequently build interest by inserting compelling story twists. I won't include any spoilers, but most people will admit to being thrown for a loop when they learned the truth about Bruce Willis' character in *The Sixth Sense* or who Keyser Soze really was in *The Usual Suspects*. But the technique is nothing new; Alfred Hitchcock shocked the movie-going world in 1960 when he killed off the main character in *Psycho* ten minutes into the film.

One of the oddest twists is in the film *Magnolia*; the story takes a twist when it unexpectedly starts raining frogs. And perhaps that's the key difference between movie storytelling and learning storytelling. If your story completely deviates from reality, you'll probably lose your audience. So your story probably shouldn't have any froggy precipitation.

For learning stories, use the "predictable unexpected." That means create events that are unexpected in the context of your story, but typical in the real world. For example, in a sales simulation I designed, you spend a long time building a relationship with a client in hope that he will introduce you to an executive. If you successfully build the relationship, the client agrees to invite you to a meeting with the executive. When you try to return his call, you receive a message that his phone line has been disconnected. He's been fired, so he's not going to get you that meeting with the executive, and you have to begin the process over again. The event was unexpected, but completely realistic within the scope of the storyline—and still completely gut-wrenching.

Architecting Your Story

How will you tell your story? Storytelling can be more art than science, but here's a simple tool that will allow you to create a story outline that will put you on the right path. It contains the following elements.

Performance Objectives

Unlike other types of learning, games, gamification, and simulations usually put the learner in an active role. The point of the game is to do something. That means that we will typically focus on performance objectives rather than learning objectives. It's not about what the player will learn; it's about what the player will do.

1. *The Situation:* Describe the situation of your story in two or three sentences. Keep it brief, as this is really just to set your direction.

2. *Characters:* Who needs to be involved in this situation? Keep the number as small as possible to keep control over your story. Sprawling epics with dozens of characters are great for five-hundred-page novels, but quickly confuse your learner in a learning game or simulation.

3. *Goals:* What are these characters trying to achieve? Break it down into small chunks or "levels." Most games have an overarching goal (rescue the princess), but several sub-goals, or levels, to achieve as part of that goal (defeat a dragon, find a potion). What are the sub-goals of your story?

4. *Metrics:* How will we measure success? What will change that will demonstrate that the goals have or have not been achieved?

5. *Barriers and Conflicts:* Conflict is the essence of storytelling. If everybody immediately obtained what they wanted, stories would be pretty dull. What will disrupt these characters in achieving their goal?

6. *Control (of the Barriers and Conflicts):* Which can the characters control, and which can they only react to? Remember, in games, gamification, and simulations, the player is your partner in story-telling. The story will be much more compelling if it is about things the player can control.

7. *"In Order to" Chain:* Work your way backward from your goal and determine what must take place to achieve that goal. For example,

if you were creating a simulation around selling a big deal, your "in order to" chain might look like this:

- In order to close the sale, we must present to the CEO.

- In order to present to the CEO, we must get on his calendar.

- In order to get on his calendar, we must convince his assistant that our product is good.

And so on, until you feel you are back at the beginning.

8. *The Predictable Unexpected:* What are some events that could occur in the story that are predictable, but may be unexpected to the characters?

To facilitate the creation of your story, try laying it out in the template in Table 6.1. Completing this template provides you with a strategic plan for your story, something you will refer back to again and again during your project.

Key Takeaways

Table 6.1 Storytelling Template for Games, Gamification, and Simulations

Elements	Description for Your Story
Performance Objectives	What will a participant be able to as a result of completing this experience?
The Situation	Describe the situation in two or three sentences.
Characters	Who needs to be involved in this situation? Keep the number as small as possible to keep control over your story.
Goal	What are these characters trying to achieve? Break it down into small chunks, or "levels."
Metrics	What will change that will demonstrate that the goals have or have not been achieved?
Barriers and Conflicts	What will disrupt these characters in achieving their goal?
Control of the Barriers and Conflicts	Which can the characters control, and which can they only react to?
"In Order to" Chain	Establish the chain of causal events; in order to achieve X, your characters must achieve Y.
The Predictable Unexpected	What are some events that would occur in the story that are predictable, but may be unexpected to the players?

7

Making the Case

CHAPTER QUESTIONS

- How do you justify the cost of a game, gamification, or simulation?
- What is the best way to justify adding a game, gamification, or simulation to the curriculum?
- How can a learning and development professional encourage the adoption of a game, gamification, or simulation into an organization?

Introduction

The information, predictions, and advice about games, gamification, and simulations can be confusing. One year an organizations is touting gamification as the next new business trend and a year later the same business publication is touting gamification as a dismal failure. Some learning and development luminaries claim that "games don't teach," while others expound on the virtues of games for teaching everything from business acumen to financial literacy to how to unload a delivery truck.[1] It is hard for an industry professional to know the right course of action, let alone develop a case for why an organization should make the substantial investment in building a game, gamification, or simulation.

The truth of the matter is that the time to invest in an ILE is when the ILE meets a real business or learning need. If a business need is met, then gaining acceptance of the ILE is much easier. There are typically three approaches that can be used to sell an ILE within an organization.

- Research-based justification
- Performance improvement justification
- Stealth implementation

Research-Based Justification

One way that some organizations have implemented games and other ILEs has been through justification based on research. Often this is called "evidence-based" training. It is a great way to justify an ILE but it does have a number of problems. First, gathering evidence and making emphatic statements based on that evidence is difficult in the social sciences. In hard sciences, like biology, scientists can often show direct cause and effect. This virus causes this disease and this antibiotic kills this bacteria. But in social sciences it's harder to claim a direct cause-and-effect relationship. Did this learner master the content because she was playing a game or because she is trying to get promoted or because she just had to use the same method to sell a major account last month?

So it is important to keep in mind that evidence-based training can guide us in the right direction, but it is not the absolute path. Exceptions can and do occur. It is also critical to remember that the results of only one research study should not dictate practice. A careful practitioner needs to look at the preponderance of evidence, the majority of findings, and draw conclusions from multiple studies. In the field of research, the process of reviewing dozens of studies to draw a general conclusion is called a meta-analysis. Results from a meta-analysis can help inform practice since they are based on multiple studies.

Supporting Evidence: Games Teach!

Not all games teach. Unfortunately, the same can be said of every type of learning delivery method. Not all lectures teach, not all students who survive a bout of the Socratic Method learn, and not all classroom discussions end in an epiphany for the learners. A lecture can be a powerful tool delivered by a skilled professor. It can also be a snore-fest when delivered by someone who speaks in a monotone, goes off topic, and fails to engender excitement or enthusiasm for the subject. Is the methodology of lecture to be blamed?

No, the fact is that the design and delivery of the lecture is the problem or the benefit, not the delivery method. Not all instructional delivery methods are effective all the time for every learner.

Researchers have been studying games for learning for decades, as shown in Figure 7.1.

There is solid research and overwhelmingly compelling evidence that games can and do teach a variety of subjects effectively. In fact, there is a rapidly growing body of empirical evidence that supports that claim. A meta-analysis study appearing in *The Journal of Applied Educational Technology* found that video games and game-like environments are conducive to deductive reasoning and hypothesis testing.[2] Another meta-analysis appearing in the *British Journal of Surgery* concluded: "Blended and interactive learning by means of serious games may be applied to train both technical and non-technical skills relevant to the surgical field. Games developed or used for this purpose need validation before integration into surgical teaching curricula."[3]

In a paper titled "Does Game-Based Learning Work? Results from Three Recent Studies," Richard Blunt who, at that time, was with the Advanced Distributed Learning (ADL) group, reported on three causal-comparative exploratory studies.[4] ADL, founded in 1997, works with business and university groups to develop consensus around standards for training software as well as associated training services purchased by federal agencies.

Figure 7.1 Researcher Hard at Work Studying Games for Learning

Image reprinted with permission of the artist, Kristin Bittner.

Blunt reported on studies conducted to examine the difference in academic achievement among students who did and did not use video games for learning. Three different video games were added to approximately half the classes of freshmen Introduction to Business and Technology courses, third-year economics courses, and third-year management courses. Identical testing situations were used in all courses, while data collected included game use, test scores, gender, ethnicity, and age. ANOVA, chi-squared, and t-tests were used to test game use effectiveness.

The findings indicated that students in classes using the game scored significantly higher means than students in classes that did not. There were no significant differences between genders, yet both genders scored significantly higher with game play. There were no significant differences between ethnicities, yet all ethnic groups scored significantly higher with game play. Students forty years and under scored significantly higher with game play, while students forty-one and older did not. Blunt indicates that "these studies add definitive research in the area of game-based learning. The DoD now has studies proving the efficacy of digital game-based learning and how it can improve learning."

Wilson, Bedwell, Lazzaru, Salas, Burke, Estock, Orvis, and Conkey concluded: "The research in this area indicates that games do positively influence trainees in terms of cognitive, skill-base and affective outcomes."[5] Connolly, Boyle, MacArthur, Hainey, and Boyle conducted a meta-analysis by reviewing 129 papers reporting evidence related to the impacts and outcomes of computer games and serious games with respect to learning and engagement. The majority of the studies reviewed—121 (84 percent) of the included papers—reported quantitative data, with eight (6 percent) reporting qualitative data.[6] One strong conclusion they reached was that the most "frequently occurring outcomes and impacts were knowledge acquisition/content understanding and affective and motivational outcomes." Certainly, knowledge acquisition and content understanding are learning—learning from games.

These findings and others from over a hundred studies both qualitative and quantitative from different meta-analyses and individual studies support the argument that games teach and positively impact motivation. The evidence is clear and compelling.

Why We Need Games

One thing people forget is that part of the need for games in learning is that our current learning paradigm is ineffective. Even the most wonderfully designed non-game intervention is not going to be undertaken by a learner if she is not interested, if she is racing through multiple-choice questions to the quiz at the end, and if she have no hands-on practice. There is little "learning by doing" either in the classroom or online.

Predominately, corporate training (and academic classes) are delivered through lectures (online or face-to-face), which are not effective for conveying knowledge and never have been. Researchers have indicated that they could not track down a single study which found lecturing to be more effective than another method for the promotion of thought. Twenty-one studies found lecturing to be less effective than discussion, reading, individual works in class, and so on. The evidence on the weakness of lectures is devastating.[7] Bloom found that during lectures students' thoughts involved attempting to solve problems, synthesize, or inter-relate information for only 1 percent of the time, while 78 percent of the lecture was spent in "passive thoughts about the subject" and "irrelevant thoughts."[8]

In 1994, Isaacs observed that "lectures are not a very effective way of teaching in higher education—especially if the aim is to teach thinking, or to change attitudes or other higher aims beyond the simple transmission of factual knowledge."[9] Ironically, games can do all these things quite well.

When a learner is being taught sales skills in a classroom and he or she then tries to transfer those skills to an actual work situation, he or she may encounter difficulty transferring the learning. First, the classroom doesn't look like the environment in which the salesperson works; second, the client doesn't ask you to raise your hand to answer a question; third, the statements made by the prospect are typically not provided in the same order as the "model" presented in class; fourth, interruptions occur that distract the prospect; and fifth, role plays are not always taken seriously or portrayed realistically.

For these reasons, among others, Sitzmann found in her research across eight studies, self-efficacy (confidence) was 20 percent higher for trainees receiving instruction via a simulation/game than trainees in a comparison group.[10] In other words, simulation games build more confidence for on-the-job application of learned knowledge than classroom instruction. Why? Part of the answer is that a game environment actually has less cognitive overhead. The graphics can be more realistic and reflective of the actual work environment than the classroom environment, the person has to apply knowledge and not passively consume knowledge, and the learner can interact in a more realistic fashion with the prospect than he or she would in the classroom.

It's not that this couldn't happen in the classroom, but it's cumbersome to conduct a good role play and give all thirty people in the class a chance to participate, its time-consuming and expensive to decorate a classroom like a prospect's office. And an online game scales more easily than a classroom role play.

Gamification Justification

Admittedly, at this point in the growth of the concept of gamification, there are few academic articles that provide insights into the long-term effectiveness of either structural gamification or content gamification.

One article indicated: "Gamification in e-learning platforms seems to have potential to increase student motivation, but it's not trivial to achieve that effect, and a big effort is required in the design and implementation of the experience for it to be fully motivating for participants."[11]

In the absence of many single studies and the subsequent absence of meta-analysis studies, the best place to look for gamification justification is through case studies that provide insights into how companies have leveraged gamification successfully. The Deloitte case study in Chapter 2 and the case studies in Section V of this book provide solid evidence of success.

It can also be helpful to look at studies that examine individual elements of games and how those impact learning. There is clear evidence that avatars, learner challenges, narrative, chance, and other game elements can positively impact learning and motivation.[12]

Table 7.1 below shows some game elements and associated research that indicates it can be effective from a learning or motivational perspective.

Simulation Justification

Perhaps the easiest of the three ILEs to justify are simulations. A simulation of an actual work process or piece of equipment is straightforward. The high fidelity of the actual environment to the simulated environment tends to make the creation of simulations justifiable if cost of the actual equipment and the danger of failure are high.

For example, flight simulators are easy to justify because the alternative of an inexperienced pilot practicing flying a commercial flight with passengers on board is unthinkable. At least the first few practice runs (and one hopes more) will take place in a flight simulator, and then the nascent commercial pilot can move to an actual aircraft.

One group looking into the effectiveness of simulations for training is ADL. In 1997, the U.S. Department of Defense (DoD) developed a

Table 7.1 Game Elements and Research Supporting the Use of Those Elements for Learning

Game Element	Impact	Research Indicating Effectiveness
Gaming uncertainty (chance)	Learners preferred activities that included an element of chance.	Howard-Jones, P.A., & Demetriou, S. (2008, September 11). Uncertainty and engagement with learning games. *Instructional Science, 37*, 519–536.
Challenge	Motivational to the learner. Caution: Too much or too little challenge will decrease learner's perception of the training value.	Wilson, K.A., Bedwell, W.L., Lazzara, El. H., Salas, E., Burke, C.S., Estock, J.L., Orvis, K.L., & Conkey, C. (2009, April). Relationships between game attributes and learning outcomes. *Simulation & Gaming, 40*(1). 217–266. Serrano, E.L., & Anderson, J.E. (2004). The evaluation of food pyramid games, a bilingual computer nutrition education program for Latino youth. *Journal of Family and Consumer Sciences Education, 22*(1), 1–16.
Assuming a role as an avatar	Changes a person's real-life perspective.	Yee, N., & Bailenson, J.N. (2006). Walk a mile in digital shoes: The impact of embodied perspective-taking on the reduction of negative stereotyping in immersive virtual environments. *Proceedings of PRESENCE 2006: The 9th Annual International Workshop on Presence.* August 24–26, Cleveland, Ohio.

Learner watching an avatar that looks like the learner	Influences the learner to perform a similar or the same activity in the future.	Fox, J., & Bailenson, J.N. (2009). Virtual self-modeling: The effects of vicarious reinforcement and identification on exercise behaviors. *Media Psychology, 12,* 1–25.
Flying around as a superhero	Influences a learner to be "nicer" in the physical world.	Rosenberg, R.S., Baughman, S.L., & Bailenson, J.N. (2013) Virtual superheroes: Using superpowers in virtual reality to encourage prosocial behavior. *PLOS One, 8*(1), 1–9.
Narrative context	Motivates learner through content.	Dondlinger, M.J. (2007). Educational video game design: A review of the literature. *Journal of Applied Educational Technology, 4*(1), 21–31.
Goals at different levels.	Motivates learner through content.	Dondlinger, M.J. (2007). Educational video game design: A review of the literature. *Journal of Applied Educational Technology, 4*(1), 21–31.
Interactivity and multi-sensory cues	Gains attention and engages the learner.	Sitzmann, T. (2011). A meta-analytic examination of the instructional effectiveness of computer-based simulation games. *Personnel Psychology, 64*(2), 489–528.
Specific, immediate feedback	Positively related to learner motivation and attitudinal valuing.	Ronen, M., & Eliahu, M. (2000). Simulation a bridge between theory and reality: The case of electrical circuits. *Journal of Computer Assisted Living, 16,* 14–26.

department-wide strategy to harness the power of learning and information technologies to standardize and modernize education and training. The strategy was called the Advanced Distributed Learning (ADL) Initiative. Since that time, the ADL has been working with business and university groups to develop consensus around standards for training software as well as associated training services purchased by federal agencies. They strive to advance the state of the art in the science and technology associated with individual and collective education, training, performance support, and assessment.

As part of that mission, the ADL has examined the effectiveness of simulations, specifically in the area of transferring knowledge from the simulation to the actual work experience. In the ADL research report on the subject of transferring knowledge, it was found that simulations have the potential to reduce the number of training hours necessary to reach proficiency compared with other methods of training. Additionally, ADL found the following:

> "The ability of simulations to teach skills that transfer to real-life, on-the-job situations seems abundantly positive, from the existing body of literature. Computer-based simulations—assessed as an alternative to other means of training, as a supplement to other means of training, as a device to combat skill decay in experienced trainees, and as a means of improving performance levels as they stand prior to training—show positive results for transfer a majority of the time: in twenty-two out of twenty-six such studies, trainees demonstrated equal or superior transfer to the control group from simulations. The remaining studies yielded mixed results; in no study did a simulation produce wholly negative results."[13]

One important element discussed in the ADL report worth noting: it is not the "psychomotor skills potentially learned during training that foster transfer, but the cognitive templates of the experience of performing the job—the steps the mind goes through when performing a task, that are directly practiced, experienced, and applied when using a simulation, no matter what the fidelity."[14]

This is important for two reasons. First, when designing a simulation, the mental steps the learner goes through in the simulation need to be as close as possible to the actual steps the employee goes through on the job. The closer the steps and actions are to the real situation, the better the transfer. Second, the fidelity or realism of the physical objects re-created in the simulations are less critical than correctly mimicking the steps the mind goes through when performing the task.

The research on transferability and the tips to follow the cognitive templates are both good methods to use in justifying why a simulation would be a good tool for learning situations. The situations that are best suited for a simulation require a high degree of realism, have high costs of failure, and are unsafe in the physical world but require individuals to practice the steps and procedures.

Return on Investment Justification

Traditionally, e-learning is sold as a method of cost avoidance or cost savings. Clients are told that if they buy e-learning, they will save thousands or millions in travel expenses. While that is effective for showing cost savings of e-learning, it is not the most effective method of selling games, gamification, or simulations. For these interactive learning events, you want to show the value to the organization, the return on the monetary investment. You don't want to show savings as much as you want to show increased performance, reduced risk, or better quality service. Show how the investment in an ILE brings money to the bottom line.

The unfortunate thing with justification is a little like "Which comes first, the chicken or the egg?" You need to have built a game, gamification, or simulation to show that the investment was worth the price. One way to do this is to start with a smaller project, show the return from that project, and then extrapolate that those types of returns will be provided to the organization given a similar game, gamification, or simulation. You can also provide case studies (many in this book) that can show returns and positive organizational benefits.

As part of your proposal to implement a game, gamification, or simulation, include a performance justification. This provides two benefits. The first is that the organization will know that you are focused on organizational performance and that you are thinking like a businessperson. The second benefit is that you can position it as a test case and not give the impression that you want to add an ILE to every type of learning challenge within your organization.

Look for a performance area where the game, gamification, or simulation can have serious impact and where you can get good numbers related to the need for the ILE intervention. These items will help you make a strong case. The benefit of a case study to show performance-based justification is that clear, visible justification can be seen. Doing this justification for one area, if successful, will help you leverage games, gamification, and simulations into other areas of the organization.

Overview of the Eight Steps

Conducting a performance-based justification involves eight steps. These are general guidelines. Typically, modifications will need to be made to each step based on your unique situation.

1. Identify the need or current training course for which you want to create the game, gamification, or simulation. Gather data that is needed to choose the right topic, course, or need. This includes tying the game, gamification, or simulation to divisional and corporate goals.

2. Determine primary goals. This is where you explore the goals of the individual with whom you are working—the sponsor from the line of business with whom you are working.

3. Operationally define how you will measure the increased performance based on the game, gamification, or simulation.

4. Dollarize the metrics. Once you determine what will be measured, put a dollar value on those metrics.

5. Conduct a baseline assessment of performance. This may involve a pre-test/post-test arrangement or it may involve using a test group and a control group.

6. Implement and deliver the game, gamification, or simulation.

7. Gather post-learning data or data from the control and test groups.

8. Calculate the performance improvements, increased revenue, reduced risk, etc., at intervals of thirty, sixty, and ninety days.

1. Identify the Need

Identify the program for analysis. Gather data to choose the right program. To determine the most appropriate training program for creating a game, simulation, or gamification for cost/benefit justification, analyze the following criteria:

- Metrics appear to be readily available.
- The topic is one that has visibility and is "cared about" by the business unit.
- The traditional stand-up version of the class is conducted on a frequent basis (quarterly, yearly).
- Links with business unit and corporate goals exist.
- It has potential for a high impact.

To decide the most appropriate training program for analysis, develop a comparison grid like the one shown in Table 7.2. The grid gives you a quick glance at the primary criteria. In each cell, indicate whether the topic being considered meets that criterion.

Metrics

When identifying the course, topic, or need, gather a list of potential metrics and identify the level of accessibility to those metrics (that is, do the metrics exist in a current report, does a new report need to be created, is the metric only available through interviews and spot-checks of processes, etc.).

Ask the following types of questions:

1. What types of reports do you use to manage this subject or need? (Obtain copies.)
2. What type of metric do you already have in place?
3. What type of problems or issues have been encountered in the past related to the training and subsequent performance?
4. How do you know when current learning events are having an impact?

Table 7.2 Selection Criteria for Justifying a Game, Gamification, or Simulation

Selection Criteria	First Topic, Course, Need Considered	Second Topic, Course, Need Considered	Third Topic, Course, Need Considered
Metrics appear readily available			
Topic has high visibility			
Stand-up version is taught frequently			
Link with business unit and corporate goals			
Potential for high return to organization			
Material appropriate for a game, gamification, or simulation			

5. What does upper management "care about" when they examine this issue or topic?

6. What type of behavior would constitute success?

7. What employee actions would result in success? What management actions?

8. What analytics would show whether the game, gamification, or simulation is successful?

9. Are there baseline analytics that suggest the need for the project?

Visibility

A highly visible need can be defined as such for a variety of reasons. For example, a topic may be highly visible because of the strategic direction of the corporation. If the corporation were focusing on increasing sales as a strategic goal, that would be a good subject area in which to look for possible games, gamification, or simulations. Another reason a program may be highly visible is due to the number of individuals the program impacts. In comparing learning programs, see which ones impact the most people.

Ask the following types of questions:

1. Is there a training program that a large number of employees must take that impacts the bottom line?

2. What program has the most visibility to upper management? Why?

3. What program would impact the most executives?

4. What program could save your organization the most money?

5. Is there a current program everyone "hates" or "loves"?

6. Which programs tie most directly to business unit objectives?

Stand-Up Version Is Taught Frequently

Determine whether there can be a direct comparison to the stand-up program (if one already exists). If a stand-up program has to be given quarterly or yearly to multiple individuals on multiple shifts, it is an excellent candidate for performance-based justification, since savings can be generated by the ILE as well as performance improvements, and you can track results throughout the year.

Ask the following types of questions:

1. How often is this training offered?

2. How many shifts or locations need this training?

3. Would you like to offer this course more frequently?

4. What are the desired results of this course?

5. Are the learners for this topic geographically dispersed?

6. Do you feel you are obtaining the desired results?

Link with Business Unit and Corporate Goals

Establish both business unit goals and corporate goals for the game, gamification, or simulation. It may be easier to establish the business unit goals and then link those goals to corporate goals. You need to ensure that the ILE can be clearly linked to goals of the organization.

Ask the following types of questions:

1. What is the ideal business outcome?

2. Are there measurable sub-goals or mid-points?

3. Are these goals mandated?

4. What are the underlying drivers?

High Return

The final step is to determine which course is likely to have the highest return if you convert it to a game, gamification, or simulation. If you do a wonderful simulation but the issue is something that doesn't bring a great deal of return, then it will be difficult to leverage the success of the effort. Although the potential is difficult to gauge, look for driving factors within each training program that point toward one program having a higher return than another.

Ask the following types of questions:

1. Is this currently an expensive course?

2. Does this program have a large number involved in its delivery?

3. Are large numbers of employees taking the class?

4. Does the material need to be updated yearly?

2. Determine Sponsor's Goals

Look at the goals of the individual with whom you are working. Corporations are filled with people who determine the success or failure of products. If a person from a line of business is supporting the creation of a game, gamification, or simulation, you need to find out what is driving him or her and manage the project to those goals.

You want to know why he or she is vested in the program and then explain how the process will benefit upper management. Explain how leveraging these numbers can provide a distinct advantage when allocating resources of time and money for future game, gamification, and simulation projects.

Ask the following types of questions:

1. What are the risks to you if the desired outcomes are not reached?

2. Why do you want to create a game, gamification, or simulation effort?

3. What is your next career move?

4. How do you see using the results of this study?

5. Operationally define the measurements.

3. Decide How to Measure

At this point, determine what baseline measure will be taken to access the impact of the game, gamification, or simulation. Determine behaviorally defined performance measurements. For example, if you created a simulation on how to safely lift materials, you could then measure days previously lost due to injury related to unsafe lifting.

This involves precisely defining what should be measured. Determine what performance results need to be measured and then find a way to measure those results. Find reports and other measurements currently undertaken by the organization. Table 7.3 shows some areas in which to look and some questions that you may want to ask.

Remember, you must develop measurements that are objective and easy to distinguish. You cannot have a measurement like "employees will understand what it means to be compliant with the regulations when selling a product in a regulated industry." You need to define what *understand* means. Something like "when faced with a non-compliant situation, employees will take corrective action and record that action on an incident sheet" is better because you can measure the number of incident sheets objectively.

You also need to determine which part of the behavior improvement is due to the game, gamification, or simulation. Sometimes, multiple sources can contribute to an improvement. With the injury example, while a game, gamification, or simulation may have contributed to decreased injuries, the fact that new procedures are put into place, posters are hung, and employees were rewarded for injury-free days may have had an impact as well—gain consensus on the improvements that were a result of a game, gamification, or simulation. This isn't always easy, but taking 100 percent credit for an improvement only works if no other efforts were undertaken.

Table 7.3 Questions Related to Performance Metrics for Games, Gamification, and Simulations

Benefit Type	Questions to Establish Performance Metrics
Improved Employee Productivity	How is employee performance measured?
	What are the current performance levels for these measurements?
	What are the performance measurement goals after the e-learning initiative?
	How can the performance improvements be quantified into bottom-line savings?
Improved Quality	How is quality defined and measured?
	What are the current quality levels and projected quality levels after the e-learning initiative?
	How does improved quality relate to business results?
Improved Customer Satisfaction	How is customer satisfaction defined and measured?
	What are the current customer satisfaction ratings and projected ratings after the e-learning initiative?
	How does improved customer satisfaction relate to business results?

4. Dollarize the Measurements

Once you have decided what to measure, assign a dollar value to it. Take the measurements from the previous step and equate them with dollars. Table 7.4 below provides some examples.

5. Conduct a Baseline Assessment

At this stage of the process, you conduct a baseline assessment of the situation. This means you record all of the existing measurements and determine the dollar value of the current costs. This is done by assembling each performance objective, assigning a dollar value to the objective, and then adding up the results.

Table 7.4 Examples of Dollarizing Performance

Type of Savings	Savings Formula
Time	
Shorter lead to reach proficiency	(hours saved × dollar value of work per hour)
Less time required to perform operations	(hours saved × dollar value of work per hour)
Less supervision required of employees	(supervisory hours saved × pay per hour)
Increased productivity	
Faster work rate	(dollar value of additional units, sales, etc.)
Time saved by not waiting for help or being idle	(hours saved × dollars per hour + hours of helpers time saved × dollars per hour)
Time saved searching for an retrieving data when could be producing	(hours saved × dollars per hour)
Improved quality	
Fewer data-entry mistakes	(dollar value of mistakes × decreased mistake level)
Reduction in errors resulting in compliance problems	(dollar value of error × number of errors)
Increased customer service	(percent increase in market share × dollar value of increase)
Better employee performance	
Avoiding the need to hire new employees	(savings in recruitment costs and salary and benefits of new employee)
Better utilization of time	(hours freed × dollars per hour × opportunity cost of freed hours)
Less absenteeism due to accidents	(hours of increased productivity × dollar value per hour + cost of hiring a temporary worker + cost of claims)

You can conduct two types of baseline assessments, depending upon the type of study you are undertaking: a two-group comparison study or a single group pre-test/post-test study.

Two-Group Comparison Study

In this case, you collect data on two groups of employees. One group, the control group, will have the same type of training as is always conducted or no training at all. The treatment group will have the game, gamification, or simulation experience. Collect the exact same performance data on both groups, both before the ILE and after; however, at this point, you are just collecting the initial data for each group.

Single Group Pre-Test/Post-Test Study

For this type of study, you need to collect data on just one group. You will compare baseline data with data collected after the ILE. The baseline data is the operationally defined and dollarized performance measurements you identified earlier. You pre-test the group on the knowledge they need to learn and you gather pre-ILE performance data on the group. You will later compare the data from before the ILE to data after the ILE.

6. Implement and Deliver the Game, Gamification, or Simulation

This is where the actual learning event occurs. This part of the process should have little intervention from the learning and development team collecting data. The idea is to naturally let the learning from the game, gamification, or simulations occur.

7. Gather Post-Learning Data and Data from the Control Group

Once the learning event has occurred, gather data on the completed learning. You need to gather the same data you did for the baseline assessment.

Two-Group Comparison Study

Break the target audience into two groups. One group will be given the ILE instruction and the other will be given a traditional learning approach. In this case, you measure performance of both groups before the learning intervention and after the intervention. After the learning intervention, collect the data and then compare the data from the two groups. Table 7.5 provides an effective means of displaying the results.

Single Group Pre-Test/Post-Test Study

The single group pre-test/post-test study collects the same data on the same group as the baseline assessment. Table 7.6 shows one method of displaying the results. Any time you collect data and record the results, you should indicate the formulas used to determine the results and state any assumptions that were made regarding the study.

For each of these measures, the values need to be converted into dollar values. In some cases, it may be difficult to assign a dollar value, but you still want to draw attention to the item. In those cases, you can simply list the improvement and call it non-quantifiable.

8. Determine the Return

Once you have established performance metrics, you can re-measure those metrics again and again at assigned intervals to determine the impact. You can also measure the impact in terms of net benefits and benefit/cost ratio. Table 7.7 includes an example of common formulas and calculations. The $60,800 is the benefit to the organization and the $25,000 is the cost.

Summary of Performance Improvement Justification

The performance-based justification is valuable conveying to other business units that the learning and development function is seriously looking at the business benefits of a game, gamification, or simulation and that, if positioned properly, the game, gamification, or simulation can provide financial benefits to the organization.

Table 7.5 Two-Group Comparison Study Results

Measurement	Control Group Before Intervention	Control Group After Intervention	Treatment Group Before Intervention	Treatment Group After Intervention
Days lost due to accidents	6	4	7	1
Hours spent in learning intervention	8	8	8	4
Number of non-compliance incidents	11	8	10	6

Table 7.6 Single Group Pre/Post Test Results

Measurement	Before Intervention	After Intervention	Benefit Calculation with Assumptions	Dollar Impact
Days lost due to accidents	2	1	$30,000 in savings	
Time spent in training	8 hours	4 hours	Assumes that all learners took the class-room training during the in-plant offering	$100,000 in savings
Number of non-compliance incidents	10	8	Number that were recorded	Non-quantifiable

Once a justification is done for an ILE, seeking subsequent funding becomes easier. The first attempt at justification may be a little shaky and require modifications to the process, but once the L&D professionals gain the skills, future justifications become easier.

Table 7.7 Costs and Benefits Calculations

Calculations	Method	Description and Calculation	Return on Investment
Net Benefit (NB)	Compares benefits to cost of the initiative	NB = Benefit − Cost	60,800 − 25,000 = $35,800 Net Benefit
Benefit/Cost Ratio (BCR)	Ratio for benefit returned for each dollar invested	BCR = Benefits/ Costs	60,800/25,000 = 2.42 Benefit/Cost Ratio*

*For every dollar invested, $2.42 was returned

Stealth Justification

Nike used to use the motto, "Just Do It." Sometimes with a game, gamification, or simulation, you just have to take the initiative and do it with a stealth approach. The status quo is too ingrained in the organization. The old paradigms of training are too entrenched.

In this case a stealth approach might be appropriate. It is less straightforward and is more organic than a performance justification or evidence-based justification and may take a little longer. The idea is that you create a game, gamification, or simulation "off-the-radar"; no one has to know what the team was working on.

Simply incorporate these ILEs into training or daily operations without much fuss. One day the sales manager distributes iPads to the sales force preloaded with a couple of games for learning how to "close" on a customer and a simulation teaching how to overcome objections and get points for moving through the content and progressing to the next level.

To find the resources for such a project, consider recruiting a team of co-workers who are familiar with games to work in their spare time or at home. If you position the stealth project correctly, you can usually find folks who are willing to experiment a little to create something that is engaging, meaningful, and has a learning impact.

Or find a business line manager interested in being innovative, a visionary. Team with this person to create the project on the sly. These types of individuals can usually "find" money, allowing the development of a game, gamification, or stimulation. Look for instances where one of these tools solves a critical business need. Implement the solution under the radar of the rest of the organization. This might fall under the category of "It's better to beg for forgiveness than to ask for permission." Once the solution is in place and successfully contributing, use the positive results to sell it to others within the organization.

Key Takeaways

The key takeaways from this chapter are

- One approach to justification for using games and simulations for learning is to use results from research studies to bolster your case.

- At the present time, little peer-reviewed research is available on the effectiveness of gamification, but you can use research describing the effectiveness of game elements to make your case.

- Focus cost justifications on the concept of performance improvement instead of cost savings.

- Using performance improvement to justify your game, gamification, or simulation will position learning and development professionals as people who understand business.

- The process for conducting a performance improvement justification is systematic but not overly complicated and can be used for justification of a game, gamification, or simulation or any type of training.

- One of the best approaches might be to just create something and launch with little fanfare. This stealth approach may be a good way to get an ILE into an organization and avoid obstacles to implementation.

8

Managing the Process

Jim Kiggens
CEO, Course Games

CHAPTER QUESTIONS

- What are the processes required to produce an educational game?

- Do you have any tips for a first-time producer or person who manages a game, gamification, or simulation project?

Introduction

This chapter highlights the processes and techniques that have been used to successfully manage a large-scale game development project. Many of the same tools, techniques, and approaches can be used to manage a game, gamification, or simulation project. For this chapter, we are going to use one my company helped develop called Survival Master˚; it's our latest educational game research product.

Survival Master˚ is a long-form educational video game (eleven game levels) that encompasses three weeks of class time in eighth grade engineering and technology education. Survival Master was developed through "Simulations and Modeling in Technology Education," a five-year National Science Foundation-funded project that is researching the potential of a hybrid instructional model that blends digital game-based learning and physical modeling using tools and materials. The research, conducted by Hofstra University, Bloomsburg University, and City University of New York, directly compares student learning and engagement in digital game-based learning with that of the more traditional physical modeling. The full details regarding Survival Master and the SMTE project can be found at http://gaming2learn.org.

The Process Required to Produce an Educational Game

Each serious game project is a unique venture, but the production requirements always share a central core. The game has to be fun and engaging, but the primary goal is to deliver the intended learning outcome. The ILE has to meet the player's expectations, but in must also be completed on time and within budget.

The contents of this chapter are drawn from and focus on my direct experience in producing/developing serious games for training and education since 1996. Due to the extensive scope of game development, it wouldn't be possible to detail every aspect of our development process here in a single chapter.

Instead, what I will do is to use selected highlights from our Survival Master project as examples that may best answer the two questions posed above. Wherever there are planning processes or documentation formats mentioned in this chapter that are not found elsewhere in this book you can visit our website (www.coursegames.com) and find each process or document detailed there.

While the terminology may vary somewhat, I think that you'll find much of this material to be common in serious game production. The hope is that you will find some or all of this to be useful for you, whether you are a first-time producer or veteran who is translating your skills and experience in entertainment game production to the unique demands of serious game production.

The reference point for our production process at Course Games is our design intention and production mantra, which is to develop effective educational games with these characteristics:

- Has an uncertain game outcome, where the learner is required to tangibly affect outcome
- Has an emphasis on learning objectives and mastery
- Provides the learner with ongoing, measurable feedback regarding progress toward the intended learning objectives
- Has rules of play, conditions of mystery, chance, or luck
- Has an overriding goal/challenge (sub-goals/challenges) with a reward system
- Requires strategy development to win or succeed
- Employs recognizable patterns of action
- Has multiple, meaningful decision paths to achieve the desired outcomes
- Is deeply engaging, captivating the learner with organized play that requires increasing mastery of skills, knowledge, and tactics
- Embodies an unfolding narrative to provide a rich, situated context
- Inspires repeated play

Our production goals are quite similar to those of an entertainment game developer, with the significant distinction that the game must effectively deliver targeted learning outcomes. That distinction has a profound impact on our production process, but it does not in any way lessen our commitment to great gameplay and a rich user experience.

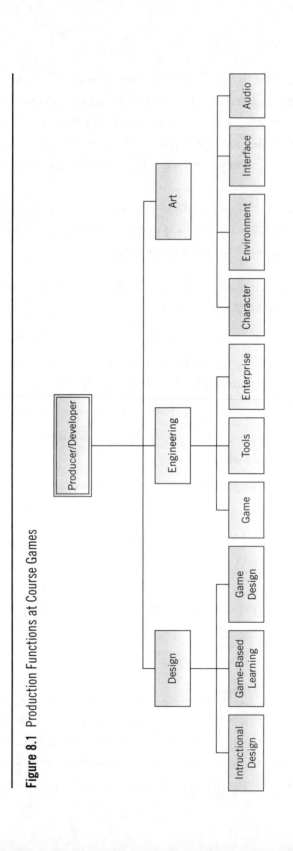

Figure 8.1 Production Functions at Course Games

Figure 8.1 depicts the functional and team organization for production at Course Games, which is the minimum functional organization required to develop a serious game. In our smallest projects, the team may only consist of five or six members, requiring that some members may have multiple or overlapping responsibilities. In our largest projects, design, engineering, and art each have a lead and the sub-functions on the lowest level each have one or more members that report to that lead. The Survival Master project falls under this last category, with the added complexity that the large team worked virtually and was geographically dispersed across North America.

Serious Game Development Process

We began the Survival Master project with our typical development process sequence: Pre-Production, Production, and Distribution. Each of the three phases in the sequence is organized with the following functional topics:

Phase 1: Pre-Production

- Concept Development
- Production Requirements Planning
- Documentation

Phase 2: Production

- Production Management
- Design
- Engineering
- Art
- Quality Assurance (QA)

Phase 3: Distribution

- Community Management
- Engineering Support
- Training

Tool for Managing Game Development

Lucas Blair

One tool I use for managing game development projects is the model in Figure 8.2.

The development model is a start-to-finish plan for educational game creation. It was initially made to introduce new team members to the process of creating educational games and later used to show clients where we were in our process. In addition, the model also has practical uses and, once tailored to meet the distinctive requirements of a project, can be a great way to stay organized.

The model takes into account the entire process from initial steps (like gathering information) to final stages (like playtesting final builds of the game). The model shows tasking for four members of the development team: project manager, designer, programmer, and artist. The model is also color-coordinated based on how heavily a team member is tasked during a particular phase of development. The color coordination comes in handy when assigning new projects while also avoiding over-tasking team members.

Take this model, cut it apart, edit it, and tweak it to match your team and projects. Print out a version of your development model for each project you are currently working on. Hang it on a cork board beside your desk and put a thumbtack in the column that currently matches where you are in the project. This will not only give you a to do list of your responsibilities, but will also let you know what your teammates are currently working on. Each column and the tasks that fall inside it can also act as an outline for team meetings that take place during each phase of a project.

Full disclosure, almost no projects ever actually work out so that they perfectly fit into a model like this. In some cases steps will be rearranged or left out entirely. Often team members will find themselves ahead or behind of the scheduled phase. If you ask any individual about the color coding referring to his or her tasking, the person will say every step should be red because he or she always feels heavily tasked. Don't be discouraged by the idea that projects don't

Figure 8.2 A Model for Managing a Game Development Project

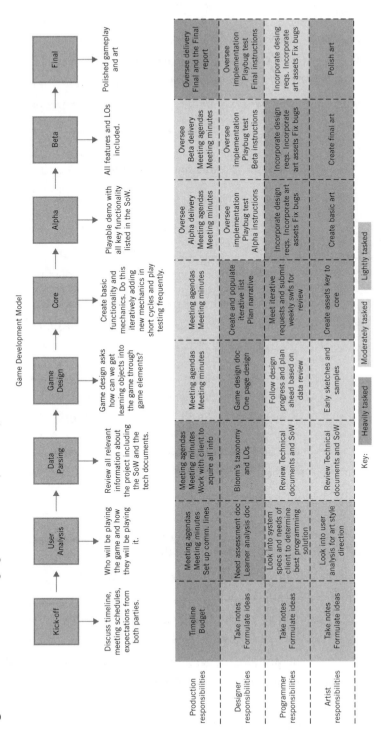

Game Development Model

	Kick-off	User Analysis	Data Parsing	Game Design	Core	Alpha	Beta	Final
	Discuss timeline, meeting schedules, expectations from both parties.	Who will be playing the game and how they will be playing it.	Review all relevant information about the project including the SoW and the tech documents.	Game design asks how can we get learning objects into the game through game elements?	Create basic functionality and mechanics. Do this iteratively adding new mechanics in short cycles and play testing frequently.	Playable demo with all key functionality listed in the SoW.	All features and LOs included.	Polished gameplay and art
Production responsibilities	Timeline Budget	Meeting agendas Meeting minutes Set up comm. lines	Meeting agendas Meeting minutes Work with client to aquire all info	Meeting agendas Meeting minutes	Meeting agendas Meeting minutes	Oversee Alpha delivery Meeting agendas Meeting minutes	Oversee Beta delivery Meeting agendas Meeting minutes	Oversee delivery Final and the Final report
Designer responsibilities	Take notes Formulate ideas	Need assessment doc Learner analysis doc	Bloom's taxonomy and LOs	Game design doc One page design	Create and populate iterative list Plan narrative	Oversee implementation Playbug test Alpha instructions	Oversee implementation Playbug test Beta instructions	Oversee implementation Playbug test Final instructions
Programmer responsibilities	Take notes Formulate ideas	Look into system specs and needs of client to determine best programming solution	Review Technical documents and SoW	Follow design progress and plan ahead based on data review	Meet iterative requests and submit weekly swfs for review	Incorporate design reqs. Incorporate art assets Fix bugs	Incorporate design reqs. Incorporate art assets Fix bugs	Incorporate desing reqs. Incorporate art assets Fix bugs
Artist responsibilities	Take notes Formulate ideas	Look into user analysis for art style direction	Review Technical documents and SoW	Early sketches and samples	Create assets key to core	Create basic art	Create final art	Polish art

Key: Heavily tasked   Moderately tasked   Lightly tasked fit into neat little boxes. We make models to give us something to strive for and to act as a pattern that we should try to consistently re-create.

To download a copy of the development model, go to the publisher's website for this book (www.wiley.com/go/kappfieldbook; password: professional).

Survival Master: Pre-Production Highlights

- Pre-production is the planning phase that lays the foundation upon which the entire project is dependent.

- The pre-production phase results in documentation that will serve the team throughout the lifecycle of the production.

- Many aspects of the documentation at this point are best estimates, with the expectation that these are "living documents" the team will continually update.

- Near the end of the production phase, these documents will be sourced to create learner support and teacher support and training documentation that will be deployed during distribution.

Tables 8.1 and 8.2 are checklists that we use at Course Games to track progress for the planning and documentation that are required to begin production.

Learner Outcomes-Driven Development

The game has to be fun and engaging, but the primary goal is to deliver the intended learning outcomes.

The first step to ensure learning outcomes are driving our game development is in pre-production, where we clarify the instructional system design to set the footprint for the game's foundation by ensuring that all team members share a detailed understanding of the learning objectives, their outcome criteria, and how the learning outcomes will be assessed. A sample of one of the objectives is shown in Table 8.3.

Table 8.1 Pre-Production Planning Checklist

Pre-Production Planning Checklist	Date	Notes
Concept Development		
Instructional System Design (ISD)		
Digital Game-Based Learning Design		
Game Story		
Level Designs		
Technology Analysis		
Competitive Analysis		
SWOT Analysis		
Production Planning Requirements		
Team Organization		
Functional Specification		
Technical Specification		
Enterprise System Design		
Production Schedule		
Production Budget		
Asset Management System		
Use Cases		
Database Model		
Outcomes Assessment Plan		
Documentation		
Concept		
Requirements		
Functional Specification Document		

Table 8.1 Pre-Production Planning Checklist (continued)

Pre-Production Planning Checklist	Date	Notes
Art Bible		
Technical Design Document		
Test Plan		
Production Plan		

The SMTE project research evaluates learner outcomes for this level with an external pre-post test instrument that has twelve objective questions that assess learning for this level.

One of the guiding tenets we hold at Course Games is that for an educational game to be successful (effective), the game-based learning must map directly to learning objectives with clearly defined behavioral objectives and accompanying specific outcome assessment criteria.

We clarify at the outset that we are developing game-based learning that leverages well-researched learning models, where the game-based learning features are harmonious with the learning models in use.

The crux is developing game-based learning features that present the learners with meaningful choices that provide evidence of the intended learning outcomes. The goal is to develop game-based learning where the learners demonstrate a level of mastery by transferring cause-and-effect gameplay experience to other concepts—especially extrinsic activities such as a traditional assessment instrument used for standardized testing.

Survival Master ISD

At the outset of the Survival Master project, we began clarifying our instructional design with the following definitions:

Audience Analysis: An analysis of the learner's current skills and how those skills map to the game's instructional content.

Entry Behaviors: Identification of the learning objectives the player must have mastered prior to playing the game to be successful. Any

Table 8.2 Pre-Production Documentation Checklist

Pre-Production Documentation Checklist	Date	Notes
Instructional System Design (ISD)		
Learning Goals		
Learning Outcomes (behavioral)		
Outcomes Assessment Design		
Reporting Requirements		
Accessibility Requirements		
Evaluation Loops		
Game Requirements		
Define Game Features		
Define Milestones and Deliverables		
Evaluate Technology		
Define Tools and Pipeline		
Documentation (Design, Art, Tech)		
Risk Analysis		
Functional Specification		
Instructional Systems Design (ISD)		
Backstory		
Gameplay Sequencing		
Level Designs/Flowboards		
Interface		
Art Direction (Art Bible)		
Art Direction		

Table 8.2 Pre-Production Documentation Checklist (continued)

Pre-Production Documentation Checklist	Date	Notes
Artistic Style		
Chroma Plan		
Character Designs		
Environment Designs		
Level Maps		
Cinematic Designs		
Lighting, Shaders, Render Requirements		
Technical Specification		
Programming Staff		
Tools Development		
Middleware		
Asset Management		
Online Technology		
Test Plan		
Q & A Staff		
Testing Plan		
Testing Checklist		
Documentation		
Outcomes Assessment		
Evaluation Loops		

skills or knowledge identified as an entry behavior will not be covered in the game. It is a prerequisite for the game.

Instructional Goals: Broad educational goals for the game.

Instructional Objectives: Performance objectives for the game. It is critical that instructional objectives be granular enough to allow for

---

Table 8.3 Learning Objectives for Educational Game

Survival Master Example: Snowshoe Race Level

Instructional Design

Key Idea: Relationship between k value and R value
Learning Goals: Students will know that:

A. k value and R value are both measures of a material's resistance to heat flow. k value relates only to the type of material where R value also takes into account the material's thickness (L).

B. Since R value takes thickness (L) into account, yet is related to k value, R, L, and k can be expressed in a relationship. The R value of a material equals its thickness / its k value ($R = L/k$).

C. The total R value (Rt) of a system of materials is the sum of each of the individual R values ($Rt = R1 + R2 + R3 + R \ldots$).

Learning Objectives

1. Given information about k value and R value, students will describe the similarities and differences between them.

2. Given information about the relationship between k value, R value, and thickness of a material, students will analyze a variety of materials to determine differences in k and R values.

3. Given k values and thicknesses for several different materials, students will calculate the R value of each material using the formula $R = L/k$.

4. Solve for heat loss using the formula $Q = A (\Delta T) / R$ given surface area, R value, and ΔT.

5. Given individual R values of several materials, students will determine the total R value of a system made from layers of those materials by summing the individual R values.

---

the diagnosing of instructional problems. At a minimum, objectives should address (1) behavior to be measured, (2) conditions under which the behavior will be measured, and (3) a minimum level of achievement needed to demonstrate mastery of the objectives.

Assessment Items: Assessment items for each of the learning objectives should be created. It is important that each assessment item test only a single instructional objective. Assessment criteria must be identifiable in gameplay regarding how they map to specific learning objectives.

Core Game Strategy: With the audience analysis, learning objectives, and game-based learning outcomes assessments prepared, we can then concentrate on how to present the necessary instructional materials to the learners in a manner that will prepare them to successfully complete the assessments. The core game strategy will drive the gameplay decisions about the game. The game mechanics in each game level and the over-arching game narrative will reflect the core game strategy.

Table 8.4 is a tracking checklist that we use at the close of the pre-production to ensure that learner outcomes are effectively driving production.

Level Design Documents

Like most game development companies, at Course Games we utilize a variety of tools to visualize the gameplay and features in each level and scene in the game. We use storyboards and maps to visualize gameplay, wireframes to visualize game GUI, spreadsheets to visualize resources and parameters, and screen trees to visualize game sequences.

In all cases, we use flowboards to visualize the logic in the level (decisions, outcomes, connections, datapoints) and each flowboard is carefully mapped to the physical model of the game database to ensure that the data input/output required for the level exists in the database design and is normalized.

We begin by drawing the gameplay logic on a whiteboard, starting with the block diagram level, and then working through the logic and flow each sequence, scene, level and feature in detail. As each of these is accomplished, we move the whiteboard drawings to digital flowboard diagrams as shown in Figure 8.3.

The model in Figure 8.4 visualizes the structure of the game data. It specifies what data tables are needed, how they relate, the primary keys, foreign keys, and helps to ensure that the database is normalized.

Survival Master: Production Highlights

In our previous educational game projects, the ISD was pre-existing and we were developing game-based learning as a new delivery approach for curriculum that was well tested. In this type of development, Waterfall was used as the game development model, which has been widely used in serious

Table 8.4 ISD to LDD Checklist

ISD to LDD Checklist	Date	Notes
Validating the ISD		
Instructional design states the learning objectives in behavioral terms, with clearly identified criteria and the method by which that criteria is to be assessed.		
ISD defines how the learning outcomes assessment is to be reported.		
Mapping the ISD to the LDD		
LDD clearly identifies the learning objectives, learning outcomes, and assessment criteria are evident in gameplay.		
LDD has detailed flowboards for each scene, level, and game feature.		
Mapping the LDD to the Game Database Model		
LDD datapoints are reflected in the game Database Model.		
Learning outcome assessment data is reflected in the game Database Model.		
Outcomes assessment reporting data is reflected in the game Database Model.		

Figure 8.3 Survival Master Game Launch Flowboard

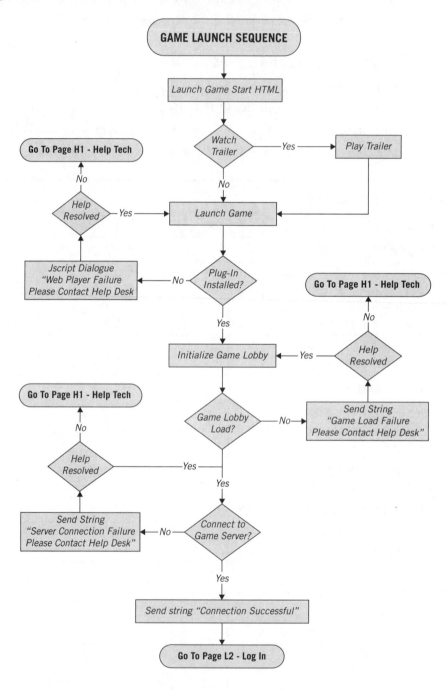

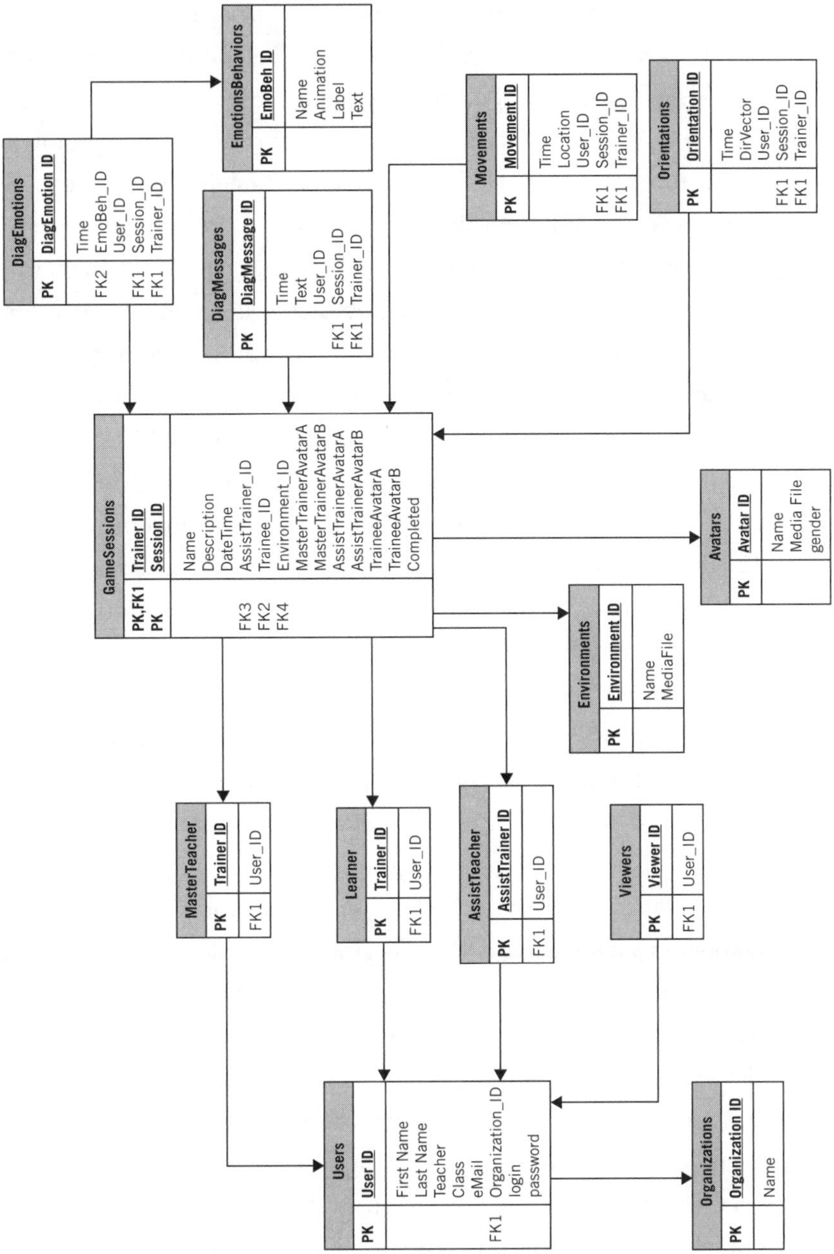

Figure 8.4 Survival Master Initial Architecture Game Database Model

game development because it aligns so well with the ADDIE instructional design model that is widely used. Our normal approach was for engineering, art, and design to begin development in parallel as soon as pre-production was completed. Designers would work on continual refinement of the level designs, artists would begin developing assets, and engineering would develop an initial architecture and a proof of concept game prototype. The goal at this point is to develop a functioning architecture and a game level prototype as quickly as possible.

Survival Master would prove to be a completely different situation. The SMTE project was conducting research using a brand-new curriculum that was intended to infuse science and math into educational technology instruction, incorporating an informed design process in the shelter engineering challenge. The project had a concrete timeline, which necessitated completing pre-preproduction and beginning production while the ISD was under constant revision. As a replacement curriculum for three weeks of class time, the curriculum scope was significant. External content and grade-level subject-matter experts worked with the team on continual refinement, often with profound changes.

In parallel, the game development closely conformed to each ISD shift and revision. Early on, this resulted in some remarkable alterations in terms of impact. For example, a large portion of the math learning objectives were eliminated after it became clear that they were beyond grade level and not feasible.

The ISD revisions were accompanied by several ongoing technology challenges of much greater impact. The original game concept called for an online multiplayer architecture, where the learners would work in small design teams of four, as shown in Figure 8.5. As a result of initial proof of technology testing, that architecture was changed to a local area network multiplayer, with the intention that using a local server would eliminate the IT obstacles at the schools that prevented the use of an online multiplayer, as shown in Figure 8.6. Months later, after the initial field testing revealed that there was a new set of IT obstacles that prevented the deployment of the LAN-based multiplayer, the architecture was altered again—this time to a single-player, team-based, social learning game that used discussion forums, real-time chat, and wiki reports for team communications, as shown in Figure 8.7.

Figure 8.5 SMTE Prototype Online Multiplayer Game Architecture, circa 2008

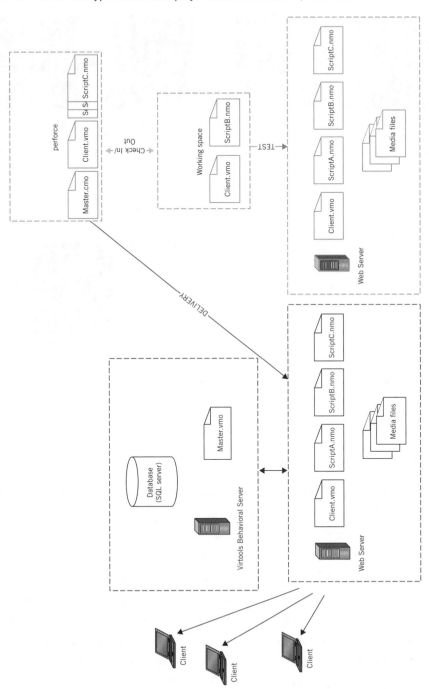

Figure 8.6 Survival Master Alpha LAN Multiplayer Game Architecture, circa 2011

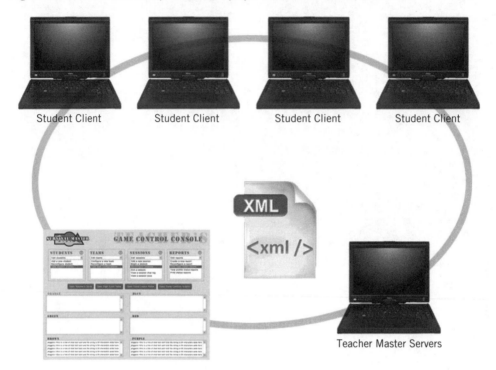

Survival Master Example: Architecture Iterations

With both the ISD and the core architecture undergoing such significant ongoing changes, we needed a unique production model that could serve all team members. This new model needed to have a flexibility not found in ADDIE and Waterfall, and it needed to be accessible to the entire team in that the processes, terms, reporting, etc., had to be understandable across a diverse range of production experience and skills.

Figure 8.8 depicts our modified Scrum development model that we have evolved to support the production of Survival Master. For more on Scrum and ADDIE, see Chapter 9 of *The Gamification of Learning and Instruction*. Using the term modified to describe our model is quite an understatement, since the modification is so deep and broad that the model would hardly be recognizable as Scrum.

Figure 8.7 Survival Master Beta Game Enterprise Architecture, circa 2013

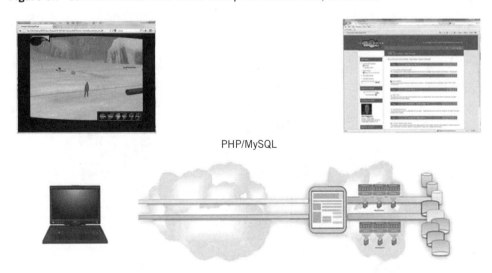

PHP/MySQL

The evolution of this production model resulted from a confluence of my need to solve production pipeline difficulties that we were experiencing in the early days on Survival Master with the coincidence that I decided to attend Scrum Master Certification Training. I wasn't expecting the Scrum Master training program to completely change my thinking about game production management, and I had no expectation that it would have any bearing on our Survival Master project.

An important aspect of our modified model as a solution is the nature of the problem that we were seeking to solve. Due to the heavy churn in the project's earliest period, the daily production management tasks felt like an upstream swim. We were trying to use a sequential, rigid model (Waterfall) to manage a project that was completely fluid.

Organizing our large team into small, self-contained units that would work intensely for a short duration, without interruption or conflicting assignments, for a short duration to complete a small working piece of our large puzzle seemed like it was the perfect solution.

Our evolved model doesn't overtly use traditional Scrum vocabulary, documents, and visualization tools, which is a decision based on resources. Some

Figure 8.8 Modified Scrum Production Model at Course Games

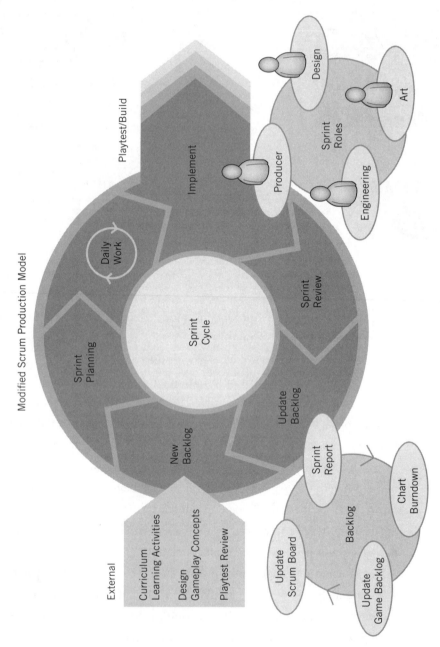

of our Survival Master team members came to the project unfamiliar with the game development process and were already stretched to the edge of their tolerance regarding production training, so adding a substantial layer of new training was out of the question because that would be counterproductive.

As we made the shift to Agile, we did so in small steps. Because it was, in fact, a good solution for our project, each new wrinkle seemed to make sense to the team and concepts like "sprints" and "backlog" were readily adapted. The fact that a large part of our Scrum process was opaque to the team at large had the unintended benefit of improving focus and velocity on the immediate tasks at hand in their sprint and almost completely eliminated team-wide rehash and debate regarding production decisions, schedule, milestones, etc.

Production Schedule Management

The lifecycle of our game development is defined by four production milestones:

1. *Prototype:* This is the first major milestone for the game. It contains representative gameplay and assets. Often, it is based on a first playable or proof of concept that was created in pre-production or early in production.

2. *Alpha:* Key gameplay functionality is implemented, assets are 40 to 50 percent final (the rest are placeholders), it runs on the correct hardware in debug mode, and there is enough working that you can get a feel for the game. Features might undergo major adjustments at this point, based on testing results and other feedback.

3. *Beta:* The game is code and asset complete. Art, design, and engineering only focus on fixing bugs that are listed in the bug database. No new assets are generated; no new features are coded; and no changes are made to existing features and functionality unless it is identified as a bug.

4. *Release Candidate:* All bugs have been addressed, the build is ready to be shipped. The code is tested against the QA test plan, and any crash bugs or other critical issues are fixed. The team is not actively making any more fixes.

Tools

Several schedule tools and formats are used for Survival Master. We use a master schedule in Gantt chart form as a high-level view of progress and scheduling for team-wide review. Internally, we use sprint burndown charts to visualize short-term progress, and a project composite velocity chart to visualize team-wide progress and tendencies, as shown in Figure 8.9.

The master schedule in Gantt chart form provides an accessible format for team members who are not familiar with the more esoteric production scheduling tools used for Agile production. A Gantt chart is easy to

Figure 8.9 Master Schedule Gantt and Sprint Burndown Chart Example

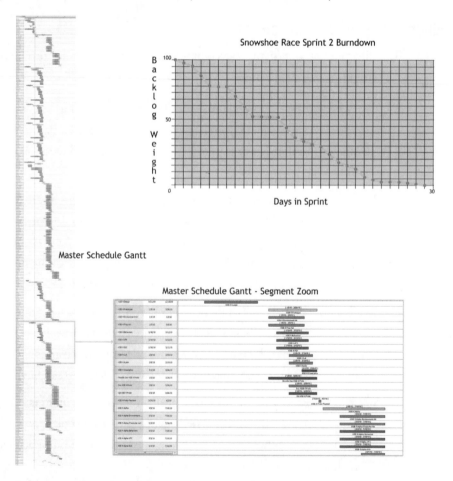

understand, and it also gives the more experienced members another way to view the backlog organized at a high level by timeline projection and depicting staffing allocations and progress points.

Sprint burndown charts are valuable diagnostics for the producer, well worth the time and effort. In our highly modified method, we organize the backlog by a parameter that we define as "weight" and the burndown charts the percentage of weight remaining across the days of the sprint.

As is the case with a traditional Scrum burndown chart, ideal production velocity would be indicated by a diagonal line from the upper left corner down to the lower right. What actually occurs is that the production velocity experiences plateaus, where no progress is made for a number of days. As a diagnostic, small plateaus are usually anticipated, while long plateaus require intervention. The project's composite of burndown charts is also a very useful diagnostic in that it frequently reveals trends that can be addressed to improve efficiency.

Level Design Concept: Snow Shoe Race

We wanted to make the game action-oriented so we spent a great deal of time coming up with concepts that would be appealing to our target audience. In Exhibit 8.1, you can see the description of the snowshoe level. In Figure 8.10 you can see a concept map for the snowshoe race.

Exhibit 8.1. Level Design Concept, Snowshoe Race

Level Description

"In the snowshoe race your mission is to get your container of liquid to the station at the end of the race, keeping its temperature hot, all while watching out for thin ice and avalanches. You transport the container by a backpack that you will choose by making tradeoffs between weight and insulation as to which is the best choice."

The player begins the level in the starting area.

Backpack Selection 1

The trainee begins the level in front of the main hut. Across from the contestants lies a wooden gazebo. Three backpacks sit on the bench. Each backpack is clickable.

Selecting a Backpack

- Each pack has a different lining and weight.
- Light backpacks lose more heat.
- Heavy backpacks provide more insulation.
- Solving R total is necessary before picking up pack.
- Lining measurements appear on the wall behind each pack.
- Click on packs to open answer menu.
- Answer menu randomizes several selections.
- Successful answers award energy.

   Once a backpack is clicked, a menu pops up giving several possible answers to each backpack.

   If the player fails to select the correct answer, the backpack is removed and the order of answers is switched. Additional choices are also changed to avoid guessing.

Sprint to Checkpoint 1

Once the player has selected a backpack, he or she must cross the starting line to begin the Checkpoint Sprint. Two paths can be taken to reach Checkpoint 1:

Thin Ice (Short Path)

- Ice paths only appear in one area along the river.
- Sprinting for more than a few seconds will break the ice.
- Player will respawn at an earlier location.

Wooden Bridge (Long Path)

- Path takes significantly longer than shortcuts.
- NPC will follow this path invariably.

Checkpoint 1 Sprint

- Player must navigate from one location to the next.
- Each leg has multiple paths to take.
- Shorter paths have traps and pitfalls.
- Longer paths are safe.
- Crossing the finish lines award large energy boosts.
- Finishing before NPCs rewards additional energy.

Backpack Selection 2

The mechanics work similarly to the first backpack challenge. These backpacks contain additional liners to account for in calculations.

Sprint to First Aid Station

Once the players have selected their backpacks, they must cross the checkpoint line to begin the Checkpoint Sprint. Two paths can be taken to reach the First Aid Station:

Avalanche (Short Path)

- A steep incline marks the path to the First Aid Station.
- Sprinting for more than a few seconds will trigger an avalanche.
- Player will respawn at an earlier location.

Rope Bridge (Long Path)

- Path takes significantly longer than shortcuts.
- NPC will follow this path invariably.

The Snowshoe Race level underwent drastic versioning from its initial concept through to Beta. In initial playtesting, teachers did not like the level because they felt that too many students were wasting class time wandering around the expanse. Some learners reported that they didn't like the level because it was too hard to find their way. Figure 8.11 and Figure 8.12 show various screen shots of the design concepts as we honed in on our final design.

Figure 8.10 Level Design Map for Survival Master Snowshoe Race Concept

Map Zoom: 3
Current Place: 4th
TIME: 03:52:07
TEMP: 104 degrees

Figure 8.11 Proof of Concept Screenshot for Survival Master Snowshoe Race Level

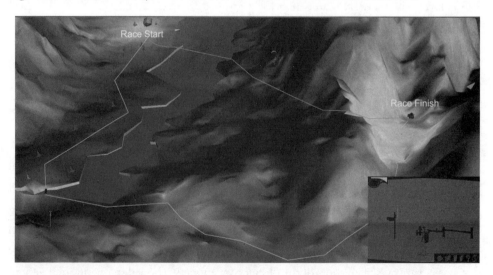

Figure 8.12 Beta Screenshots for Survival Master Snowshoe Race Level

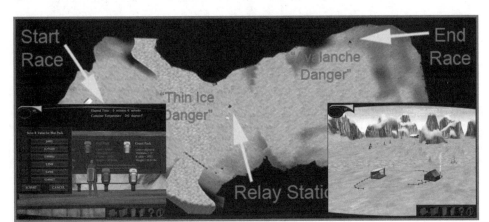

Coupled with that, learning outcomes were disappointing, especially compared with the traditional workbook format that the research was comparing with non-game classes. The level had been designed to give the learners the choice to calculate the values of the various backpacks, using the reward system to incentivize that behavior. The incentive wasn't strong enough for many students, with teachers reporting that the students who needed the calculation practice the most were the ones who were ignoring it.

In our next version, we reduced and simplified the level map. We altered the art direction by changing from reduced palette, with a dark, snowy ambience with reduced visibility, to a high key palette with bright daylight and unlimited visibility.

We also added a second-leg segment to separate learning objectives regarding Rt and added practice calculating R from k and L.

Most importantly, the next version required calculations to pick a pack for each segment, with enhanced rewards for calculating all packs. Also enhanced was the risk versus reward for taking dangerous paths, encouraging replay.

Over the lifecycle of the Survival Master development, each of the eleven game levels underwent similar (or more significant) versioning. Through these iterations, game balance and learning outcomes remarkably improved.

Each versioning cycle also led to enhancements that improved team efficiency and effectiveness in using the modified Scrum production model developed for this project.

Tips for a First-Time Producer

A producer in game development parlance is a person who is responsible for overseeing the development of a video game. In instructional design circles it is called a project manager. Here are some things you'll want to think about if you are going to manage an educational game, gamification, or simulation development project.

Is this the right project? I've learned to carefully consider whether I "know what I don't know" when I'm evaluating the opportunity to take on a new project.

For example, if a potential project would require development for a delivery platform that is unfamiliar, look closely to determine what you will need to learn (aka don't know), listing new skills, software, etc., that would be required and whether the new capacity would be something that your company would benefit from in the long term.

In short, seeking to "know what I don't know" is a method to identify and organize my sense of opportunity cost, potential obstacles, and risk.

Next, does the project align with our company's core goals and objectives? Does this project fit into one of the categories that we feel is something that we do well?

Do not ignore alignment during the initial evaluation of a project, no matter how attractive the funding or potential visibility may be. It may be a terrific opportunity in a general sense, but it might not be a good opportunity if it isn't a good fit, if we may not be successful, or if we are dissatisfied in doing the work.

Go beyond these initial questions, then evaluate the aspects that are external to your company, where you may be dependent and where that dependency may not be an acceptable risk.

Engaging with a large-scale educational game project entails working closely with new external team members, and most likely also includes dependency upon new and unfamiliar institutions. Do these new team members realistically understand what will be required to complete and deploy their game? Do these new institutions have the capacity to adequately support the project over the long haul of a large project?

If the project budget appears sufficient, look for risks that may be present, who actually controls how the budget will be allocated, whether there are external commitments that may drain the available funds for development, and who is in direct control of paying you. If the project team is not in direct control of the budget, you are taking on the added risk of payment delays, staff reductions, changes in scope, changes in process, and changes in contract terms.

The serious game industry is vibrant and there are many opportunities available. I've learned to avoid work that isn't a good fit. Not only don't you enjoy the work, but if you are under contract on bad work, then you're unavailable for new projects that do align.

Managing the Virtual Production Team

You don't all need to be in the same physical location. For the last seven years, across four large serious game projects, I've worked on production teams that were entirely virtual, dispersed across the United States and several other countries. I've worked comfortably with and enjoyed getting to know team members I didn't meet in person until many months had passed on the project.

As the producer of a virtual game development team, life can be something of a study in contradiction. In one sense, you have a great deal of schedule freedom since you are not time- and place-bound. However, that also means that you may have very little schedule freedom because the team has access to you 24/7/365; the team never shuts off. We use a combination of email, discussion forums, chat, and both scheduled and ad hoc live web meetings to communicate, with a phone call being the choice of last resort. Infrequently, we enjoy the luxury of meeting face-to-face. From my studio in a remote, rural location in California I'm connected throughout the workday to the team that is spread across thousands of miles, various time zones, languages, and cultures.

I've found that the skills required to be successful on a virtual team are those that typically describe the best team members in a face-to-face situation: self-reliance, self-confidence, strong problem-solving skills, a thirst for self-training, strong time management, the ability to intensely focus, routinely paying attention to detail, and the ability to communicate clearly.

Develop an Appreciation for Pre-Production

To begin the pre-production phase, an absolute minimum requirement is that your team must have expertise in each of the function areas shown in Figure 8.1. One or more team members may have overlapping expertise, but it is essential that each functional area be represented. If the project begins pre-production with a team that lacks expertise in any functional area, it will result in deficient or defective production planning that will have a profound negative impact on the final product. It is the producer's responsibility to prevent this from happening.

To begin the production phase, the planning and documentation that were completed in the pre-production phase will limit the efficiency and effectiveness of production. Where the planning was left unaddressed or incomplete, it will come back to cost the production much more than any perceived savings that might have been calculated back in pre-production. Again, it is important that the producer prevents this from happening.

Playtest

Playtest early, often, use the feedback, be sure to measure the learning outcomes. Also, make sure you playtest under the worst case in terms of delivery technology, not the best. Equally important, make sure the entire team is playtesting.

Using playtest results to balance and tune gameplay is an aspect that typically leaves the producer feeling that the game will never actually be done. In a certain regard, this has an element truth. You don't actually finish, you just run out of resources (time and money). Don't be discouraged if you discover during playtesting that a game level or feature that you thought was strong isn't what you hoped for; it is the nature of the beast.

It is important that you observe and act upon the feedback, resisting the temptation to discount or blame the playtest. Conversely, there are tremendous opportunities to be found in playtesting if you are open to the serendipity. Testers do the unexpected, sometimes with wonderfully surprising results.

Learner's Advocate

The team and the product benefit greatly if there is at least one team member whose nature and professional interest is to be a spokesperson who advocates for the best interests of the learners as players. This is typically a strong game designer who doesn't wilt in the face of strong leadership or team undercurrents (peer pressure).

Low Game Literacy

Something that is somewhat unique and common to large-scale serious game projects is the likelihood that some team members may have extremely low or non-existent video game literacy. This is especially true in large corporations, as managers, subject-matter experts, and others will not be highly versed in games. In academic institutions, this may include administrators, teachers, researchers, clients, and faculty members. The impact of this can range from a mild distraction to major dysfunction. This is a situation that is either managed by the producer or manages the producer.

One method to assess the game literacy of an unfamiliar team member is for the producer to arrange a time to play a game with him or her. It is truly the only way that the producer can assess a team member's game literacy. This literacy assessment can play an important role in team management, because it helps inform the weight and risk of the project that should be entrusted to that team member that pertains in any way to the design, development, or testing and deployment of the game. For example, feedback from "casual experts" is a common result of low game literacy, surfacing when a team member contributes unsolicited playtest feedback from their children, friends, colleagues, or anyone else that they happen to know who is a gamer and has seen the project's work in progress.

It is important to note that low game literacy isn't a defect to be solved; it is simply a symptom. It is one of many characteristics that the producer needs to know about all team members to put them in the best position to contribute to the project in harmony.

Managing Expectations

As the producer of the project you will either manage the expectations of all stakeholders, or they will manage you. If the project involves team members who have no prior experience with digital game-based learning production, there will be several critical points in the life of the project when managing expectations will be vital. This is a distinction from low game literacy in that this regards a lack of experience with the game development cycle.

Pre-production can be troublesome for large-scale serious game projects, where there may be team members who lack the skill and experience to appreciate the information in the production planning documentation. As a result, their contribution is minimized in that they don't consider the downstream ramifications of decisions that they agree to. The producer needs his antenna tuned to this likelihood to uncover the opportunities to explore cause and effect in terms that they can understand and appreciate.

Playtesting early, by putting "proof-of-concept" and "first-playable" builds in the hands of all of the team members is a double-edged sword in that it is critically important for the team but is also another aspect that can have similar challenges. If you were fortunate enough to be able to pay professional game testers for these early playtests, they would evaluate the build in the context of the current production phase. If you are testing a pre-alpha vertical slice of a level, they would know what to expect. But if your project includes members who do not have that type of skill and experience, their first inclination is to compare the build to finished commercial products that they have played. Even when you explain in advance that the purpose of the playtest is to evaluate a core feature, learning outcomes, etc., they will be disappointed and concerned by the way that the game looks and whatever usability issues they may experience due to the lack of GUI/UI. I've found that there are two mitigations that the producer can employ:

- Show and explain an example sequence from a previous project: design concept, prototype, alpha, beta, and the final release product. Use the example sequence to briefly highlight the milestone definitions that the team has agreed to for each phase. If this is your first project and you don't have an example sequence, then use an outside example.

- Provide detailed structure for the playtesting. Distribute and explain a detailed testing checklist that will ask them to focus their attention on the criteria under testing.

Summary

Do you really want to take on the responsibilities as producer/developer?

I have a passion for producing/developing serious games. I couldn't imagine myself doing anything else. On each project, there are new demands; I'm constantly self-training. Every day is a new set of optimization problems, creative demands, frustrations, and joy in accomplishment.

On all but the mega-budget serious game productions that have sufficient team size to ensure that each phase of production is complete to the last detail, the producer/developer ends up filling in many blanks, making critical decisions regarding specifics for level design, engineering, art, etc. This can be both the most rewarding aspect and also a maddening churn cycle that can seem to go on without end. Typically, the closer you are to a milestone, the more profound this becomes.

The work requires an ease with and passion for detail. It demands constant reorganizing, reevaluation, and reprioritization. You must be willing to quickly reduce and solve complex problems. Every aspect of game development is reiterative, from start to finish. For the producer, this means that nothing is ever actually "done," as any aspect of the project that may have been considered completed can resurface for revision at any time. The success of your project is directly dependent on your willingness do this and your ability to it quickly and effectively.

How can you know whether this is for you? One idea is to first work as a subordinate team member on at least one game, gamification, or simulation project from start to finish to hone your skills as a producer.

Key Takeaways

The key takeaways from this chapter are

- Spend as much time as you need in pre-production. Pre-production is the key to success.

- Use checklists to keep the team on track. Document the requirements.

- Make sure your course objectives and goals are well determined before creating a game, gamification, or simulation.

- Determine whether the potential game, gamification, or simulation project would require development for a delivery platform that is unfamiliar; look closely to determine what you will need to learn, listing new skills, software, etc., that would be required and whether the new capacity would be something that you would benefit from in the long term.

- Playtest early and often, use the feedback, and be sure to measure the learning outcomes.

- Playtest under the worst case in terms of delivery technology, not the best.

- Make sure the entire team is playtesting.

- Use playtest results to balance and tune gameplay.

- It is important that you observe and act upon playtest feedback, resisting the temptation to discount or blame the playtest for things you don't like.

- If you find low game literacy in some of your project team members, encourage them to play games.

- Manage expectations carefully. You aren't building the next Halo; you are building an educational game, gamification, or simulation.

- First work as a subordinate team member on at least one game, gamification, or simulation project from start to finish to hone your skills as a producer.

Design Considerations

Where to Find Ideas

CHAPTER QUESTIONS

- How do I find an idea for a game, gamification, or simulation?
- Are there brainstorming techniques that can help with this process?
- Once we have an idea, how do we record our thinking?
- How do we convey the ideas to others so they understand?

Introduction

Often the most difficult task in the entire process is figuring out what ideas can be used to create the game, gamification, or simulation. On the surface it seems easy to sit down and develop an interactive learning experience, but the reality is that it takes a great deal of hard work and thought process to develop engaging and meaningful experiences. There are several ways to start; the first is to play games. This provides a foundation upon which you can build a learning game. Then you want to brainstorm ideas to gain a sense of how the interactive learning experience will work from a learner's perspective.

At this point, creating a paper-based prototype is often a good idea. The next step is to playtest your prototype. At this point, it is time to develop the game and create the first digital prototype. To share ideas and to solidify the team's thinking about the game, gamification, or simulation, you'll want to create a design document to help you talk about the idea and make revisions. This can be a one-page document or can be more formal. Finally, if time is of the essence, you can try a Shazam session, where an entire game is conceptualizes, prototyped, and tested in one week's time.

This chapter explores various methods for creating games, gamification, and simulations to help you go from idea to game, gamification, or simulation, as shown in Figure 9.1.

It explains how to capture those ideas on paper so others can understand what the team is doing and gain insight into the final version of the game, gamification, or simulation.

Play Games

The best place to start is to play games, lots of games. In today's modern online and video games, the elements of gamification and simulation abound. The simulated environments of Call of Duty games are highly realistic to the point of almost being a simulation. The elements of socialization and leveling up in games like Farmville and the points progression in games such as Angry Birds all serve as excellent examples of elements that can be used within games, gamification, and simulations for learning. Even playing board games with the perspective of a game designer can provide ideas.

However, you can't play these games for fun. You need to play them as homework. You are gaining insight into what the game developers are doing and how they are holding your attention, directing you from one place to another, and providing you with the information you need to be successful.

Figure 9.1 Moving from Idea to Finished Game, Gamification, or Simulation

Image reprinted with permission of the artist, Kristen Bittner.

Examine the help system, the feedback provided, and even what happens when you fail to accomplish a goal at a certain level. These insights will guide you as you play the game. You must also resolve to play different types of games. Most people gravitate toward one game genre or another. Some people just like to play casual games like Bejeweled or Angry Birds, some people like Farmville-type games, while others like first-person shooters. Regardless of the types of games you like, branch out. Make it your mission to play a different type of game every day. Record what you like or don't like about those games. The more you play games and the more you get into the heads of the developers, the more insight you'll gain into creating games, gamification, and simulations for learning.

Choose a game type from the list in Chapter 3. Choose to play games that have the activities of:

- Collecting/capturing
- Allocating resources

- Strategizing

- Building

- Puzzle solving

- Exploring

- Helping

- Role playing

Some recommended games to play to get a sense of the different types of games include:

- Civilization V (PC game)

- Myst (PC game)

- Railroad Tycoon (PC game)

- Angry Birds (mobile device)

- Darfur Is Dying (web browser)

- Uncharted Series (PlayStation)

- Halo Series (Xbox)

- Wii Sports Games (Wii Systems)

- Fruit Ninja (mobile device)

- Risk (board game)

- Settlers of Catan (board game)

- Chutes and Ladders (board game)

Questions to ask yourself while playing these games include:

- What is the objective of this game? How do I know?

- What type of tutorial or instructions did I receive prior to playing the game?

- What type of feedback am I receiving during this game?

- What activities am I doing in the game that are of value? How do I know they are of value?

- What rewards do I receive for accomplishing the tasks of the game?

- What rewards are expected? What are unexpected?

- What type of help is offered? Are there "lifelines" or advice given by non-player characters along the way?

- How many levels are in this game?

- What is this game teaching me?

- What elements in the game are like elements in a simulation?

- What elements are like gamification elements? Is there a leaderboard?

- Are there both single player and multi-player modes? Are they the same or different?

Answering these questions and playing these games will provide you with an excellent foundation from which you can brainstorm ideas for your own learning games, gamification, and simulations.

Simulation Specific

Simulations have an extra dimension; simulations re-create real-life environments, so identifying real-life scenarios is key to generating simulation ideas. Simulations use key measures of performance or metrics to determine success. Ask yourself the following questions when brainstorming ideas for a simulation:

- *What are your metrics and what drives these metrics in real life?* For example, if one of your metrics is "customer service," what are the real-life drivers of customer service? Once you've identified these drivers, it will be easier to use one of the idea-generating techniques below to come up with good scenario ideas.

- *What makes the tasks or behaviors in the simulation difficult to do in real life?* For example, statistics show that new leaders in businesses often fail in the first year, typically due to unrealistic expectations about what their jobs will be like. They experience conflicting instructions from their bosses, resistance from their team members, and demanding schedules that make prioritizing their days difficult. Figuring out these categories will also help you generate simulation ideas and will make your simulation more difficult—and more realistic.

- *Where am I in time?* Time is a big driver in simulation. Think about what would happen at each point in time. For example, in the retail world, late summer is always back-to-school. Late autumn is the beginning of the holiday rush. These time-based events tell you the kinds of decisions that have to be made in your simulation.

Brainstorming Techniques

Many techniques can be used for brainstorming the creation of a game, gamification, or simulation. It is usually best if you can have a cross-functional team involved in the process. If you can find some people who are instructional designers, programmers, artists, subject-matter experts, and others, you will then have a variety of ideas generated. If the group is too homogeneous, you'll have too many similar ideas.

Choose the technique that you are most comfortable or familiar with or that the company or organization uses. When brainstorming about an interactive learning experience:

- Keep the business and learning goals in mind. Write them down so everyone can continually refer to them.
- Interactivity is the key to a successful learning ILE.
- Balance "fun" with learning outcomes.
- Keeping those items in mind, choose your technique to begin brainstorming.

Gamefest

One quick method of generating a lot of ideas is to have a gamefest. To conduct a gamefest, you need a large conference room with a table in the middle and then space for board games and laptops for playing computer-based and web-based games. Some games will be multiplayer and some single player.

In the room, place a flip chart and sticky-notes. The idea is that each player has fifteen to twenty minutes to play a game to which he is randomly assigned. After the play time, the players go to the flip chart and write down a major idea they would like to include in a game, gamification, or simulation.

Once everyone has written down a major idea, they switch games and play a new game for fifteen to twenty minutes. After that play time, they again write down ideas on the flip chart. If major ideas are already taken, the players then can write refinements or smaller ideas on the sticky notes and add them beside the major ideas.

This method is especially effective if the individuals working on the game, gamification, or simulation are not overly familiar with games. The forced play exposes them quickly to many different game mechanics and game elements. Use the list of recommended games above as a starter for the gamefest.

Mind Mapping

The mind-mapping process is used to display thoughts visually for examination and to create connections among items. Typically, a mind map is drawn with a single idea, concept, or word in the center and connections drawn from the center out.

For game, gamification, or simulation design, you can place the learning outcome in the middle and diagram the actions, activities, or tasks that are required to help a person learn the desired outcome. Mind maps work best for concepts, problem solving, and human relations skills such as negotiation or sales. Mind maps aren't as effective for procedures, as a more linear approach such as a flow diagram is typically more applicable.

With the ILE team in a single room with a large whiteboard, list the focal item, word, phrase, or learning outcome in the middle and brainstorm game ideas around the focal item, as shown in Figure 9.2. One method is "forced" brainstorming, during which each person takes a turn adding one thing to the mind map when it is his or her turn. This can be done in a "lightening" round fashion and provides a quick way of capturing ideas and first impressions. Once the contributions slow down, the ideas can be refined.

Figure 9.2 Creating a Mind Map for a Sales-Oriented Interactive Learning Experience
Image reprinted with permission of the artist, Kristen Bittner.

When using a whiteboard or computer-based software for the mind map process, consider using different colors to represent different information and connections. The goal is to bring together ideas for the ILE in one visual image and then to drill down into the areas map that make sense for the development of the game, gamification, or simulation.

Affinity Diagram

Another way to brainstorm ideas for a game, gamification, or simulation is to create an affinity diagram, as shown in Figure 9.3. Again, the entire team gets into the same room (it could be a virtual room with today's software tools), and they generate ideas. This works well after a gamefest but can be used at any time. The team members generate ideas, write ideas on sticky notes, and place them on a whiteboard or other surface. Then the team members group similar ideas together.

Figure 9.3 Creating an Affinity Diagram on the Wall of the Conference Room

Image reprinted with permission of the artist, Kristen Bittner.

One advantage of an affinity diagram is that concepts will surface as critical to the design process. Look carefully at the ideas that receive a large number of notes and have strong relationships.

Paper Prototyping

Once the idea is formed and has a little more substance than just a concept floating around a mind map, the next step is to create a paper prototype. This step helps to avoid miscues later in the process. A game, gamification, or simulation can only be truly assessed for playability, engagement, and learning when played. Figure 9.4 shows a development team playtesting a prototype.

This is a good process to start early because, even when you are playing the first version of the paper prototype, you'll notice opportunities for fine-tuning the environment, rules, and structure. Paper is great because it is so flexible, and there are no expectations of permanence. You want to make this

Figure 9.4 Playtest a Prototype Before Full-Scale Development

Image reprinted with permission of the artist, Kristen Bittner.

as basic as possible. Don't get caught up in the aesthetics; instead, focus on the interactions and activities that are occurring.

The paper prototyping process should work as follows:

1. Once an idea is agreed on, write up a player interaction with the ILE. How does a player first enter into the ILE? What does he do? What does he see? This is called a "player walkthrough."

2. Write the rules. It is amazing that as you begin to write rules you'll discover new rules that need to be written. For example, when does a learner earn points? What is the highest possible number of points that can be earned? How does the player know how to move around the simulation? How many different environments are going to be used within the simulation?

3. Spend extra time documenting the scoring and points process. People become concerned when points don't add up or they sense an unfair rule. Carefully consider how all the interactions will work.

4. Design a paper environment or environments that mimic the environments for the ILE. This could be a board if it's a board game

or it can be a rough drawing of an office or piece of equipment for a simulation, or for gamification it might be the website interface that helps a learner "level up." The drawings don't need to be 100 percent accurate but should depict the general idea. In the case of simulations, you may want to snap photographs of the machinery or equipment used within the simulation. If you want, you can take the environments to an office supply store and have them laminated.

5. If required, create paper characters and non-player characters that interact in the ILE space. These "game pieces" are how the learners will interact within the ILE space you've developed.

6. Now that you have the game pieces, environment, and rules, play the game, gamification, or simulation. Observe what happens; make changes and modifications. You should run through three or more iterations with just the design team before taking it any further in the testing process.

7. While testing the game within the design team, look for certain problems. These include inconsistencies in scoring, difficulties with what to do in a certain situation, complications with piece movement, and other issues.

8. The next step is to incorporate a group from outside of the design team to playtest the game.

Playtesting Your Paper Prototype

Sharon Boller, President Bottom-Line Performance, Inc.

Here's what to assess as you prototype and playtest:

- Is the game achieving the learning objectives defined for it?
- Is the game achieving the desired player experience? In other words:
  - Is the game "fun?" (Remember, fun is a lot of different things. Fun can be problem solving, strategizing, exploring, collecting, being immersed in a story, competing, achieving, etc.)

- Is the game "balanced" in terms of difficulty?
- Are the rules clear?
- Are the rules logical and well aligned with the learning objectives?
- Is the game goal clear to players?
- Are the game aesthetics compelling and engaging?
- Who should my playtesters be?

Involve your target "player" or learner early. A game can seem great to a bunch of subject-matter experts and totally bore or frustrate a target player. In early playtesting, involve a group friendly to you who can offer supportive feedback.

Once you are past those first paper prototypes—but well before you've put high-end production values on your game—pull in some strangers who can give honest and frank feedback.

How to Do a Playtest

As scary as it sounds, you hand a group of players the rules and let them set up and play your game. If they get totally stuck, that is, they absolutely cannot continue without intervention, then help them just enough to keep them going. Let them know going in how long you expect them to play. It may be until someone achieves the game goal or it may be for a specified amount of time. After the playtest, you can use these questions to debrief the experience:

1. Give me a one-word description of your gameplay experience.
2. Was the game engaging to you? On a scale of 1 to 5 with 5 being "extremely engaged," how engaged were you in the gameplay? Did this change for you at any point in the game?
3. Were the rules clear and realistic to learn?
   a. If not, when were you confused?
   b. Would you suggest any other rules or the elimination of any rules?
4. What, in your words, was the objective of the game?
5. If you had to describe the game to someone who hasn't played, what would you say?

6. What information do you wish you had while playing the game that you did not have?

7. Was there anything you didn't like about the game? What was it?

8. Was anything confusing? What was it?

9. Here were the learning goals for the game. On a scale of 1 to 5, rate how well do you feel the game enabled you to achieve each goal.

You need to be careful in a playtest. You aren't really looking for your players to tell you how to redesign the game. You may have very compelling reasons for a design decision—or you could have abandoned a game element or mechanic based on a previous round of playtesting—so you don't want to invite commentary on what else to do with your game. You want to assess what worked and what didn't—and then take this information back with you to determine any redesign you need to make. Importantly, when creating a learning game, you can't just assess the fun factor; you have to assess how well it helped you meet the learning objectives you defined for the game.

Shazam Session

One way to quickly develop a game, gamification, or simulation is to create a Shazam session. If you recall, Shazam is a comic book character created by Bill Parker and C.C. Beck for Fawcett Comics. He is an ancient wizard who gives a young boy named Billy Batson the power to transform into the superhero Captain Marvel. Because DC Comics has billed Captain Marvel's adventures under the name *Shazam!* since 1973, the superhero is often mistakenly referred to by his mentor's name. Because of this, in 2012 DC officially changed Captain Marvel's name to Shazam.[1]

The name Shazam is actually an acronym containing the initials of the first letters of the names of six ancient heroes. Each letter empowers Captain Marvel/Shazam with certain attributes:

- S for The wisdom of Solomon

- H for the strength of Hercules

- A for the stamina of Atlas

- Z for the power of Zeus

- A for the courage of Achilles

- M for the speed of Mercury[2]

For the purposes of rapidly designing, prototyping, and playtesting a game, gamification, or simulation, the name seems perfect.

In the Shazam session, a team is assembled of different individuals with different skill sets. You'll need an instructional designer, developer, artist, subject-matter expert, and anyone else who can contribute to the design of the ILE. Then the following process is undertaken over a week-long period:

- *Preparation:* Creation of learner personas, creation of agenda and schedule, coordination of learner focus group, and research related to the needs of the particular session. Discussion of games and gamification for learning is conducted by a facilitator. Creation of work teams and assignment of each individual to the work team.

- *Day One: Facilitated, Live Session:* The first part of the session involves presentation of the needs of the learners, discussion of the personas, understanding the Shazam session workflow, facilitated gameplaying to level set the team (online and board games), discussion of week's objectives, and a short work session to begin the process of rapid prototyping.

- *Day Two: Facilitated, Live Session:* Team meets briefly to discuss progress and lessons learned from yesterday's session. Morning consists of two hours of prototype followed by a "stealing" session. The participants are able to view progress of other teams and steal best ideas to facilitate the creation of an even better version of the prototype. Ideas are incorporated. Afternoon session involves more prototyping and one or two more rounds of stealing.

- *Day Three: Facilitated, Live Session:* Final prototype form is agreed on. Development of paper prototype.

- *Day Four: Facilitated, Live Session:* Test/focus group does a "think aloud" walkthrough in one-on-one sessions to surface issues, problems, and gameplay hiccups.

- *Day Five: Facilitated, Live Session:* The team incorporates the ideas learned from Day Four into a final prototype version of the game or gamification. Debriefing discussion of experience, meta-lessons from overall experience.

The idea of the Shazam session is that at the end of the week a viable prototype has been created. The prototype is validated by a test group of learners and the ideas can then be developed further. This technique has helped to create a number of successful game, gamification, and simulation projects.

Sharing Output

Regardless of what process is used, once a game, gamification, or simulation is developed, there is going to be a need to articulate the design, goals, and outcomes to an audience outside of the project team. This typically requires the use of some type of design document.

Traditional Design Document

In many environments, a design document is used so that a team has a common framework for the creation of a large-scale training effort. Table 9.1 shows elements that should be contained within a design document and provides an example of the type of information provided in the design template. The left column is basically an outline of what should be contained within your design document.

One-Page Design Document

An alternative to the full-fledged design document is something Stone Librande, the creative director at EA/Maxis dubbed the "one-page design document." Stone's argument is that people tend not to read long, expansive

Table 9.1 Elements of a Design Document

Design Template Element	Example
Overview of Concept	The concept is to create a web-based single-player online game for pharmaceutical sales representatives that provides engaging, relevant, and personalized learning on the topic of opening and closing a conversation with a physician. Topics covered in the game are tied to our ABC engagement model. The game is based on a realistic setting of a physician's office. The game will happen from a third-person perspective and the learner will be evaluated on credibility, affability, and the ability to become an information source for the physician.
Outcome	Pharmaceutical sales representatives will properly use the ABC model to gain more time with the physician and become a valuable resource to the physician.
Instructional Objectives	At the end of the game, the learners will be able to:
	Properly apply the three steps of an ABC opening
	Properly apply the two steps of the ABC closing
	Appropriately prepare for a call on a physician
	Be affective
	Behave in a warm, friendly, professional manner toward the physician
Description of Character(s)	The learners will be able to customize an avatar in terms of eyes, skin, and hair and be able to select different styles of clothes. The learners will interact with six NPCs, three female and three male, each representing ethnic and personality diversity. The NPC physicians will each have different amounts of time they are able to spend with the sales representative.
Environment	Home office for the learner and then six different offices. Learners will walk their characters to a car that has a map on the passenger seat. The map has images, each representing a different physician's office location. The learner will click on the map to arrive at the front door of that location. Six physician offices need to be created.

	Office one: Rural small family practice. Older filing cabinets, small waiting room space with six chairs.
	Office two: . . .
Description of Gameplay	Upon entering the learning management system and launching the game, the learner is placed into an office where customization can occur. After learners customize their avatars, they hear an audio of a phone ringing. They must click on the phone to answer it. At that time, the voice provides them with instructions on how to navigate through the game. At the end of the call, instructions are given as to the next step. When the call is over, the learners must click on the computer to view a list of physicians. Each image and name is clickable to receive more information. The learners must then prioritize the list to decide in what order to visit the physicians. Next . . .
Reward Structure	The points in this game will be based on three variables: credibility, affability, and the ability to become an information source for the physician. Each will be scored separately and then an overall score will be provided, the "engagement score." Within the game, focus will be on a mastery orientation toward the goal. This means each learner works to master the content in the game and the overall score is not related to any other learner's scores. Feedback will be provided immediately with an unobtrusive popup accompanied by a longer explanation available after play.
Look and Feel of Game	The goal is to provide a realistic-looking avatar in three dimensions. The players will be able to see both the front and back of the avatar through a spinning function. The environment will contain 3-D objects that are typical colors, black phone, gray computer terminal, brown briefcase. The heads-up display will contain six elements. The first is. . . .
Technical Description	This game will be developed using Caspian's Thinking Worlds software to provide the 3-D environment that is required. The game will be accessed via the corporate intranet and will not require any client downloads. The results need to flow into our learning management system when the player completes the game in a compatible format. Additionally, ...
Timeline	This can be a Gantt chart or other method of showing the estimated time to complete the project.

design documents and they are typically written by the design team and then never looked at again. He believes that a simple, one-page document discussing the major elements of the gameplay would be a better solution.

The one-page design document is easier to comprehend, provides an opportunity to make visible changes to the design of the game, gamification, or simulation, and is a great jumping-off point for discussions about the ILE. Figure 9.5 shows a sample one-page design document.[3]

The premise behind the one-page design document is simple: use lots of white space and include a title and a date. You'll also want illustrations of the basic environment of the game, gamification, or simulation. You may want smaller diagrams as well to provide more detailed information. You should also include short description of navigation and gameplay, callouts of important information, and navigational information.

Figure 9.5 One-Page Design Document

Create a document that can be viewed quickly and easily by a team and use to vet the idea with stakeholders once the idea takes more shape. You can make the one-page document more artistic and formal. Also, some organizations create both the one-page design document as well as the larger formal document. The formal document is to keep track of all the information about the game, gamification, or simulation and the one-page is to share and gain "buzz."

Key Takeaways

The key takeaways from this chapter are these:

- To gain ideas for designing games, gamification, and simulations, play a lot of games. These should be board games, video games, mobile games, and any other type of game you can envision.

- When playing games, study them. Think about and record what the game designer was thinking when he created a certain gameplay element. The idea is to learn as much as you can from different games.

- Simulations re-create real-life environments and use key measures of performance, or metrics, to determine success. Ask yourself what drives these metrics in real life.

- Use brainstorming sessions to develop the concepts you would like in your game, gamification, or simulation. It doesn't matter what technique you use, but choose a technique and brainstorm ideas.

- Once an idea is developed, create a paper prototype. The paper prototype allows for a great deal of flexibility when testing an interactive learning experience.

- Test first with the design team for several interactions and then test with people who are not part of the design team. Playtesting is a critical element of the development of an ILE.

- If you have a short period of time, use a Shazam session, where creating, prototyping, and testing are crammed into one week of vigorous activity.

- When a game idea is fleshed out and a direction to proceed has been established, create a design document.

- Design documents can either be long with lots of sections to help the design team understand the direction of the game or can be one-page design documents.

- Often teams use the longer design document for internal team use and create a one-page document to share with individuals outside the team.

Games

CHAPTER QUESTIONS

- How do you create an instructional game?
- How do you choose the right game type?
- What are personas? How can they help in game design?

Introduction

Prerequisite knowledge for this chapter: an in-depth knowledge of current game genres and mechanics.

In this chapter we will go step-by-step through the process of making an educational game. Outside of the steps that will be covered in this chapter, the best advice any aspiring educational game creator can take is to play many games. Play card games, board games, and especially video games. I hope that you play these games because you enjoy them. If you don't enjoy games, it is unlikely that you will ever design them successfully. Even though this chapter will give you a set of tools, make sure that you ask the right questions, and help you create a mental model of the process, it cannot teach you the most important aspect of effectively designing games.

The most important tool a designer has is the language of games, which is the product of a rich history of characters, stories, rule sets, feedback, and mechanics. This language can only be learned by experiencing it first-hand by playing the games. Anything that a designer creates is always influenced by what he or she has experienced. The more games a designer has played, the more options he or she will have when coming up with ideas.

Conversations between designers often sound like this:

> "Hey we could try a game from this genre, except we could replace this mechanic with this one."
>
> "Oh yeah, that reminds me of this game. . . ."
>
> "And we could use the scoring from this other type of game. . . ."
>
> "And maybe the feedback system from this game. . . ."
>
> "Oh and I love the mechanic in this game, let's tweak it to do this though."

If you cannot see yourself participating in a conversation like the one above, filling in the gaps with your own experiences, you need to build your general knowledge of games before attempting to make them.

Designing a Game from Start to Finish

What are we teaching?

The first question that must be answered before any actual design can take place is "What are we teaching?" Or more directly "How will the players be different after playing this game? The answer will enable you to ask other important questions and lay the groundwork for all of the design decisions that are to come. The answer is not as simple as a few words or sentences. The information you need must include the following:

- Terminal learning objective(s) (TLO)

- Enabling learning objectives(s) (ELO)

- The type of learning for each learning objective (Bloom's Taxonomy)

- The knowledge, skills, and attitudes (KSAs) that support the enabling learning objectives

While organizing this data it is also a good time to list learning objectives (LOs)by their difficulty and the order in which they must be learned. Organizing LOs this way will make it easier to match them up with gameplay and properly scaffold them when we are at that point in the process.

After you have established what you are teaching, you must determine whether the game is supposed to teach or test. Whether you or a client make the determination, it is very important to establish what you want the game to accomplish. The difference between teaching and testing with a game really comes down to the designer's assumptions about the player's prerequisite knowledge. In many cases games are used in conjunction with some kind of traditional learning. You will need to understand all of the content that the players will receive in the classroom or online module before playing.

Other important questions to ask that pertain to the learning material:

- How is it being taught now?

- What are they doing right?

- What are they doing wrong?

- Why do they need a game?

- Will a game make it better and how?

- What is the best platform to deliver the game?

- How long will they play this game?

- Will they be expected to play multiple times?

Designer Notes

Ideas will rush into your head when you first hear about the subject matter or problem. Write these ideas down, but do not get hung up on any single idea. Wait until you have a grasp of the instructional material and situation before you commit to ideas.

Start organizing your LOs into a flowchart. Show them in the order that they should be learned and connect them to one another to illustrate a logical flow.

KSA	→	ELO		
KSA	→	ELO		
KSA	→	ELO	→	TLO
KSA	→	ELO		
KSA	→	ELO		

And then make the flowchart more linear by thinking about the specific order that items should be taught in. This is not final and will likely change once you begin to account for gameplay and narrative.

K A S → ELO K S → ELO K A → ELO A K S → ELO K S A → ELO → TLO

Later in the process when you are planning out gameplay or a narrative, it is useful to refer back to this flowchart and create other flows/storylines that run in parallel with this one.

Who are we teaching?

The next important piece of information that you need before you can begin the design process is who your audience will be. *Who* you are teaching is just as important as *what* you are teaching. It is your job as the designer to assess the audience's capabilities and consider what you know about them while you are creating a game. Another important piece of information that can be lumped into your exploration about the intended audience is the environment that they will they be learning in. When you playtest your game you will want to do the testing with players similar to your intended audience and in a setting like the one that your game will eventually be in.

Other important questions to ask that pertain to the audience:

- What is their knowledge level?

- What is their tech level?

- Are they gamers?

- Are there any other considerations like disabilities, age requirements, play time, or hardware?

- Where will they be playing the game?

- What is the best platform for the learning environment?

One design tool that is very helpful with this step of the process is a persona. Personas are representations of your players in archetypal forms, as shown in Figure 10.1. It is a great way to organize information about your intended audience and a reminder that the work you are doing now will affect real people. When creating personas give them names and back stories that are representative of your intended audience. Be sure to include things like disabilities, diverse educational levels, and varying experience with technology.

Game Design

At this point you should have a good grasp on what you are teaching and who you are teaching. Now it is time to start putting more thought into the game ideas you wrote down while you were learning more about the game content and the learners. When designing, never lose sight of the learning objectives and your learners. Remember that you are trying to create an experience for them.

If you are making a game to test:

If you are making a game that is going to evaluate players on knowledge that they should have going into the game, it is important to

Figure 10.1 Personas Are Helpful for Keeping Your Audience in Mind

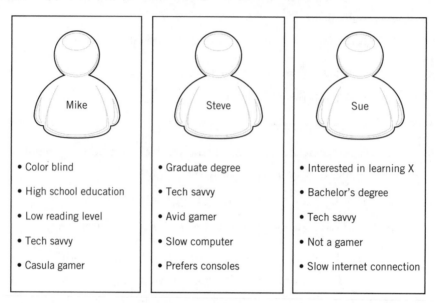

Mike	Steve	Sue
• Color blind	• Graduate degree	• Interested in learning X
• High school education	• Tech savvy	• Bachelor's degree
• Low reading level	• Avid gamer	• Tech savvy
• Tech savvy	• Slow computer	• Not a gamer
• Casula gamer	• Prefers consoles	• Slow internet connection

have a firm understanding of the prerequisite knowledge. If you are evaluating skills, you will likely be making a game that is closer to a simulation because you want the players to be able to perform and practice as they would in the real world. If the game is intended to test declarative knowledge, then the game can be a little more abstract. However, keep in mind that even when testing declarative knowledge, it is important to create an environment that is close to the one they would need to access the information in.

If you are making a game to teach:

The first step is to break down the task into its component knowledge, skills, and attitudes (KSAs) and match them with game mechanics, feedback, and rules.

Knowledge can be taught through narrative, dialogue with game characters, or system messages. Just relaying the information to players is not enough. Ideally, you want the players to have to act on the information or utilize it in some way. Don't just re-create the classroom experience where players are obtaining the information through a document in the game. That is the kind of delivery we are trying to improve upon.

- *Example:* A phone center where the player takes calls and answers questions.
- *Example:* A game where a player must gather information through questing.

Skills should be modeled after the actions the player would perform in the real world. It is important to match learning objectives to game mechanics that are complementary to them.

- *Example:* How to operate within or coordinate a team.
- *Example:* How to navigate a space using maps or clues.
- *Example:* A puzzle game where putting something together or taking it apart matches a real-world skill.

Instilling attitudes in players can require some creativity. It is a little more abstract than giving players some piece of knowledge or letting them perform a skill. It is important not to be heavy-handed when trying to convey an attitude. Try to represent the attitude by presenting the information or gameplay from a certain perspective. You can also accomplish this by having the players interact with characters in the game who may have a story the player can relate to.

- *Example:* Playing as an avatar is a great way to allow players to see things from another person's perspective.
- *Example:* Having players make an extremely difficult or impossible choice that others have had to make.

Theming and Story

Many games have some kind of theming or story that is independent of the genre and mechanics. Theme and story should be decided on before or concurrently with the genre and mechanics. Having an interesting theme or original story can actually make the design process easier because it constricts the possibilities and can give you a direction to start in.

Choosing a Game Genre/Type

In many cases your learning objectives will choose the genre for you. You will start with a set of learning objectives and some mechanics that address them. At that point it is acceptable to see whether the mechanics and environment that you have chosen fall into one of the accepted genres. Do not pick a genre too early in the process. Every game type comes with baggage, such as extra unnecessary mechanics, that may not fit into your game. You can, however, draw inspiration from other games with similar play. The type of game you decide to make and the genre that it falls into will be dependent on several things. The first thing to consider is the limitations on your design possibilities created by topics like timeline, budget, and your team's capabilities. After accounting for those restrictions, it is time to start thinking about what game types your KSA/mechanic/interaction combinations fit into. This is where your experience playing games will be very important. There are too many game types to fully list, but the following are some of the most popular genres:

- 2-D Platformers
- Driving/Racing
- Fighting Games
- Massively Multiplayer Online Games
- Music Games
- Puzzle Games
- Real-Time Strategy
- Role-Playing Games (many types)
- Shooters
- Social/Casual Games
- Sports Games
- Stealth Games
- Survival Games
- Tower Defense

Designer Notes

To further complicate the situation, most of these game types, or certain aspects of them, can be combined to create something new.

Don't just get hung up on the question "What kind of game am I making?" Better questions to ask include:

- What game mechanics best represent the skills I am trying to teach?
- What theming will best represent the setting?
- What feedback will change player behavior to meet your objectives?
- What rules can I use to limit the player in an effective way?

When you have a few genres or mechanics in mind that you think could be a good fit for your game, it is good practice to find a few examples and play them. Do this with your entire team if possible. It is good to collect multiple perspectives on the games. Try to look at the games critically as you play them. In addition to your own experiences, read reviews about them and see what people liked and didn't like. Make note of what rules, feedback, and UI the games used. Playing games like this will always give you some additional ideas.

Looking at a wide range of sample games will help you determine the best game to develop. Here are a few examples. Figure 10.2 is modeled after a tower defense type game called Garden Defense. Players earn currency by answering questions. Figure 10.3 is called Devil's Advocate; it is a stealth game where players identified automatic thoughts and replaced them with logical thoughts in soldiers suffering from post-traumatic stress disorder (PTSD). Figure 10.4 is Bullseye Trainer, an arcade-style game that teaches the Navy's bullseye system. These sample instructional games are courtesy UCF RETRO Lab.

Designer Note

The order of the next few sections: Wireframing, One-Page Designs, Paper Prototyping, and Storyboards are not written in stone. You do not have to do them in that order or even do them all. Do what works for you or for your particular situation.

Figure 10.2 Tower Defense Type Game (Garden Defense)

Figure 10.3 2-D Stealth Platformer (Devil's Advocate)

Figure 10.4 Arcade Game Bullseye Trainer

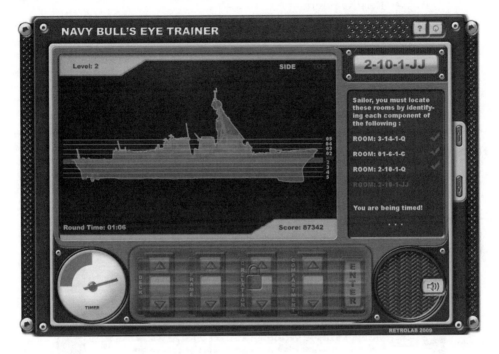

Wireframing

Wireframes are like a blueprint for your game. They can be as simple or complex as needed and usually go through many revisions. When creating them, use simple line drawings to reflect the interface and menu structures. There are several popular tools available just for wireframing, as well as more traditional vector-based illustration tools.

It is good practice to create your wireframes on a canvas that is the same size as the final product will be. This will ensure your spacing and arrangements will all fit when a prototype is made. If you are designing for a specific platform like mobile devices, it is common practice to have the basic shape of the phone or tablet surrounding the wireframe.

Information you are trying to convey:

- Basic shapes and sizes

- Relative positions

- Notes on basics functionality and movement

- Location and type of information displayed

Figure 10.5 is an example of a wireframe for a tablet application.

Figure 10.5 Sample Wireframe for a Mobile Device Game

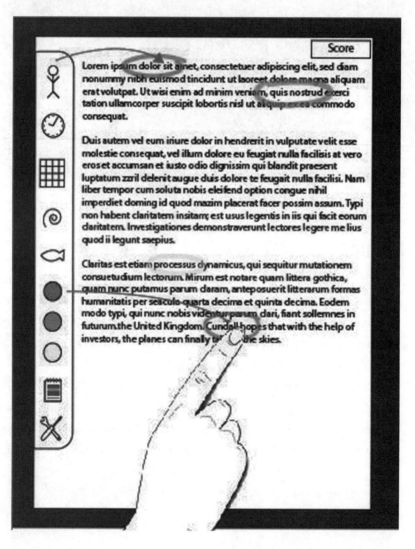

One-Page Design

While doing this initial planning, I recommend creating a one-page design document. This idea was popularized by the game designer Stone Librande. One-page designs are great for planning out the basic gameplay, user interface, and interactions. "One page" refers to a single surface, not a single sheet of paper. Sometimes one-page designs can fill up an entire board or an entire room. The point is that your team should be able to look at it and see a design in its entirety.

Designer Note

When meeting around a one-page design at a whiteboard, we like to have the designers, artist, and programmers use different colored markers. This makes it easier to distinguish between important notes from each group.

A one-page design combines the benefits of illustration with the organization of a design document. Think of it as an "infographic" for your game. It is important to be as visual as possible and show how things are connected. Use callouts where needed to add detail to sections. You should be able to talk someone through the game experience from start to finish using the one-page design document as your guide.

When creating your one-page design, don't just think about it as a snapshot of gameplay. Remember to take into account how long and how often you expect the learners to play your game. Think about how you will keep players challenged for their entire experience. There are many ways to do this, including levels, more challenging enemies, faster timers, or higher requirements for winning. Making another flowchart that takes this challenge scaling into account and matching it up with your learning objectives flowchart from earlier can be helpful.

Information to include:

- Notes about rules and scoring
- Ideas about levels/challenge

- Notes about how learning objectives are addressed
- Callouts with details
- Some indications about the proper order of operation
- Arrows indicating flow, movement, and interactions

Figure 10.6 is an example of a one-page design and Figure 10.7 is what the finished game screen looks like that was created from it.

Paper Prototyping

Once you have your one-page design to a point where you can talk through the gameplay and it makes sense, it is time to start having other people play through the game. Paper prototypes are great for this because you can quickly iterate on your design and gather feedback. Another important aspect of paper prototyping is that it is relatively cheap compared to actually creating the assets digitally. There are several techniques that go into paper prototyping.

Figure 10.6 One-Page Design Created on a Whiteboard

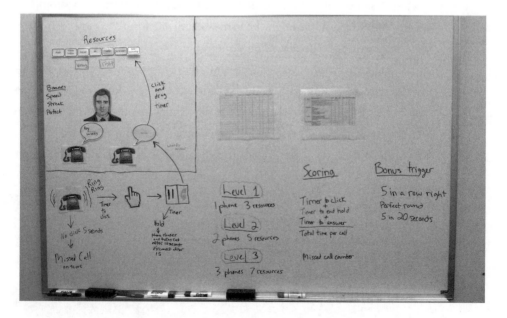

Figure 10.7 Finished Game Screen Based on the One-Page Design Document

Re-create your UI and basic game functionality on paper, as shown in Figure 10.8.

Use your flowcharts, wireframes, and one-page design document as resources. Do not just sit a tester in front of a paper prototype and say "Go." You will have to be an active participant in the process by acting as a puppeteer. Because it is a paper prototype, nothing will move on its own. So when a tester pushes a button you will have to move the pieces around for the proper response to happen. This is also great practice for you as the designer because to successfully move the pieces around for a tester you will be required to have an in-depth knowledge of the interactions. A popular technique for prototyping mobile interfaces is to create all of the possible states of the application on one piece of paper. You will then move a frame from illustration to illustration for the tester to work in instead of moving individual pieces. Sometimes you will have to re-create mechanics with whatever objects you have available, for instance using a twenty-sided die for a damage or movement roll.

Figure 10.8 Using a Paper Prototype to Test Gameplay

Paper Prototyping To-Do List

- Create your interface in paper with moveable pieces or create multiple states.

- Create a list of objectives for the tester to accomplish.

- Do not talk to the user during the process. Do not answer questions or help the person.

- Have the tester speak out loud about what he or she is doing.

- Take notes about where the tester becomes lost or where he intuitively thinks things should be.

Storyboards

The purpose of storyboards, as their name implies, is to tell a story. They are comparable to the blocks that make up a comic book page. Each block has a piece of text and some illustrations that follow a narrative and contribute to a larger story. They are used to show art direction and to show how well a project flows. They are a good way to present early ideas to a client because they are usually presented linearly, which makes them easy to give a presentation around.

Storyboards are where you can expand on the story that you told with your one-page design. The flowcharts that you made to organize your learning objectives, gameplay, and story should be your main source of inspiration. Get all of the flow charts in one place and circle large parts of each that are representative of a key idea or interaction in your game. All of the content inside each of the areas you circled will go into a single storyboard. Storyboards do not have to be completely linear. Having a section that branches to illustrate where a player could have made a choice and the consequences of the choice will help your team better understand your intent. Two storyboard examples from Devil's Advocate are shown in Figures 10.9 and 10.10.

Figure 10.9 Storyboard Example from Devil's Advocate

Figure 10.10 Storyboard Showing a Number of Thoughts from the Devil's Advocate Game

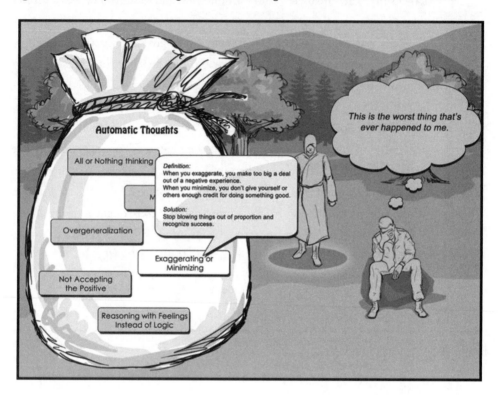

Design Document

A full design document is where all of the information from your working documents will be collected. These documents are usually pretty big and are a good way to gather everything in one place. Design documents are not that great as working documents though. You cannot just give a fifty-page document to programmers and artists and say, "Make this." Design documents should instead be a way to put all of your important information in one place.

See Chapter 9 of this book for additional information and examples of design documents.

Key Takeaways

Key takeaways from this chapter are as follows:

- You must have an in-depth knowledge of current game genres and mechanics.
- Know what your game is teaching and who you are teaching.
- Use personas to keep in mind your target audience for the game.
- Know whether you are creating a testing or a teaching game.
- Choose the right theme and story for your game.
- Use tools like wireframing, a one-page design document, and paper prototyping to test and retest your games before you begin programming.

Gamification

CHAPTER QUESTIONS

- How do I design a gamification experience?

- Are intrinsic and extrinsic motivation mutually exclusive?

- What factors weigh into my decision to design a gamification experience?

- What types of elements are contained within gamified learning?

- How can we avoid cheating in structural gamification?

Introduction

As mentioned in Chapter 3, gamification is "using game-based mechanics, aesthetics, and game thinking to engage people, motivate action, promote learning, and solve problems" and there are two types of gamification—content and structural. In this chapter, we'll explore how to create learning experiences using each type. The goal is to provide a framework for you to create a compelling gamified experience for learners. Keep in mind that elements of content gamification and structural gamification can be used interchangeably. It is possible to add a character to structural gamification, and it is possible to add points to content gamification. The discussion in this chapter is for clarity of concept, but the reality is that the two often overlap.

Controversial Nature of Gamification

Some people don't like gamification because they feel it is manipulative and relies too much on extrinsic motivational factors. Extrinsic motivation is usually defined as some behavior undertaken to obtain some reward or avoid punishment.[1] It is seen as artificial and, it is argued, the impact won't last. The alternative, intrinsic motivation, is seen as good because a person undertakes an activity for its own sake, for the enjoyment it provides, the learning it permits, or the feeling of accomplishment it evokes.[2]

An example sometimes given of the good of intrinsic motivation versus the bad of extrinsic motivation is using a "star chart" to motivate children. A star chart is a poster or piece of paper that lists all the chores a child needs to perform for each day of the week. On the first day when you tell your child to brush her teeth, she runs up stairs and brushes her teeth immediately to receive the star. At this point, you think you've discovered the secret to parenthood. Who knew it could be this easy?

Then about a week later, you tell your child to brush her teeth and receive a star, she tells you "no." She doesn't want to brush her teeth for one star, she wants two. It is escalating. Soon after, stars are not enough. She wants a bigger reward for brushing her teeth. Until finally it escalate to a level where to get her to brush her teeth, you have to give her a candy bar. Proof-positive, the critics say, that gamification doesn't work and that extrinsic motivation is all bad. (See Figures 11.1 and 11.2.)

However, human motivation is not that simple. Human motivation is not black and white—intrinsic is always good while extrinsic motivation is always bad. In reality, intrinsic motivation and extrinsic motivation actually work side-by-side and can provide positive motivation for learners.

Figure 11.1 First Day with the Star Chart—Secret to Parenthood

Image reprinted with permission of the artist, Kristin Bittner.

Figure 11.2 Second Week with the Star Chart—Giving Out Candy Bars to Get Kids to Brush Teeth

Image reprinted with permission of the artist, Kristin Bittner.

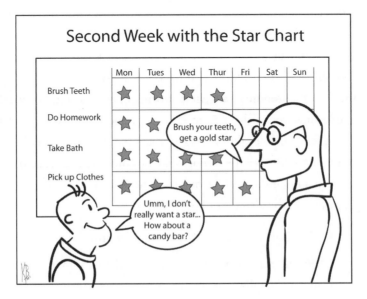

Extrinsic Motivation

Researchers have discovered a number of interesting elements about extrinsic motivation, intrinsic motivation, and how the two work together. When designing gamification for learning, it's important to understand these relationships.

Extrinsic motivation can be effectively used in the following manner:

- To increase a learner's expression of task enjoyment and free time spent performing a task. This results from using performance-contingent rewards, that is, rewards given depending on the performance of the learner.[3]

- To strengthen the perception of freedom of action. This results when rewards for high performance appear.[4]

- To engage a learner when the activity is one that learners do not find of inherent interest or value.[5]

- To engage learners when they initially view the activity as low value.[6]

- To narrowly focus attention and to shorten time perspectives.[7]

Intrinsic Motivation

When considering developing for intrinsic motivation, one widely cited theory is called "self-determination theory (SDT)." This is a macro-theory that explains human motivation to perform a task or an activity as being internally driven.[8] SDT addresses three elements that drive human motivation. The first is "autonomy," a feeling of being in control and being able to direct your own actions. The second is "competence," the concept of mastery. A person feels capable of mastering a situation or the content to be learned. The third is "relatedness," the feeling of being connected or "related to" others.

By mapping the three elements of intrinsic motivation onto a design for gamification, the elements of SDT can be used to:

- Give learners a sense of choice and control

- Provide learners with confidence in their ability to meet a challenge and accomplish a goal

- Provide learners with a clear path to content or skill mastery

- Reward learners for incremental learning as well as for learning terminal objective

- Help learners feel connected to other learners through leaderboards, challenging of friends, and other methods of social interaction

Intrinsic and Extrinsic Co-Existing

From a practical standpoint, it is difficult to separate intrinsic and extrinsic motivation. Let's say a person is seeking to become a Certified Professional in Learning and Performance with credentials from ASTD.[9] She may be seeking certification because it "looks good on a resume" and because it will increase her earning potential when seeking a job and she will receive verbal praise from her friends (extrinsic motivators). But she could also be seeking certification because she is interested in the subject of learning and development and wants to learn more to prove to herself that she "knows her stuff" (intrinsic motivation). More often than not, humans are simultaneously internally and externally motivated. One of the problems with much of the research on the subject is that the measurement instruments are designed to make the two mutually exclusive.

One widely used scale to measure intrinsic versus extrinsic motivation was created by Harter, who designed a scale with three subscales for intrinsic motivation and one scale of extrinsic motivation.[10] The scale is "designed in such a way that it is not possible for children to report themselves as simultaneously intrinsically and extrinsically motivated. [In fact], a perfect negative correlation between the two sales has been built into the scale."[11] When measured separately, not on the same scale with one measure on one side and the other on the other side, the relationship between intrinsic and extrinsic motivation was only moderately negatively correlated. People can be intrinsically and extrinsically motivated and motivation should be viewed as two mutually independent constructs rather than opposite ends of a single dimension. Intrinsic and extrinsic motivation do co-exist.[12]

What this means to a person designing a gamification experience is that you need to strive to create both internal and external motivators to move the learners through the content. Don't rely just on rewards and points; include elements like learner control, a sense of challenge, and a visible path toward mastery.

Structural Gamification

Structural gamification is the application of game elements to propel learners through content with no alteration or changes to the content. The content does not become game-like, only the structure around the content does. The primary focus behind this type of gamification is to motivate the learners to go through the content and to engage them in the process of learning.

Affordances

The use of structural gamification provides a number of affordances to the designer and the learners. These affordances help the learners to gain the knowledge, skills, and abilities (KSA) they need while simultaneously allowing them to have control over when they learn and how they decide to approach the learning process. When designing structural gamification experiences, keep these elements in mind.

Clear Goals

Goals are important because they add purpose, focus, and measureable outcomes. Clearly establishing goals for the learner allows them to know what needs to be accomplished and the final outcome. In structural gamification, goals should be specific and unambiguous. There should be no doubt about whether or not the goal was obtained. This requires clear measurement and objective criteria. The goal sustains the activity and keeps the learners moving forward.

A goal should provide learners with the freedom and autonomy to pursue it using different approaches and techniques. Goals are not prescriptive in that they do not tell the learners what to do, they only tell the learners what the final outcome needs to be and the learners determine how to get there.

Incremental Goals and Rewards

A goal that is too ambitious or seems too challenging will not motivate someone in a gamification experience; in fact; seemingly impossible goals can actually be demotivating. To help a player move toward the ultimate goal, incremental goals are used.

Create a well-structured and sequenced series of mini-goals that lead the learners toward mastery. The learners should be rewarded for accomplishing these mini-goals. The reward provides motivation and keeps them on track toward the next mini-goal. Ideally, each mini-goal becomes increasingly more challenging and difficult and builds on the accomplishment of previous mini-goals. In instructional terms, you create a series of enabling objectives that ultimately leads to the terminal objective.

Providing rewards for each mini-goal means a learner doesn't have to wait until the end for the big "payoff." This helps to avoid frustration and provides a sense of accomplishment as the learner moves from one reward to the next. The celebration of incremental success brings the final goal just one more step closer as the learner progresses through the content. The concept of moving from goal to goal can be thought of as progression.

Progression

Moving from Point A to Point B is an integral part of structural gamification. The concept is that the learner is able to "see" progress. The progress might be in the form of a character moving across a board or an image of how close the learner is to the next level. In structural gamification, cues are provided giving the learners an up-to-the-minute indication of how far they are within the content and how far they are from completing the learning goals.

Progression within the module or curriculum serves to indicate where the learners are and to provide them with motivation to move toward completion. The motivational aspects are most effective when the progression is in small, easy-to-manage parts of the course that lets them finish learning a small piece of content and then move on to learning the next small piece of content. The learners keep progressing.

Real-Time Feedback

Design the structural gamification experience to maximize feedback. What has the learner accomplished to date? Where were mistakes made? What does the learner need to do next? The hallmark of any well-designed structural gamification effort is the inclusion of immediate, corrective, and informative feedback. When learners are successful, they are immediately rewarded; when they are unsuccessful, the feedback is provided right away. No need to wait for the end to see that you earned 6/10 on the quiz; you know as you are proceeding.

Feedback in a structural gamification design is multifaceted. The learner receives points and badges and moves from level to level in the experience. The learner can visually see progress or lack of progress and can typically observe his or her progress in relation to others. This type of feedback guides actions, moves learners toward goals, and incrementally provides direction. Well-designed feedback systems allow mid-course corrections to learner misconceptions, tangents, and incorrect responses.

Transparency

Structural gamification designs should provide data to all learners and participants equally. The progress, setbacks, and achieved goals should be transparent. This doesn't mean that everyone has to see everyone else's progress all the time, but it does mean that everyone has the same access to data and information. The point system is clearly designed and understood. The rewards are consistent and how to achieve them is equally clear or unclear to all learners. The system should allow progress to be tracked at that moment and as it relates toward the long-term goal.

On the back end, structural gamification provides a wealth of data and statistics about learner behavior, click patterns, and the number of correct or incorrect choices. The idea behind a well-designed structural gamification platform is that every click can be recorded, every wrong answer noted. This is in sharp contrast to many learning management systems that only provide the number of correctly answered questions. With a structural gamification platform, an administrator can have access to see where the learners spent their time, what links they clicked on, what pop-up windows they close immediately, and what efforts they undertake to gain coins. The data can be used to determine the effectiveness of the design as well as which areas of instruction are most beneficial and which require modification.

Status

Humans like to be noticed. From the proverbial corner office to wearing designer clothes with huge logos, people want others to know where they stand in the pecking order. Structural gamification provides visible notification of knowledge and mastery of topics. When developing a structural gamification system, include the ability for people to indicate their status. It can be through badges they can post within the gamification platform or it can be badges or achievements that can be shared outside the system.

There is a story of a gentleman who was working for a company and was partaking in a structural gamification program to learn programming, although his job was not in programming but in human resources. However, in his free time at home and on weekends, he pursued his passion of learning to program. Every time he reached a new level, he posted his status on his Facebook page. One day when the information technology department was looking for a new programmer, they noticed that this gentleman had a number of impressive badges on his Facebook page, even though he had absolutely no formal training in programming. They hired him to be a programmer within the company. The indication of status helped him land a new job.

Status is an important element when designing structural gamification. It provides an opportunity to make skills and learning visible. Often the skills, talents, and abilities of individuals within a company are invisible. The use of structural gamification and the display of badges and achievements can surface those talents and abilities and make them visible.

High Stakes/Challenge

If the structural gamification platform is too easy, no one will care. The goals, challenges, and reward structure all must convey a sense of difficulty and high stakes. If a person doesn't think the experience will be challenging or interesting or result in a large enough payoff, he or she will not engage. The challenge could be related to the number of points that need to be achieved, finding hidden badges, or reaching the final level. Each of the challenges not only needs to be related to structural gamification items but also must be tied to learning complex ideas, concepts, and skills. Achieving the final level within the gamification environment must equate with having mastery and above-average competencies in the actual work or learning environment. There has to be alignment between the two.

Time

Structural gamification should be designed to roll out over time. A quick one-and-done is not the most efficient use of structural gamification. One of the advantages of structural gamification is the ability to engage learners with the content over a longer period of time. One of the most powerful tools of structural gamification is the use of the concept of distributed practice.

Distributed practice is the concept distributing study or learning efforts over multiple short sessions, with each session focused on the subject matter to be learned. The advantage is that short bits of information provided to the learners over time allows them to learn content that was missed earlier in the learning process or the first time it was presented; it helps the learners remember the content because it's reviewed; and it reinforces what was learned the last time the content was presented. Distributed practice helps learners retain access to memorized information over long periods of time because the spacing promotes deeper processing of the learned material.

Elements

To make the affordances effective within structural gamification, a number of game elements are used. These elements must be designed carefully to positively impact learning and propel the learners toward the goals of the instruction. A number of elements are often associated with structural gamification, including rules, reward structure, leaderboards, points, currency, and badges.

Rules Rules within structural gamification keep all the learners on a level playing field. They provide the context and guidelines under which learners progress toward goals. Rules keep everything fair and balanced. Rules are what make all the other elements of structural gamification work, the badges, the rewards, the points, even the leaderboard. Every item is dictated by a rule.

Designer Notes

- Keep the rules simple.
- Once you implement the rule, experience the gamification for yourself to see whether there are any unintended consequences.
- Let the learners know the rules are for them to gain the maximum from the experience. .
- Periodically monitor and police the rules so the learners know that the rules have to be taken seriously.

Reward Structure A reward structure consists of all the ways learners are rewarded for activities within the structural gamification platform. This can include earning points, badges, and moving through levels. It can also equate to unlocking new content or being given new challenges.[13]

Designer Notes

- Use measurement achievements instead of completion achievements to increase intrinsic motivation through feedback.
- Reward players for boring tasks and give them feedback for interesting ones. Make achievements for interesting tasks that focus the players' attention on important lessons or strategies used for that task.
- For complex tasks requiring creativity or complicated strategies, try to instill a mastery orientation. For simple or repetitive tasks, instill a performance orientation. Try to keep new players who are still learning how to play in a mastery orientation.

- Primarily use expected achievements so learners can establish goals for themselves. Make sure achievement descriptions accurately reflect what needs to be done and why it is important. Unexpected achievements can be used sparingly to encourage exploration and engagement.
- Try to give new players immediate rewards and give more experienced players delayed rewards.
- To prevent learners from being excluded because of their lack of experience, create achievements for learners who take other learners under their wing.
- Don't use negative achievements as a punishment for failure. Provide feedback within the system that can assist struggling learners.
- Use incremental and meta achievements to hold the learners' interest for longer periods of time and guide them to related activities. Make the spacing between incremental achievements, both in time and location, separated enough so that learners don't feel too controlled.
- If competitive achievements are used, make them available only after learners are comfortable with the gamification environment and no longer learning the ropes. To foster a cooperative environment, offering achievements for more advanced learners to assist less experienced learners is an option.
- Groups for cooperative achievements should be kept relatively small to decrease social loafing and process loss. The metrics used for earning achievements should assess individual performances within the group setting.

Leaderboards A leaderboard is a list of the individuals who have the highest scores or most points or who have achieved higher levels. It is a list of top players in structural gamification, so whoever else is involved can see everyone else's name or initials and score. It can be a powerful motivator and a chance to interact socially in discussions around the leaderboard. It provides social capital to the individuals who are at the higher levels.

When designing structural gamification, there are a number of considerations for creating the most effective leaderboard. If the organization is large, having an unedited list of everyone in the organization in order from best score to the worst score may not be as motivating as you had hoped. For example, if you like to run on the weekends, being on the list with the world's fastest runner would not be motivational. In fact, it might be demotivating because there is no way an average person could catch the world's fastest person. However, being on a leaderboard with a group of friends might be highly motivational because those are people you are able to compete against.

Designer Notes

- Allow learners to choose their own friends to place on a personalized leaderboard.
- Structure the leaderboard by territory or department to allow individual contributions to a larger goal.
- Only show a relative position on the leaderboard. This could mean showing the five scores above and the five scores below the individual learner.
- Regardless of what you show to the learners on a regular basis concerning their positions on the leaderboard, always allow access to the top twenty-five scores so that you provide transparency (no need to show lower scores to "everyone").

Points Points can be used in a variety of methods for structural gamification. They can be used to reward progress and correct answers, they can be a way of achieving social status, they can be used to unlock content, and even spent as currency to obtain virtual or physical goods.

Designer Notes

- Don't overwhelm your learners with complicated point systems. Keep it simple.
- Design the point system first; points tell the learners what's important. Use points to focus attention and drive learning.
- Redeeming points for physical items can be complicated logistically and sometimes legally; avoid physical and redeemable points if possible.
- One method in a timed exercise is to tie points to time. This works well in a countdown scenario. Start the timer at 60 seconds, which equals 60 points. The learner receives the number of points based on time. If it took 30 seconds to answer the question, the learner receives 30 points. Add on a bonus point structure for correct answers so the learner is not just rushing through the questions.
- Provide points for everything you want to manage. For example, if you need to manage correct answers and speed, give points for both so one doesn't overshadow the other. Aim for balance.
- Use points as currency to give learners more autonomy over how they are rewarded for their efforts.
- Test out the point system before you implement on a large scale. If there are ways to exploit the point system, you want to find out early and fix those areas.

Currency Currency can be thought of as a specialized kind of points—points that can be used to acquire other items. Currency within structural gamification has no value without having items of value to purchase. These are often called virtual goods. These provide the incentive for learners to earn currency so they can purchase virtual goods.

If you decide to design a currency system, make sure that the currency system doesn't overtake the learning goals. If the focus of the learners' efforts becomes too fixated on purchasing virtual goods and showing them off to others, then the potential for learning is diminished.

Designer Notes

- Offer learners currency for completing tasks instead of rewards to give them a greater sense of control.
- Use a currency system to enhance the gamification experience, but don't attempt to make currency acquisition the main reason learners engage in an activity.
- Carefully examine and test the currency system within the game to ensure that currency is not too difficult or easy to obtain.
- If you have a currency system, you must have something for the learner to purchase with the currency. Make sure the items are of sufficient interest that the learners want to spend their currency on them.

Badges A badge is a visible symbol of accomplishment. They can come in the form of ribbons, trophies, or other symbols. Many learners enjoy collecting badges, while others will like to show them off to others. (See Figure 11.3.)

Figure 11.3 Collecting Badges

Image reprinted with permission of the artist, Kristin Bittner.

Designer Notes

- Give learners the opportunity to go over their earned achievements using some kind of stored list. Digitally tangible rewards are a great incentive, but won't keep the learners around after a reward is earned.
- Provide a mechanism to show off a badge to others within the learning environment.
- To prevent learners from being excluded because of their lack of experience, create achievements for learners who take other learners under their wing.
- Making earned achievements viewable to other learners is a powerful incentive. Let learners display a few achievements they are proud of to increase motivation.
- Badges are good for showing non-linear progress through content; levels are good for showing linear progress.

Leveling Up

In video games, leveling up typically means moving from one area of a game to another while the level of difficulty correspondingly increases. In structural gamification, the term "leveling up" means gaining enough points to go to the next area of content, earning a new badge or series of badges, or even mastering a certain portion of the curriculum. In structural gamification for learning, each level is typically associated with one overall learning goal supported by sub-goals within the level. Once the ultimate learning goal is achieved at a level, then a learner can move on. Sometimes the gamification is simply related to one chunk of content. Learners demonstrate that they have learned certain contain and they then move to the next level.

As a designer of structural gamification, creating levels lets you control the progress of the learners. It allows you to move them from basic knowledge to more complex knowledge and allows for certain checkpoints they have to obtain. From the learners' perspective, knowing how many levels helps them to realize how far they are into the learning process and how far they need to proceed.

Designer Notes

- Levels are good for showing linear progress through content.
- Tie each level to a specific learning objective.
- Let the learners know how many levels they must move through to reach the end.

Social Sharing

In structural gamification there are many social aspects. Showing off badges is a way to share accomplishments and achievement of non-linear goals. Even the element of competition is a social construct. The leaderboard allows for the sharing of progress and success. The social aspects allow for the socialization of a single learner experience. If the learner goes through the structural gamification on his or her own, social artifacts like a leaderboard or previous learner's score allows for the sharing across time and distance.

Designer Notes

- Store previous learner answers or actions on a task and, when a new learner comes along, use the stored information to have the two learners "play" against each other, even though they are not actually playing at the same time.
- Provide opportunities to share achievements and badges outside of the gamification space.

Avoid Learners Gaming the System

As with most human endeavors, the opportunity to cheat or "game" the system is available in structural gamification. The main point of any interactive learning experience is to provide the learners with a more engaging and meaningful opportunity to learn. Unfortunately, some folks will be more interested in winning than learning.

No designer of structural gamification or anyone else, for that matter, is going to change the human tendency of some people to cheat. The remedy isn't to stop cheating; the remedy is to design the system to minimize the impact of cheating or to make the cheating conducive to learning.

A few years ago in a computer hacker contest, a hacker cheated the system and won the contest. The idea of the contest was that the hackers had to hack through a series of computer servers. Each server was progressively more difficult in terms of security and anti-hacking software. Each server that was hacked gained points for the hacker and the hacker with the most points at the end of the contest would win.

One clever hacker decided not to waste his time hacking through all the servers; instead, he hacked into the server that was keeping score. He then made his score the highest, even though he hadn't hacked any of the servers in the contest. His out-of-the-box thinking allowed him to win the contest.

In fictional lure, the famous "cheat" by Captain James T. Kirk, known as the Kobayashi Maru, stands out as one of the greatest cheats of all time. Captain Kirk turned a computer simulation that was supposed to be unwinnable into a winnable situation by reprogramming the simulation. He changed the conditions of the test and even received a commendation for his original thinking.

Commendations and achieving victory aside, most often you are going to want to make your structural gamification as bulletproof as possible. One remedy to the inevitable cheat is to make the avenues for cheating aligned with the goals of the learning as accomplished by our hacker friend and our galaxy-hopping captain. Unfortunately, in most cases, that is not an option. If everyone hacked or reprogrammed our structural gamification, the outcomes would be miserable.

Fortunately, other remedies can help. One is to test and re-test the structural gamification system. See whether you and your team can cheat it yourselves. If you can figure out how to cheat, you can be sure others will as well. Find all the ways to cheat and then fix those before wide-scale release.

Once you have found all the possible ways to cheat, ask an outside group to find more. They will. Tell them it's impossible to cheat and then let them go at it. If you tell them it's impossible, that just might be the motivation they need to exploit unexposed weaknesses in the system. You want to have unbiased people looking at the gamification. See whether they can increase points without learning anything. If they can, you need to go back to the drawing board. If no learning occurs, the structural gamification is a failure.

No matter how much you test structural gamification, once it's out in the open, the clever learners will find additional ways to cheat—ways you never even dreamed of. So once the gamification platform is released, you still must be vigilant for cheaters. Look for unusually high scores, completing tasks in unbelievable times, gaining currency at an incredible rate, or any other outlier that indicates something is amiss. Constant tracking and attention to what is happening within the system will help spot cheaters. Most people are not going to cheat unless the opportunity is so obvious and so easy and, in that case, it's the fault of the designer. For the most part, if someone is cheating, you'll be able to spot it because the person will be so far ahead he or she will draw attention.

Finally, keep in mind that your structural gamification is only a wrapper around your content. If you don't have engaging or interesting content and if the content doesn't seem relevant to the learners, they are going to look for shortcuts or ways to game the system because they'll think it's a waste of time. The number one defense against gaming a gamified learning system is to have compelling, engaging content, which brings us to the subject of content gamification.

Content Gamification

Content gamification is the application of game elements, game mechanics, and game thinking to alter content to make it more game-like. For example, adding story elements to a compliance course or starting a course with a challenge instead of a list of objectives are both methods of content gamification. The idea is not to create an entire game but to add elements and concepts from games to the instruction. Many of the concepts in Chapter 5 can be used to provide content gamification to learning modules. The basic elements of games are the basic elements for creating content gamification.

Elements

While many different game elements and mechanics can be added to traditional course content to make it more game-like, the most common elements for turning typical learning content into gamified content are

- Story
- Challenge
- Curiosity
- Character
- Interactivity
- Feedback
- Freedom to Fail

Story Research indicates that learners remember facts, terms, and jargon more easily when they learn that information in the form of a story rather than from a bulleted list.[14] Stories evoke emotions, provide a context for placing information, and are the way humans have handed down information for centuries.

Creating a story for your compliance training or sales training provides the learners with an engaging way to learn about the content you are teaching. Using a story is similar to using a case study or a scenario, but the focus should be on building a story that is meaningful and has some emotional pull that brings the learner along. Involving a learner in a story can make the learning more powerful and memorable. A well-crafted story focuses on helping learners to solve problems, educates the learners, and is easily recalled when the actual situation arises or when a learner is in a similar situation.

Good stories have characters the learners care about. Take the time to craft a character that the learner can sympathize with and someone they will like. Often it is a good idea to have the character the learner is following in the story be slightly ahead of where the learner is and the learner can then observe what the character does.

As an example, if the training module is for new hire training, have the character in the learning module be on the job for three months. Then that on-screen character in the story can provide advice and counsel to the learner because she has "been there, seen it, done it." An important point is that you don't want a huge cast of characters because you don't want to confuse the learners and you aren't writing an epic novel—keep the number of characters manageable. To help you keep track of the characters you are creating use a chart like the one shown in Table 11.1.

Next, the story has to have a plot. Something has to happen. This should be the intriguing part of the story. This should draw the learners into the story and rouse their curiosity. Here are some plot considerations based around various learning scenarios:

- Salesperson need to close the big sale to make numbers.

- A compliance violation has occurred; learner must investigate the cause.

- A form didn't make it to the right person. Where is that form? Who is the right person?

- An employee injured himself on a piece of equipment. How could this happen? What did he do wrong?

- Company expenses are through the roof. How can they be brought under control?

The use of questions works well for a plot. Most interesting stories take an average day and then throw in an extraordinary event. Look at your training and determine how you can write a plot that is engaging to the learners.

When the plot is unfolding, a key element is building tension. This is when two or more things are in conflict or are not working well together. Tension builds within the story because someone is

- Doing something wrong

- Confused about what he or she should be doing

- Hiding something

- Receiving false information

Table 11.1 Use a Chart Like This to Keep Track of the Characters You Add to a Learning Module

Name	Role/Position	Gender	Attitude	Attire	Represents
John	Potential Customer	Male	Friendly	Shirt, tie, suit-no jacket	Elusive potential customer
Mary	Sales Representative	Female	Helpful	Business casual	Proper procedure for initiating potential customer contact
Lou Ann	Co-Worker	Female	Unfriendly	Business casual	Provides critical information regarding pre-qualification of potential customer
User	New Sales Representative	N/A	N/A	N/A	Person who needs to pre-qualify John during the case study

Use these elements to build tension within your story. The tension should be related to something that is being taught within your learning module. Arrange the story so that the tension can only be alleviated by learning the content you are teaching within the course.

Relieving that tension is called the "resolution." This is where the learning occurs. Ideally, the resolution occurs because the learner learns the information needed to relieve the tension. After the content is applied, there has to be a brief review of the learning that took place so the learners can solidify that information in their minds.

Designer Notes

- To find ideas for stories with mystery and intrigue, watch medical mysteries or detective shows.
- Look at some of your favorite games and examine the conventions and techniques they use to move the plot forward.
- An opponent or nemesis always makes for good tension; just make sure that device is appropriate for your learning environment.
- To learn more about good storytelling, look into the Hero's Journey or the Monomyth, which describe how many stories unfold.

Challenge In content gamification, challenge plays a big role in engaging learners. Research indicates that challenge is a strong motivator in learning.[15] Think like a game developer and start a module with a problem the learners have to solve immediately before any instruction. Tell the learners something like "You are a manager and an employee has informed you that a co-worker has been leaving work early for the past month. What do you do?"

As the learners try to figure out what to do, provide guidance and assistance. Be supportive of the learners, but only provide information when they encounter obstacles to solving the problem. Create the need for the learners to seek or require the information you want them to learn. This creates motivation and aids retention because people like a challenge and they will remember how they solved the challenge much more easily than remembering an abstract bulleted list titled "Five things to do if you suspect an employee is leaving work early."

Too often, learning events start with the answer in the form of objectives. When you start with a learning objective, you are giving the learners the answer. Instead of giving them the answer, give them a question or a challenge. The learners will be more engaged and will work hard to answer the question.

Designer Note

- Turn a learning objective like "You will learn three methods for properly reporting your time" into a challenge like "Can you properly report your time three different ways in five minutes?" or "Do you know the three different ways in which you can report time?" Simply turning an objective into a question can challenge a learner.

Curiosity Inevitably, when playing a video game, players become curious. They explore the game-space to see what happens. "What if I don't slay the dragon and just run away?" "What if I tax my populous at 50 percent?" "What if I run in a straight line to that building?"

People are naturally driven by curiosity, so game developers take advantage of that by creating different levels and places to explore within games. Game developers allow players to do tasks or take actions more than once so they can explore different alternatives. Curiosity is used to motivate players to stay in the game and to engage them with the game environment.

Most e-learning does not use curiosity to drive learners through the instruction, but rather tends to be based on telling learners what they need to know in bulleted lists or paragraphs on the screen. Telling learners what they need to do throughout an entire e-learning module doesn't motivate action or create a desire to continue through the learning.

Leverage learners' natural sense of curiosity by providing a novel or exciting environment. Highlight areas of inconsistency, incompleteness, or even inelegance in the learners' knowledge base. Give the learners an activity for which they want to find the answer, want to learn the correct process, and want to solve the problem. Setting up these types of learning experiences taps into the curiosity of learners and will propel them through the instruction in the same way video game players are propelled through a game. For example, give learners various choices and then let them replay those choices to see what would happen if they chose an alternative or give them a space to explore and to discover new information and content.

Character Add characters to the learning. Even if you don't create a fully fledged story with plot and tension, simply adding a character can help to deeply engage learners. Research involving characters provides some interesting results. On tests involving different word problems, the group that had a character explain the problems generated 30 percent more correct answers than the group with just on-screen text.[16]

It seems that having an avatar appear on the screen can be motivating to learners because they somehow feel more accountable to a "person" than to a computer. And the character on the computer doesn't even have to be realistic. Additional research has indicated that a "realistic" character did not facilitate learning any better than a "cartoon-like" character. The indication is clear that simply using the video game technique of having characters and adding them to your content will make your content more engaging and help learners learn more.

In this case, it also turns out that two characters are better than one.[17] Research indicates that the best way to employ characters for teaching is to have one character provide content and learning information and to have another avatar encourage the learners. The thought is that it allows the learners to attend to the specific character and know that content from one character will be highly relevant to what they need to learn.

Designer Notes

- Add a character to learning to more fully engage the learners.
- Blue, green, and purple characters work just as well as other characters. Don't be afraid to have some "fun" with the characters.
- Remember, however, that characters are there to convey knowledge; don't let the characters take over and distract from the learning.
- Two characters are better than one—one to provide content or teaching information and one to provide support and encouragement.

Interactivity A hallmark of content gamification is interactivity. Encouraging learners to engage with content is what leads to deeper levels of learning. There are many advantages of having learners interact with the subject matter they are learning. Studies, as well as common sense, indicate that interactivity helps the learners retain information as well as increasing learners' willingness to spend time with the material.[18]

Games are filled with interactivity and content gamification should mimic that amount of interactivity. People tend to learn more richly and quickly when they are engaged and interacting with content than when they are passive viewers of content.

Designer Notes

- Examine your content and find information that can be used to engage the learners.
- Force the learners to interact with the content to gain richer understanding.
- Interaction can be moving a character around a screen, it can be dragging and dropping items from one place to another, or it can be clicking on objects to learn more.
- Play some video games and see how they handle interactivity; borrow liberally.

Feedback One of the features video games, board games, and other types of games have over traditional learning environments is the frequency and intensity of feedback. Feedback in games is constant and is a key element in content gamification. See Chapter 5 for more detailed information on feedback.

Research shows that feedback is a critical element in learning. The more frequent and targeted the feedback, the more effective the learning. Unfortunately, in many learning programs feedback is not frequent or specific. Provide continual feedback to learners in the form of self-paced exercises, visual cues, frequent question-and-answer activities, a progress bar, or carefully placed comments by non-player characters. Even something as simple as having a learner summarize the content just covered as a review is effective for providing feedback to her about her level of comprehension.

Freedom to Fail In content gamification, make failure an option. In many environments, learners are objectively scored and either they are right the first time or they fail and do not pass. Few people enjoy failing in traditional learning environments, and most will do everything they can to avoid failing. This means that most learning environments do not encourage exploration or trial-and-error learning. Learners have little insight into the real consequences of wrong answers or incorrect decisions other than being told they are not correct. Answering a question wrong to "see what happens" is frowned upon in most learning situations.

Content gamification should encourage failure. Alter instruction to allow learners the freedom to fail. This is not the same as allowing multiple guesses on a four-item multiple-choice question. This involves encouraging learners to explore the content, to take chances with their decision making, and to be exposed to realistic consequences for making a wrong or poor decision. The risk of failure without punishment is engaging. Learners will explore and examine causes and effects if they know it's okay to fail. In many cases, they will learn as much from seeing the consequences of their failures as they will from a correct answer.

Create instruction that forces a learner who enters the wrong code in a piece of software to do the actual work to correct the error. Don't simply provide feedback like "No, that data doesn't belong in that field" show the consequence, illuminate the cause and effect.

If the learner doesn't treat a client properly in an online role play, show the company losing a sale, losing money, and the person being fired. Then give the learner another chance. Allow him to try again so he can keep the customer, make a bigger sale, help the company make more money, and, most importantly, keep his job or even receive a promotion. Don't trap the learner into always being correct because that doesn't happen in real life and it's not engaging. Take the lesson from games and encourage learning from failure.

Key Takeaways

The key takeaways from this chapter include:

- Extrinsic motivation does have a place in learning and development.
- Intrinsic motivation consists of autonomy, competence, and relatedness.
- Intrinsic and extrinsic motivation should not be considered polar opposites. The best gamification includes both.
- Structural gamification is the application of game elements to propel learners through content with no alteration or changes to the content.
- Structural gamification has the affordances of:
  - Clear goals
  - Incremental goals and rewards
  - Progression
  - Real-time feedback
  - Transparency
  - Status
  - High stakes/challenge
  - Time

- The elements of structural gamification are rules, reward structures, leaderboards, points, currency, badges, leveling up, and social sharing.

- Avoid cheating in structural gamification by testing, retesting, and monitoring the activities within the system.

- One way to avoid cheating is to build some type of cheat into the rules of the structural gamification.

- Content gamification is the application of game elements, game mechanics, and game thinking to alter content to make it more game-like.

- The elements of content gamification are

  - Story

  - Challenge

  - Curiosity

  - Character

  - Interactivity

  - Feedback

  - Freedom to fail

12

Simulations

CHAPTER QUESTIONS

- What makes simulations unique?
- Why are simulations valuable for learning?
- Where do I start when designing a simulation?
- What are best practices for simulation design?

Introduction

In this chapter, we'll cover simulations, a topic we could easily spend the whole book on. We'll cover quite a bit of ground in this chapter, with an emphasis on the practical—how do you actually design and build a simulation?

In that spirit, I've called on some of the best simulation designers I've ever met to provide some input. Throughout this chapter, you'll see tips from Stacie Comolli, Alan Kumor, Carrie Marcinkevage, and Ken Spero—talented designers who have hundreds of simulation designs among them and a lot of valuable insights to share.

With that being said, here are the most important points to take away from this chapter:

- *Simulations are about doing.* Everything in your simulation needs to be behavioral, about *doing* something. If you can't assign a behavior or an action to your content, you're probably not designing a simulation. If your goal is to have your learner "think about," "consider," or "understand," you may want to consider a different learning method. Simulations are about doing.

- *Simulations are driven by metrics.* When we design simulations, our first question is always: "How will we measure success?" Simulations re-create real-world processes and behaviors; those processes and behaviors have outcomes that are measured, called metrics. Those metrics tell us what the simulation needs to be about. Metrics tell us when a job is being done well or poorly; a good simulation helps us understand the behaviors that drive those metrics.

- *Simulations are grounded in reality.* Unlike games, which can be very abstract or fanciful, simulations need to be grounded in the realities of the tasks and behaviors being simulated. While too much detail in a simulation can actually be distracting, the essence of the job must be captured, or the simulation won't feel real.

- *Storytelling is a critical component to simulation (but metrics come first).* Like virtually any type of learning game, simulations need to tell a good story. However, since simulations are grounded in reality, that story needs to be realistic. It's important to allow your metrics to drive your story, and not the other way around. It's tempting to come up with a great story idea and try to shoehorn it into your simulation; however, then you risk having a story that doesn't drive your metrics. Instead, look at your metrics and ask yourself: What story do I need to tell to drive these metrics?

Why Simulations Are Valuable for Learning

In Chapter 3, we defined simulations and talked about some of their key attributes. But what makes simulations uniquely suited to learning environments?

In Bloom's Taxonomy, simulations don't really fit into the Knowledge or Comprehension categories. Since they are about *doing*, they fall clearly into Application, and because they exercise and develop critical thinking and decision-making skills, they also fall into Analysis, Synthesis, and Evaluation.

Simulations build sense memory—the feeling that we've done something before and we're conditioned to do it again, just as a tennis player may practice her serve thousands of times until the action is so natural that her muscles "remember" it and a great serve can be executed without having to think about it. Simulations build sense memory for our decision-making skills, allowing us to practice until good decision making becomes a natural part of our thought processes.

How do simulations do that? Well, in a world filled with acronyms, I apologize for creating another—although, to be fair, I created this one a while ago.

I've been building simulations for a long time—since 1985, actually [this is author Rich Mesch]. Now, while that's a long time to be doing anything, I really have found simulation (and simulation-type activities) to be perhaps the most effective way to deliver application-based learning. And here's the reason why: so much of learning is focused on knowledge transfer. You have a bunch of stuff in your head, and you want it to be in my head, too, so you shovel it in there. Then you probably want me to take a test to prove that I learned it. Which I pass, and then we assume I know all this knowledge—which I probably do at that particular moment in time. But what happens when I actually need to use that knowledge? Will I be able to?

What's the point of gaining superpowers if you can't use them?

That's the problem. A lot of content is easy to understand, but not nearly so easy to implement. So we end up with a lot of good knowledge that we aren't able to use, and often we revert back to the old way. Bridging the Learn-Do gap is one of the oldest challenges of learning. That's why I'm such a big fan of simulation—because it's not about knowledge transfer; it's about knowledge application. It's about behavior, not about content.

Why does simulation do such a good job of bridging the Learn-Do gap? Because it provides:

- *Context:* How does this behavior impact my role and the roles I interact with?

- *Application:* When and where do I use this behavior on the job?

- *Practice:* Try the behavior in a low-risk environment to gain confidence and perspective.

- *Example:* What does it look like when I do it right? What does it look like when I do it wrong?

Simulation allows you to leap over the Learn-Do gap in a single bound, by allowing you to use new behaviors in a low-risk environment and providing the Context, Application, Practice, and Example you need to succeed in the real world.

Put it all together, and you have a CAPE that will help you get your superpowers off the ground.

Designing a Simulation

How do you begin designing a simulation? Remember, a simulation is a representation of process or behaviors that occur in the real world. Processes and behaviors have outputs, and those outputs are measured by metrics. The goal of any process or behavior is to impact metrics. In a flight simulator, you might have metrics like altitude, stabilization, or even something as basic as safe takeoff and safe landing (Figure 12.1).

In business simulation, you have business metrics, including macro metrics like revenue, cost of goods sold, market share, and stock price, and micro metrics like sales by product, employee retention, or job satisfaction.

Figure 12.1 Practicing Takeoffs and Safe Landings with a Flight Simulator

Image reprinted with permission of the artist, Kristin Bittner.

So begin the process at the end: What do you plan to measure? To know this, you need to answer the question: "What is the desired outcome of what I am simulating?" For a sales simulation, for example, it might be something like customer retention, deal size, or new product sales. Once you know what you are measuring, you can ask the question: "What actions or behaviors will move these metrics?"

Carries Marcinkevage suggests

"Start with the learner, not the expert. Figure out what the learner needs to know and do, and go from the basics up. Don't start with the expert and go down."

Stacie Comolli shares

"My top three tips for designing a simulation—anchored in the things you DON'T want to hear learners say:

1. **"My score doesn't make any sense. What does this feedback even mean?"** Knowing what you want to simulate, start by turning your performance goals into decision points and then determine the variables you can score to track learners' performance in the sim.
2. **"Wait—who is that, and why do I care what they're saying to me?"** Next, figure out the characters, locations, and information required to set up each decision, and pull the story from decision to decision.
3. **"This looks nothing like my job."** Before you put pen to paper and start writing, talk to high performers (in addition to your SMEs) to hear how the simulated process plays out in the real world."

The Illusion of Complexity

Carrie Marcinkevage suggests

"Resist the urge to overcomplicate. The player will always assume the game is much more complex than it actually is. Start simple and only add levels of complexity that add substantively to the learning."

Designing a branching storyline scenario can be daunting; new designers often become caught up in the complexities of geometric progressions. If a decision has four options, each of which results in four outcomes, and each of those outcomes has four new options, and each of those has four outcomes, and each outcome. . . .

Well, you get the picture. Using a geometric progression, a simple five-decision simulation would require over one thousand individual outcomes and the result would be something like Figure 12.2.

Figure 12.2 Flowcharts Can Become Exponentially Complex

Image reprinted with permission of the artist, Kristin Bittner.

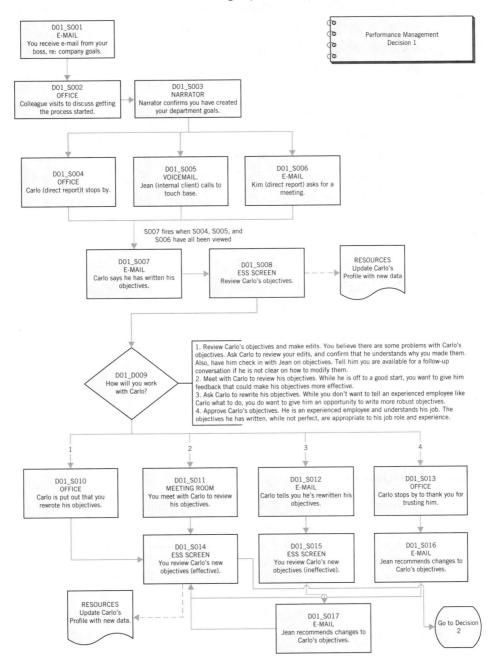

My word of advice: Don't.

Motion pictures don't move at all. They are a series of still frame pictures, projected at twenty-four pictures per second. They seem to move because our brains fill in the information between the still pictures, causing the perception of movement. So, too, will learners fill in the information in a well-designed simulation. They will believe that the simulation is more complex than it really is.

Perhaps the simplest way to simplify your simulation design is considering the learners' experience. Do they need to see every possible outcome of their decision? Or do they simply need to see a positive outcome and a negative outcome? If that's the case, even if you have four decision options, you only need two outcomes. Your flowchart just became a lot simpler.

In some scenarios, you may have decision choices that have minimal learning value, because in the real world they would not actually be implemented. For example, if the learner makes an inappropriate decision to fire an employee, that decision might be corrected by human resources before the employee was actually terminated. So rather than playing that decision choice out to its conclusion, it's perfectly reasonable to have a simulation character step in and tell the learner that he can't make that decision. That effectively terminates that part of the flowchart and prevents you from having to design out that part of the storyline.

Using Flowcharts

No matter what type of simulation you are creating, you will want to create flowcharts to keep track of your process flow. Simulations are inherently non-linear, so linear design tools like storyboards are really insufficient to track the flow. And trying to keep your process flow in your head is difficult for simple simulations and downright impossible for more complex ones. Figure 12.3 shows a very simple simulation decision flowchart—they can become very complex.

Figure 12.3 Sample Simulation Flowchart

There are plenty of good flowcharting programs out there. For Microsoft Office users, Microsoft Visio is a great flowcharting tool, with all the basic features you'll need and way more extended features than you'll ever use. For a budget option, Edraw Flowchart is bargain-priced and still has all the features you'll need for simulation flowcharting. For real bargain-hunters, Diagram Designer has its quirks, but it will get the job done, and you can't beat the price—it's free.

Another good tool is called Chat Mapper. It's technically not a flowcharting tool; it's actually a tool for writing and editing non-linear dialogue. It allows you to test branching and dialogues without having to create the entire simulation first and it gives you a much better feeling of how a branching simulation would work than trying to use paper. It even let's you test the actual dialogue to see how it flows.

Storytelling for Simulations

For information on storytelling in general, refer to Chapter 9 earlier in the book. All the guidelines for storytelling discussed there apply to simulations. Additionally, here are a few pointers that are specific to simulations:

- *You can control time.* One of the first decisions you need to make when designing a simulation storyline is how you will handle time. A simple systems simulation might simulate just a few minutes in the life of a system. A job process simulation might simulate a "day in the life." A complex business process simulation might simulate ten years or more. As a designer, you can compress or expand time as necessary. How long does it take for decisions to have an impact? If a decision takes two years to really play out, your simulation will need to cover at least two years.

Ken Spero observes

"**Simulations accelerate time**. One of the key limitations to learning from our real-life experiences is that the consequences do not always unfold right away, so it hampers our ability to connect the consequence to the action. Simulations allow the designer to accelerate time so that the learner can make a decision, implement it, and experience its consequences all within the same exercise."

- *Play on their emotions.* You want people to have an emotional connection to your story. Think about what makes the job frustrating, joyous, miserable, frightening. Think about how the learner will interact with other characters in the story. If you can engage the heart, your learner will care about how the story turns out. Then he or she will start making decisions the same way he or she does in real life—and you'll have a real learning moment.

Carrie Marcinkevage recommends

"Like your characters. If your simulation includes people, give them back stories and depth, even if it doesn't come out in the game. The more real they are to you, the more real they will feel to the player."

- *No robots, please.* Simulation storytelling works best when events happen the same way they do in real life, and people talk the same way they do in real life. Unfortunately, sometimes characters in simulation stories end up talking like robots. "This new selling process is really helping me close sales! Thank you for helping me implement this new process!" *Nobody* talks like that, and that kind of dialogue kills the immersion for your learners. Listen closely to how people talk, and replicate it as closely as possible.

Alan Kumor suggests

"Create buzz with subtleties. Nothing sells a simulation better than hearing how awesome and life-like it was from your co-workers. Add subtle gestures, attire, dialogue, and backgrounds in which learners can relate. They'll pick up on these details and become immersed in the experience. If they can relate to the experience, they'll want to tell their friends."

Creating Decisions for Simulations

Simulation decisions take many forms. For example, in a machine simulation, part of your decision making will involve replicating the controls and gauges of the machine. However, the overarching decision structure will probably not be on how to use the machine, but why to use the machine. Typically, you will create scenarios, small chunks of storytelling that establish the need for critical thinking and decision making.

Branching Simulations

In branching simulations, there are several decision types we can use, including:

- *Multiple Choice (of several choices, choose one):* this is the most common and most familiar decision type. Learners are presented with a selection of options and select the one they feel will achieve the most appropriate outcome. We'll talk about how to write these in a moment.

- *Multiple Select (of several choices, choose one or more):* Similar to multiple choice, a multiple select decision can be much more challenging. In multiple choice, the learner concludes that there is only one "right" answer and therefore sets about eliminating choices that she feels probably aren't right. Rather than encouraging critical thinking, multiple choice can encourage process of elimination and educated guessing. However, multiple select implies that more than one answer can be right; in fact, it's possible that all of the options are necessary to create a good outcome. It's much more difficult for the learners to do process of elimination, so they are forced to think harder about the tradeoffs.

- *Ranking (Ordering):* One type of ranking decision is when you take a list of events and put them in the order in which they should be completed. For example, if you had five options, you might ask the learner to put a 1 next to the correct option.

- *Ranking (Prioritizing):* Another type of ranking decision is to put choices in priority order; which is most important, which is second most important, and so on. It may also be useful to think about the ranking from an effectiveness perspective; which would be most effective, second most effective, and so on. These are often good for leadership scenarios, where it may not be possible to do everything in a day so the learner must prioritize what *must* be done.

Exhibit 12.1 shows some examples of the different types of decisions.

Exhibit 12.1 Different Types of Decisions in a Simulation

Scenario: Hector is an account manager for a business services outsourcing company. The company traditionally sold specific human resources services to HR managers. However, the new company strategy is to sell broader business services to CEOs and other top executives. Hector's job is to set up a meeting with the CEO of ClientCo, Inc.

Multiple-Choice Decision

How should Hector set a meeting with the CEO?

A. Call the CEO and ask for a meeting.

B. Send the CEO an email and tell her you will follow up with a phone call.

C. Ask for an introduction to the CEO from a member of her staff.

D. Attend an industry event where the CEO is speaking and talk to her afterward.

Multiple-Select Decision

Which steps should Hector follow to get meeting with the CEO? Select one or more options:

A. Call the CEO.

B. Send the CEO an email.

C. Invite the CEO to a company event.

D. Ask a contact at the company for an introduction.

Ranking (Ordering) Decision

The options below represent the steps that Hector could follow to set a meeting with the CEO; place the steps in the order that Hector should complete them:

A. Call the CEO.

B. Send the CEO an email.

C. Invite the CEO to a company event.

D. Ask a contact at the company for an introduction.

(*continued*)

Ranking (Prioritizing) Decision

The options below represent the steps that Hector could follow to set a meeting with the CEO; prioritize the steps from the most critical to the least critical:

A. Call the CEO.

B. Send the CEO an email.

C. Invite the CEO to a company event.

D. Ask a contact at the company for an introduction.

Tips for Writing Decisions

When writing branching storyline simulations, one of the toughest challenges is writing good decision sets. We've been conditioned by multiple-choice tests to feel there must be one right answer and several wrong answers. In real life, we rarely deal with rights and wrongs, but with shades of gray. What makes one decision better than another? Here are few tips for writing good branching decisions:

- *Decision choices should not be bad and good, but good and better.* We want our learners to engage in critical thinking, not process of elimination. If you show your learner several choices, all of which seem like reasonable approaches, you force him or her to do some deep thinking around why one might be more favorable than another. This helps the learner develop judgment skills.

- *Real-life tradeoffs.* For decision choices to be compelling, you need to create the same tradeoffs that exist in real life. Why is the decision difficult in real life? Is it hard to be a good manager because I hate giving my team members bad news? Is it hard to be a consultative salesperson because my boss pressures me to close, close, close? If you incorporate these conflicts into your decisions, your learners will feel the same pressures as they do in real life—and react the same way.

- *Every right is wrong again.* Often your learners will look for patterns and general rules to apply. They try to "game the system" by guessing what the designer had in mind. That conflicts with critical thinking, which requires you to evaluate each situation on its merits. A simple way to address this is to make an approach the "right" choice in one decision, but the "wrong" choice in another. For example, in a leadership scenario, coaching may be the right choice for an experienced team member, but the wrong choice for an inexperienced one.

- *The basics*. Here are a few decision-writing pointers that may seem pretty basic, but are still good to remember:

  - The order in which decision choices are presented is important; for example, nobody expects the first choice to be the right choice.

  - Try to make all of choices about the same length. People assume that the longest or most detailed choice is the right one. Of course, you can confound that expectation by writing a "wrong" choice that's long and detailed.

Creating Simulation Feedback

Ironically, a lot of learning content focuses on right answers and wrong answers. The truth is, life is rarely that simple. Very few activities have an absolutely right way and an absolutely wrong way to do them. So rather than focusing on right answers and wrong answers, we should be helping our learners to focus on critical thinking skills, problem solving, and weighing alternatives.

All simulations utilize some kind of feedback, and most use several types. Generally speaking, there are three types of feedback:

- *Intrinsic Feedback:* Intrinsic feedback is part of the story. As you make decisions you will receive feedback in the way the story changes, and from the reactions of characters within the story. Of course, negative feedback from other characters does not always indicate a poor decision; the behavior may indicate a resistance to change. This type of feedback not only helps learners gauge their success throughout the simulation, but also gives them a sense of how people will react when they try these behaviors in the real world.

- *Extrinsic Feedback:* Extrinsic feedback typically comes in the form of numeric reports or as a written analysis of the decisions a learner makes. Reports should be as close as possible to the actual reports that a learner will receive when doing the job in the real world. If the learner is measured on safety statistics in the real world, then there needs to be a safety report available at the end of the simulation. Written feedback should focus on:

  - Why the learner's decision was appropriate or inappropriate,
  - The likely outcome of the decision, and
  - Suggestions for improved performance.

The most effective feedback does not focus on "right" or "wrong" answers, but rather on actions and consequences and tradeoffs. If learners receive feedback on the likely outcomes and impacts of the decisions they have made, they can do some critical thinking and planning around how to incorporate those behaviors on the job.

- *Peer/Facilitator Feedback:* Simulations are often implemented as self-paced experiences, but they may be even more effective as collaborative experiences. Collaborative simulations allow for additional feedback from peers and facilitators. Following each simulation segment, participants can review their experiences and decisions with their team members. They identify where they felt they did well and where they did poorly and determine whether their feedback was expected or unexpected. Team members can also be brought together for a group debriefing with a facilitator, where they can share their experiences. This session is sometimes called a "bridging" session, since the goal is to bridge between the experience in the simulation and how that experience can improve performance back in the real world.

Simulation Design Tool

This tool is designed to help gather information from subject-matter experts to design simulation scenarios shown in Tables 12.1 and 12.2. Use these categories as guidelines when interviewing subject-matter experts. If all of the information on the worksheet is gathered from the client, you will have enough information to build the simulation scenarios. Use one worksheet for each scenario.

Decision Design Guidelines

Metrics: What metrics will reflect success or failure in the process or behavior we have chosen to simulate? (*Note:* Metrics tend to be for the entire simulation experience, not for each decision.)

Behavior: What behaviors will drive the metrics above? What do we want the participant to learn, reinforce, or test the participant's knowledge of?

Issue: Tell the story of this decision. What is the issue, and why should the participant be concerned?

Setup: How does the participant learn of this issue? (i.e., he receives a call from his boss; a direct report brings it to his attention; she receives a call from an angry customer)

What options does the participant have for handling this situation?

Designer Notes

Decision choices should all appear reasonable, so the participant cannot automatically eliminate some of them. Decision choices should focus on real-life tradeoffs and on the pressures that exist in the real world that prevent people from making the "right" decisions.

- What are the impacts on the measures of performance for each decision choice? Which measures does this decision impact? Are the impacts positive or negative? Are there tradeoffs (i.e., one metric goes up, but another goes down)?
- What are the short-term and long-term outcomes of selecting each of the decision choices?
- What would happen? How would you find out what happened (you see bad numbers in your reports, a team member calls to complain, your boss calls to congratulate you, a customer thanks you for your help)?
- Why do these outcomes happen? Describe the "behind the scenes" events that happened between the decision and the outcomes.
- What feedback would you give to the participant about each of these choices?

Simulation Design Worksheet

Metrics: What metrics will reflect success or failure in the process or behavior we have chosen to simulate? (*Note:* Metrics tend to be for the entire simulation experience, not for each decision.)

1.

2.

3.

4.

Decision Design Worksheet

(Complete one worksheet for each scenario.)

Scenario Number _____

Metrics: Which of your previously selected metrics will this decision focus on?

Behavior: What behaviors will drive the metrics above? What do we want the participant to learn, reinforce, or test the participant's knowledge of?

Issue: Tell the story of this decision. What is the issue, and why should the participant be concerned?

Setup: How does the participant learn of this issue?

Decision Choice 1 Text:

Decision Choice 1 Impacts: *What are the outcomes of selecting this option? Consider both short- and long-term implications.*

Decision Choice 1 Feedback: *Rather than "right or wrong," what were the impacts, the tradeoffs, and the consequences of this decision?*

Decision Choice 2 Text:

Decision Choice 2 Impacts: *What are the outcomes of selecting this option? Consider both short- and long-term implications.*

Decision Choice 2 Feedback: *Rather than "right or wrong," what were the impacts, the tradeoffs, and the consequences of this decision?*

Decision Choice 3 Text:

Decision Choice 3 Impacts: *What are the outcomes of selecting this option? Consider both short- and long-term implications.*

Decision Choice 3 Feedback: *Rather than "right or wrong," what were the impacts, the tradeoffs, and the consequences of this decision?*

Decision Choice 4 Text:

Decision Choice 4 Impacts: *What are the outcomes of selecting this option? Consider both short- and long-term implications.*

Decision Choice 4 Feedback: *Rather than "right or wrong," what were the impacts, the tradeoffs, and the consequences of this decision?*

Key Takeaways

The key takeaways from this chapter are listed below:

- Storytelling is critical for simulations but metrics come first.
- Simulations are about doing—not telling.
- Simulations need to be grounded in the realities of the tasks and behaviors being simulated.
- Simulations build sense memory.
- Resist the urge to over-complicate the simulation.
- Use simulations to accelerate time and shorten feedback loops.
- When asking learners to make decisions, the decisions should not be bad and good, but good and better.
- Design questions, situations, and branching to force the learners to think critically.

- Consider long- and short-term consequences.

- Decision choices should all appear reasonable, so the participants cannot automatically eliminate some of them.

- Decision choices should focus on real-life tradeoffs and on the pressures that exist in the real world that prevent people from making the "right" decisions.

Development

13

Technology Tools

Helmut Doll

CHAPTER QUESTIONS

- What types of tools are available to develop instructional games?
- What types of tools are available for gamification efforts?
- What types of tools are available for creating simulations?
- Do mobile games require special considerations?

Introduction

So you have decided to use games, gamification, or simulations in your instruction and have designed the experience for the learners. Now the technical issues are becoming an overwhelming obstacle. It does not matter whether you are not involved in the development or you are a one-person shop where you have to cover every step of the project: You will have to be able to address some of the most difficult questions yourself or be able to communicate key issues in your discussion with the project leads or developers. When considering the development of an ILE, you must weigh complexity of development against the ease of customization, as shown in Figure 13.1. Here are some of the questions you have to ask yourself:

- Are we creating a game or are we adding game elements such as badges and leaderboards?
- What game genre are we looking for?
- Who is going to develop the game? Will it be the instructional designer or do we have a specialized game developer?
- What platforms do we have to support?
- Is mobile included?

Developing an Interactive Learning Experience

Due to the user's expectations from playing commercially available video games and due to the complexities of those types of games, it is important to keep the scope for a game, gamification, or simulation effort within reason. A full commercial-scale video game is beyond the capabilities of an e-learning developer or even a single game developer. A full-fledged video game development team can consist of one hundred full-time people for a game like Call of Duty or even as many as a dozen people working full-time and part-time for a game like Angry Birds.

Most of the time there will be a need for specialized game programmers, artists, game designers, and sound editors in addition to the common instructional design project team. For an e-learning game project, these roles will have to interact with the instructional design team to create a valuable learning experience as well as a rich game, gamification, or simulation experience. For large scale games, this will frequently require the outsourcing of the actual game development steps.

However, for a smaller scope ILE with a targeted learning objectives, there are tools available that can make game, gamification, and simulation development feasible. When a project is carefully designed and targeted for the learners' needs, a small team can use available tools and techniques to develop a highly effective learning game, gamification, or simulation.

Development Terms

First, let's look at some common terms that are important for understanding the development side of games, gamification, and simulations:

- *3-D game*—A game that uses three-dimensional graphics and allows movement in all three dimensions.

- *2-D game*—A game for which the graphics and movement are limited to two dimensions. Platform games are a good example of 2-D games.

- *Collision detection*—Detecting whether two objects in your game are intersecting. This could be the player touching an enemy or the player moving into a wall or a weapon hitting an enemy. Detecting collisions is very resource-intensive. It is frequently handled by the game engine.

- *Game loop*—The central component of the game program. How many times per second the game checks for user input, moves players, checks for collisions, redraws the screen, plays sounds, etc. This is one of the tasks that is handled by the game engine.

- *Artificial intelligence (AI)*—The logic that gives the illusion of intelligent decisions by computer-controlled characters in the game.

- *Sprite*—A game graphic frequently consisting of a grid of several images that show a game character in different positions. The animation of the character is created by displaying the individual images in rapid succession.

Figure 13.1 Chart of Customization vs. Learning Curve

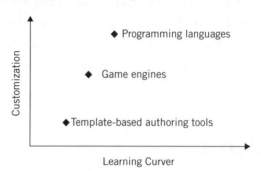

Template-Based Authoring Tools/ Arcade-Style Games

Many games that are currently used for instructional purposes are based on a few common types of game mechanics: Hangman-style games, Jeopardy-style games, Who-Wants-to-Be-a-Millionaire games—to mention a few. Since these game types are reused so frequently, there is a wide range of templates available to generate a game with your own content. These can be in the form of a PowerPoint template for a Jeopardy game, which can be found at many locations on the web such as Jeopardy Labs, which provides a chance for you to make your own Jeopardy-style game without the need for any special software. In fact, PowerPoint with its branching capabilities can be used to create many types of simple games and branching scenarios. Another example is the website ActiveDen, which has many Flash templates for such games as a Hangman puzzle game and a matching game, allowing the addition of your own content using an XML file. If you just want to add characters to an e-learning module as a form of gamification, tools like CodeBaby allow you to create characters that can be placed into e-learning courses.

The website eLearning Brothers has a number of HTML5 games that can be customized for a variety of subjects. Another customizable game template can be found at The Knowledge Guru, which provides a specific game environment in which an originator can place his or her own questions.

Selected Game Templates

- ActiveDen
- C3 Softworks' Bravo
- eLearning Brothers
- Jeopardy Lab
- Knowledge Guru
- Raptivity

Selected Character Animation Software

- CodeBaby
- CrazyTalk
- Media Semantics
- NOAH

Many of these templates are stand-alone games that have to be integrated into courses individually. Some e-learning authoring tools are including game templates that allow the quick addition of games to courses. For example, Raptivity's Games Turbopack includes many templates (interaction models) for games ranging from Million Dollar games to Snakes and Ladders quizzes. Implementing a game in these authoring tools involves choosing the templates and modifying the parameters of the game using a built-in interface. Because these authoring tools are specifically for the learning industry, they also frequently are SCORM compatible and are starting to support the Experience API.

The development time and learning curve is therefore very short. The tradeoff is that the game mechanics are pre-programmed and only the game content and some interface elements are customizable. Additionally, these tend to be testing games and not teaching games, as explored in Chapter 3. Other e-learning authoring tools such as Articulate Storyline, Captivate, or Lectura are not geared toward games using a template approach, but are flexible enough to support the programming of games, so third-party game templates have also been created.

The output format for most authoring tools is still Flash-based, but the number of options for HTML formats, which will be compatible with mobile devices, are growing.

Selected Authoring Tools for Creating Games

- Articulate Storyline
- Adobe Captivate
- JeLSIM Builder
- Lectora
- Quandary
- What2Learn
- ZebraZapps

Game Engines

If one of these preplanned games is not what you are looking for, you may be closer to designing and programming a game, gamification, or simulation from scratch. However, the development of almost all ILEs shares common tasks:

- Displaying the constantly changing graphics (rendering engine)
- Reacting to user input with keyboard, mouse, touch screen, or other devices
- Making the character movement look natural, reacting to accelerations and gravity (physics engine)
- Determining when game objects collide (collision engine)

Because these tasks are shared by so many games, game development software has prebuilt components for them. These software packages are called *game engines*. In the large number of game engines that are available, the biggest distinction is whether they are used to build two- or three-dimensional games.

While 2-D games have declined in popularity due to the increased graphics power of modern computers, their simpler controls have generated new interest for games on mobile devices. For example, platform games are still a very popular game genre. YoYo Games GameMaker, GameSalad, Scirra Construct2, and Stencyl are some of the popular game engines that excel in the creation of 2-D games. They all use a simple and visual drag-and-drop approach for the creation of the game, but can also be programmed using scripting languages to expand their functionality.

Selected 2-D Game Engines

- YoYo Games GameMaker

- GameSalad

- Scirra Construct2

- Stencyl

While some of these 2-D game engines have expanded to also include some three-dimensional game functionality, 3-D game development is usually reserved for a separate set of specialized game engines that excel in their expanded graphics rendering and physics capabilities.

Selected 3-D Game Engines

- CryEngine

- ThinkingWorlds

- Torque 3D

- Unity3D

- Unreal Engine

The creation of advanced games in 3-D engines requires programming in C#, C++, Lua, and other programming languages. In addition to the specialized programming skills, the creation of three-dimensional models to be used for the game world and game characters is also usually reserved for specialists in 3-D modeling software. Below is a list of some criteria to help you decide on the best game engine for your game development:

- Learning curve

- Networking support

- Multiplayer support
- Platform support
- Functionality supported
- Licensing

Game development engines are not geared for the instructional market. So features such as SCORM compatibility are not directly supported by most of the engines. However, especially for game engines that publish to a web player or in HTML5 format, SCORM—and in the Experience API—compatibility can be implemented through custom approaches. It is also worth noting that most 3-D game development will require the creation of three-dimensional models for characters and the game worlds.

Due to the popularity of immersive 3-D learning environments, especially for simulations and military training, customized 3-D authoring platforms for serious learning games have appeared. Caspian Thinking Worlds is one such tool. Thinking Worlds integrates many features from 3-D game engines with the special needs of the instructional designer. In addition to the realistic interactions of the game characters with the three-dimensional environment, there are also building blocks for instructional elements such as quizzes. It also supports SCORM interactions directly.

Other Development Tools

In addition to the tools listed above, a number of other tools can be used for the creation of games, gamification, and simulation. These tools include:

HTML5

The decline of the Adobe Flash plug-in has created a renaissance of HTML as the main delivery method, especially on mobile devices. The term HTML5 is often used and refers in this context to a combination of new features in HTML5, new methods in JavaScript (also much improved performance of the browser JavaScript execution), and—to a smaller degree in interaction development—the new features of CSS3. Such web-based content is competing with native applications in the mobile area. Both approaches have advantages and disadvantages, but almost all e-learning authoring tools and many of the game engines that were mentioned earlier are either offering HTML5 output as one publishing option or are purely HTML-based.

In addition to authoring tools and game engines, an experienced JavaScript developer can also use JavaScript game libraries such as EaselJS, Box2D-JS, or ImpactJS to create a game. While there are still difficulties with browser compatibility, performance, and audio issues, the multi-platform advantage of HTML5 is a compelling argument to develop games using web standards.

Adobe Flash

Flash? Yes, despite the disappearing browser support, Flash can be an option for game development. Adobe is emphasizing game development and has added additional game development frameworks that integrate with Flash. Flash games can be published as AIR apps for iOS and Android and still run through the plug-in on desktop browsers.

Gamification Platforms

In addition to different development tools for creating games, a number of platforms can be used for adding points, badges, or leaderboards to content that you've created. These platforms don't change the content you provide but add elements around the content to propel the learners through it. This is what is known as "structural gamification" and is highlighted in Chapter 2 in the description of the Deloitte Leadership Academy. Additionally, a number of plug-ins or software add-ins exist for such platforms as WordPress, which includes Captain Up and Punch Tab.

Selected Gamification Platforms

- Axonify
- Badgeville
- BigDoor
- Bunchball
- GamEffective

- Gamify
- Mozilla's Open Badges project
- MindTickle
- OnPoint Digital
- Knowledge Guru

Mobile Games

Mobile devices require special considerations in game development; this is due to a variety of unique aspects of mobile devices. Mobile devices are everywhere and can play a variety to games, as shown in Figure 13.2.

Technical Differences

Mobile devices have technical differences that require design changes. They traditionally have limited processing and graphics power. Since games and simulations tend to place especially high demands on the hardware, game designers and developers may have to limit the game complexity and use

---

Figure 13.2 Mobile Games Are Everywhere

Image reprinted with permission of the artist, Kristin Bittner.

available optimization strategies. Most often gamification does not produce such demands, but if it is heavily integrated with graphics and processing, it can require extra resources from mobile devices.

However, as smart phones and tablets continue to have more powerful processors and graphics cards, many of these limitations disappear. Screen size on smart phones is still an issue While the resolution of mobile screens has caught up with desktops through the use of high-dpi displays, the physical size is still small. Since interface elements also have to be sized for the touch of our fingers instead of the point of a mouse click, the interface has to be simplified. In addition, the traditional game controls using the keyboard or joystick are not readily available in mobile games. When mobile game developers create games, they rely on input methods such as touch gestures, including swipes, pinching, and tapping.

Learner Behavior

Learner behavior is different on mobile devices. Mobile learners will most likely play their games, gamifications, or simulations for short amounts of time. Because of this, levels in mobile ILEs are usually shorter than for their desktop counterparts. Since the learner may be interrupted more frequently, the ILE should save its state automatically and allow continuation at a later time.

Delivery of the ILE

Game delivery to mobile devices is either through an application (app) or HTML5. The app stores are the only alternative to web-based content written in HTML5. Many of the game engines offer output in HTML5 format in addition to a publishing option as an app for mobile platforms. Since apps are platform-specific, this approach requires multiple versions for iOS, Android, Windows 8 Mobile, and possible future operating systems. One alternative offered by some e-learning authoring tools is to create one "player" app for each platform, which can then load the individual modules or games in one standardized format.

Adding Leaderboards or Badges

In addition to full-fledged games, the most common request is to add game elements such as leaderboards or badges to instructional activities. The tracking of achievements requires back-end development in addition to the coding in the game or training itself.

While the display of the game elements will be handled in the platform of the learning environment, the points and data have to be recorded in a server database, which is accessed using server-side software such as PHP. The addition of such a server-side structure and the communication with the training site on the client can be custom programmed by an experienced developer, but—if the data does not need to remain in-house—Cloud-based gamification platforms are an additional option. They can track all the achievements and frequently also allow the creation of rules and goals for the training. For an excellent overview of the choices and questions to ask in order to compare different offerings see A Checklist for Evaluating Gamification Platforms by Enterprise-Gamification.com.

A third approach is offered by Apple, Microsoft, and others through their Game Center or Xbox Live services, which allow game developers and designers to hook their games into the company's game tracking and rewards system. This approach may also not be feasible if data cannot be shared in the Cloud.

Key Takeaways

The key takeaways from this chapter include:

- Developing games, gamification, and simulations for training may require an organization to seek additional technical expertise and tools.

- Most of the current crop of e-learning authoring tools is not geared specifically toward the creation of games or the implementation of gamification elements into the training modules but, with skilled programmers, can be molded to meet some basic game needs.

- For the most common types of instructional games, a template-based authoring tool is the fastest and easiest approach to create and integrate games.

- Game engines (both 2-D and 3-D) can provide more flexibility for the creation of games, gamification, and simulation. They cover a broad range of popular game types that can be used in instruction.

- There is not one engine that is the best choice for all genres. 3-D games require a different engine than 2-D games; a tool that is a great choice for platform games is not necessarily good for role-playing games.

- The most sophisticated level of development is to program using C++ or other languages.

- Games, gamification, and simulations built for mobile platforms require additional technical and design considerations.

14

Storyboarding

Kevin Thorn

CHAPTER QUESTIONS

- What is storyboarding?
- Why is storyboarding important for games, gamification, and simulations?
- How does storyboarding work?
- What are some storyboarding techniques?

Introduction

We hear of the term "storyboard" often in the world of online learning or e-learning. The name itself leads us to believe its a noun, a tangible product, a thing we can store on a shelf when not in use. A storyboard is in fact a noun. The term is also used as a verb, for example: "I need to storyboard this project." What exactly is a storyboard? Before we attempt to define it, let's go back in history and learn where the term originated.

If we break the word in half as "story" and "board," we can better visualize where it all began. One sunny afternoon at the Disney Studios in southern California in the early 1920s, the first storyboards were used to illustrate the story and concepts in the animation sequences for Disney shorts "Plane Crazy" (1923) and "Steamboat Willie" (1929). These storyboards were essentially a series of single-page sketches arranged on a board to show the sequential path to the story.

Draw a stick figure on a piece of paper and hang it on the wall. Now draw that same stick figure on another piece of paper but this time with its arm raised waving. Place that piece of paper next to the one already hanging on the wall. Keep going until you assemble your "story." In this case I suppose it would be called a storywall, but you get the idea.

Disney actually credited one of its own animators for coming up with the idea of the storyboard. Webb Smith suggested drawing scenes on separate pieces of paper and pinning them to a bulletin board to show the storytelling in sequence, according to *The Art of Walt Disney*.[1]

Let's recap. The "storyboard" process was born out of an existing process by placing a series of *story* sketches, on a *board*, in sequence, presented in comic-book style, to aid in the pre-visualization of a Disney animation. In Henry Holt's 1956 book, *The Story of Walt Disney*, Diane Disney Miller describes the first known complete set of storyboards created in 1933 for the Disney short, "Three Little Pigs."

Today, it's a widely used technique for designing and developing all sorts of media, including e-learning, game design, filmmaking, theater, simulations, marketing, and, of course, animation. *Gone with the Wind* (1939) was the first film to be completely storyboarded. Since that film, the 1940s process of storyboarding films grew widely popular and today is considered an essential part of the creation process.

How does that all relate to e-learning, games for learning, and gamification? If you're involved in any part of the creation process, storyboarding should relate to your role. There is no right or wrong way to storyboard. It's a process and a style. And there can be more than one storyboard per project. Some examples of the various types of storyboards found in typical online learning projects are

- Instructional narrative
- Audio narration script
- Video shot list
- Production storyboard

Let's take a closer look at each.

Instructional Narrative

An instructional narrative might be the best way to describe what an instructional designer may already be producing. This type of storyboard is usually developed in word processing software such as Microsoft Word or Apple's Pages. Usually, each scene (slide, screen, etc.) is displayed in a table format with a header for title, subtitle, and scene number. Additional rows/columns depict such things as on-screen text or images, narrator script, animations/annotations/interactions, and production notes for actions or navigation. Microsoft PowerPoint or Apple's Keynote are also widely used for instructional narrative storyboarding, as they can be designed visually to resemble the look and feel the project will take on in final production.

Audio Narration Script

Often the narration or audio script is included in an instructional narrative storyboard. However, separating the audio narration script specifically into its own storyboard becomes an efficient way for audio talent and recording studios to better organize the final output. Additionally, splitting out the audio from the main storyboard eliminates "noise" so the audio talent can focus on the text associated with the script.

Video Shot List

The video shot list or the video storyboard is similar to the audio narration script storyboard where specific instructions on how a video is to be produced reside on its own storyboard separate from the instructional narrative. The Instructional Narrative storyboard usually has a brief description of the desired video for a particular screen, but a specific shot list depicts such things as camera angle, lead-in footage, trailing footage, and other stage set-ups. Once post-production editing is complete and the desired video format is published, it's inserted into the project as described in the main instructional narrative storyboard.

Production Storyboard

A production storyboard is similar to the audio and video storyboards, yet written specifically for the developer or development team. In some cases an animation sequence or a complex interaction requires more details on how it is to be produced than what would fit in the main storyboard. Instructions such as when a user clicks a certain button several actions occur or various calculations must be updated. Production storyboards are an effective tool for interactive serious comics, simulations, and serious games, as there are typically more "behind the scenes" actions happening simultaneously and this type of storyboard is a good way to capture those notes.

The four types of storyboards described above are just a few examples of how simple or how complex the process of storyboarding can be. There is no right or wrong way to storyboard. To answer the big question "What is a storyboard?" is to say it's a process by which the creative design can be translated into a set of production steps and instructions. However that works for you is best.

Why Storyboarding Is Important

One can argue that storyboarding has many benefits or that it's an extra amount of time that's not necessary. Whatever your view on the level of effort to storyboard a project, the single most valuable benefit is documenting the development process. In terms of e-learning or any project that's instructional in nature, whether a serious game, serious comic, simulation, etc., the shelf life in today's global workforce is twelve to eighteen months. Information is updated, policies change, performance goals change based on the change of the business, and a myriad of other reasons exist for why an online project should include ongoing maintenance and updates.

There is nothing worse than revisiting a project you worked on the year before only to learn you don't quite remember how something was developed. In some cases, the question arises as to why certain instructional paths were developed in that one-year-old course. The business practice covered at that time isn't relevant any longer and an entire section may have to be removed. If there are no original storyboard documents to study prior to updating the project, you may find yourself spending an unexpected amount of time working out a solution.

Because storyboarding began with pre-visualizing a sequential story, I'd like to share a story about what happens when you don't document a project while working in a multi-person team.

Several years ago when working for a Fortune 500 company in the training department, we were approached by the safety department to help solve a problem with a training issue, specifically around driver training. Our company had a fleet service and employed nearly four thousand drivers. They had invested in a massive driver safety campaign the year before that included monthly marketing posters, job aid tip sheets, and an online program that focused on a different driver-related safety topic each month.

This was pre-learning management system (LMS) days, so they had an external company build the online piece, which was essentially a website that looked like e-learning. I won't share how much was invested in that single year, but let's just say it was ridiculous and their budget would not allow them to invest in the same project for a second year.

The project was quite simple in scope. Create a new look and feel for a driver safety awareness and training program that published a new topic each month. Each topic should be very short and be no more than five to ten minutes in duration. Each module presented the safety hazard, the safety consequences for not adhering to it, the benefits to the driver and the company of following the safety guidelines, a short challenge quiz at the end of the module, and, most importantly, a way to track completion by every driver in the company. Remember, this was pre-LMS days.

The project seemed simple enough in design, but the scope could have become an asset management nightmare. Twelve separate modules to be published on a monthly schedule meant a one-year project plan had to be implemented. Building the first module would be like starting any new project beginning with a new UI (user interface), colors and branding, an instructional model that could be copied, and a database for collecting data. Once that was in place it was just a matter of modeling the production of a module over time broken out by a four-week production cycle: (1) instructional design, (2) develop, (3) QA and testing, (4) pre-publish and communication. By the first week of the next month the module would go live and the next module would go into its production cycle.

The plan was in place. Or so we thought. When the storyboards and asset management documentation of the previous year were requested, one would have thought we were speaking a foreign language. No one had a clue what we were requesting. It turns out that none of the previous year's project was documented by this third-party contractor. No one knew where anything was, how it was developed, or how to access any of the raw data that had already been collected.

We had to start from scratch. It took approximately three months to reorganize, build a new database, and put new processes in place before we could even begin the new design and development. In just one year a project that was off and running was tagged as useless because there was no way to pass the storyboard documents from one development team to another. This was a big lesson in how valuable and important it is to document the entire design and development of a project, no matter the size. One never knows how it will impact the business in the future.

Storyboarding is an invaluable tool not only when a third-party contractor must pass an ongoing project to an internal team but when an internal team with two or more people is working on a project. The time spent regrouping a project equals lost time that could have been prevented. My story was nearly a decade ago without the technological advances we are afforded today. With today's Cloud-based services such as Dropbox and Google Drive, storyboard documents can all be saved in one place, backed up, secure, and protected from loss.

Along with the collaborative tools as those services provide, everyone can participate, be informed, and contribute collectively to the same set of documents at the same time.

The moral of the story is that there is no reason not to storyboard today.

The Storyboarding Process

Again there are no right or wrong way ways to storyboard; however, there are certain methodologies that aid in the process within certain genres. Within any instructional design model, several approaches are available to help the learner gain knowledge and skills. All are fundamentally instructional in nature.

The difference or the process is slightly different when designing the following:

- Games for learning
- Gamification
  - Structural
  - Content
- Simulations
- Serious comics

We'll start with the most difficult or most challenging, *games for learning*. These are challenging not in terms of skill level, but in terms of instructional flow. Games in themselves are not hard to design. I'll bet you've designed several and didn't even realize you did. Teaching a child a new task and creating a game out of the learning experience is probably something every parent can relate to.

Not to go too deep into game design, game genres, or game mechanics here, but let's look at the fundamental basics. A game is a challenge. The challenge is to perform tasks or overcome obstacles. The user is awarded points, badges, health, and so forth when a task is accomplished or an obstacle is overcome. The user is also reprimanded or faces a consequence if the task is not accomplished in the prescribed order it was intended, time runs out, or other factors indicate failure. In its simplest form, that's it. That's a game.

Tying a learning event to the game is the creative part of the process and where mapping out the flow of instruction becomes critical. That map is your storyboard. Designing a game can be a rewarding experience; however, a game for learning is not something one can slap together in a few weeks. In addition, time and cost are invested into the game play that may or may not end up in the final product. It's a necessary part of game design to put a lot of time into the project to learn that it just will not work for the intended outcome. Documenting the game design and its entire process in a storyboard is critical regardless of whether everything is used or not.

Storyboarding in Action

I designed and developed a course that used structural gamification titled "MISSION: Turfgrass." I wrapped a military theme around a course where learners were taught about domestic lawns and lawn care. The course was broken down into four paths, or missions:

1. Differences among the types of grass,
2. Differences among the types of weeds,
3. Tools and equipment used to care for a lawn, and
4. Care and maintenance of a lawn.

The course was linear in its instructional path but employed structural gamification aspects such as leveling up (rank) and earning badges (items to put in your ruckpack). I wanted to engage the learners in a way that motivated them to go through the content, but I still wanted to control the path in a linear fashion.

At the beginning learners start at as "privates" with empty rucksacks. To teach learners about how to be promoted to the next rank and earn a piece of gear for their rucksacks, they were awarded both after the initial "Mission Brief." The gamification technique taught the learners early in the course how to be promoted and earn more gear. After each mission they would be promoted to the next highest rank and earn another piece of gear. By the end of the course they would have full rucksacks and earn the highest level military rank.

Figure 14.1 shows the visual storyboard in its original pencil sketch on graphing paper. Figure 14.2 shows the visual storyboard in its production states.

Notice in the production visual storyboard (Figure 14.2) the bolder lines indicate the linear path. All navigation away from that main path is what I refer to as spider-branching or navigating away from the main instructional flow with a single bi-directional path—out and back in with no other path than back to the main path.

Storyboarding a course using structural gamification, while more complex in terms of design, is not as difficult because the content doesn't change. Your design is centered on a theme and gamification elements to motivate the user through the content.

Content gamification is equally as complex yet differs from structural gamification because you have to design gamification elements into the content during the design of the instruction. One example is a course that challenges learners at the beginning to rate their aptitudes on the topic. For those scoring higher on the initial challenge, the instructional path may be shorter but more difficult. For those scoring lower on the initial challenge, the instructional path may be longer to ensure competence but may not be as difficult.

Another approach to content gamification is treating the content as easy, hard, or epic, with each choice proportionate to the path a learner chooses. Within those paths additional challenges can be presented, which could further alter the content as it's presented depending on the design of rewards versus consequences.

Each type of gamification adds a level of interest to instructional design, both with the end goal of motivating a learner through the content. Structural gamification design is intended to motivate learners through content, while content gamification design is intended to challenge learners about the content. Keep that in mind, as both can be extremely effective but

Figure 14.1 Pencil Sketch of a Storyboard

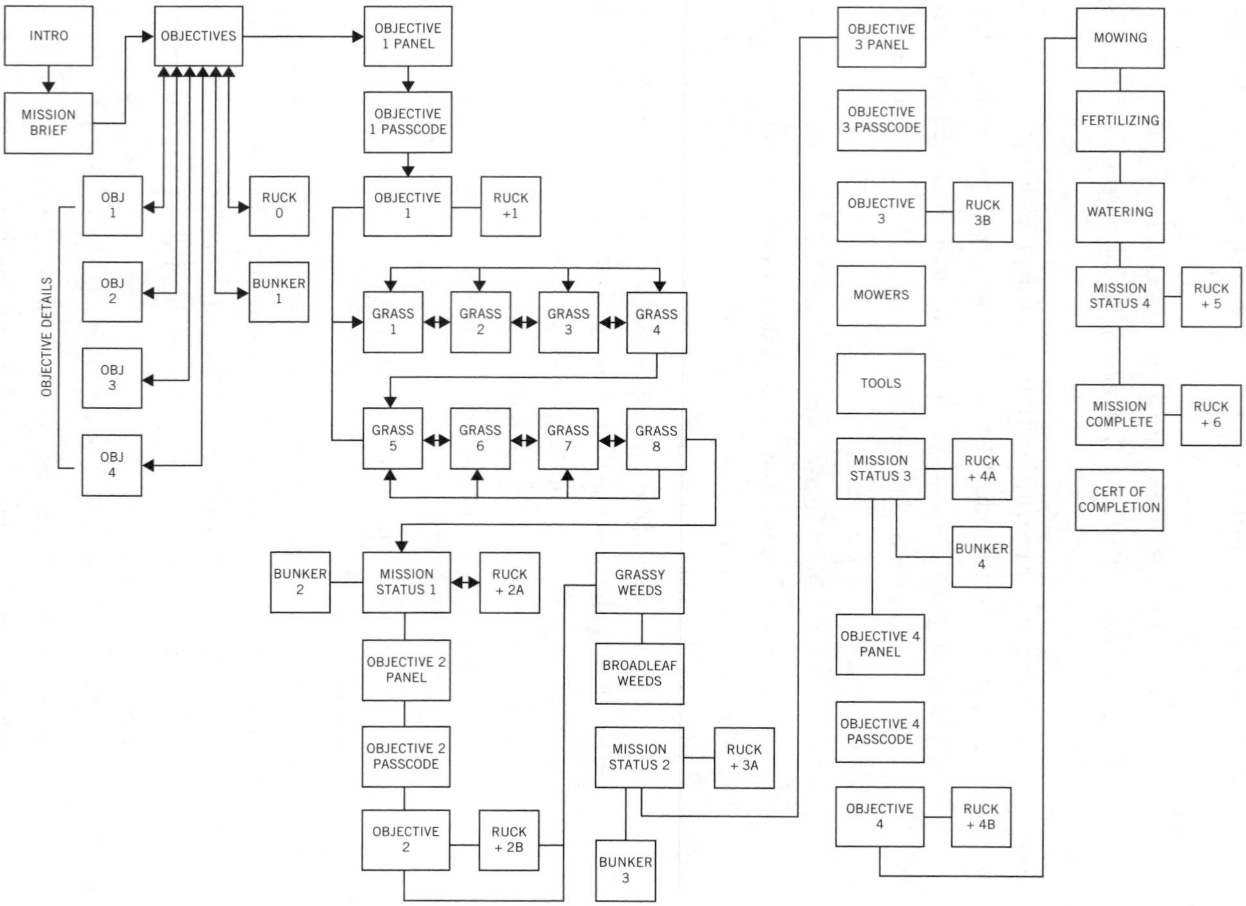

Figure 14.2 More Formalized Storyboard

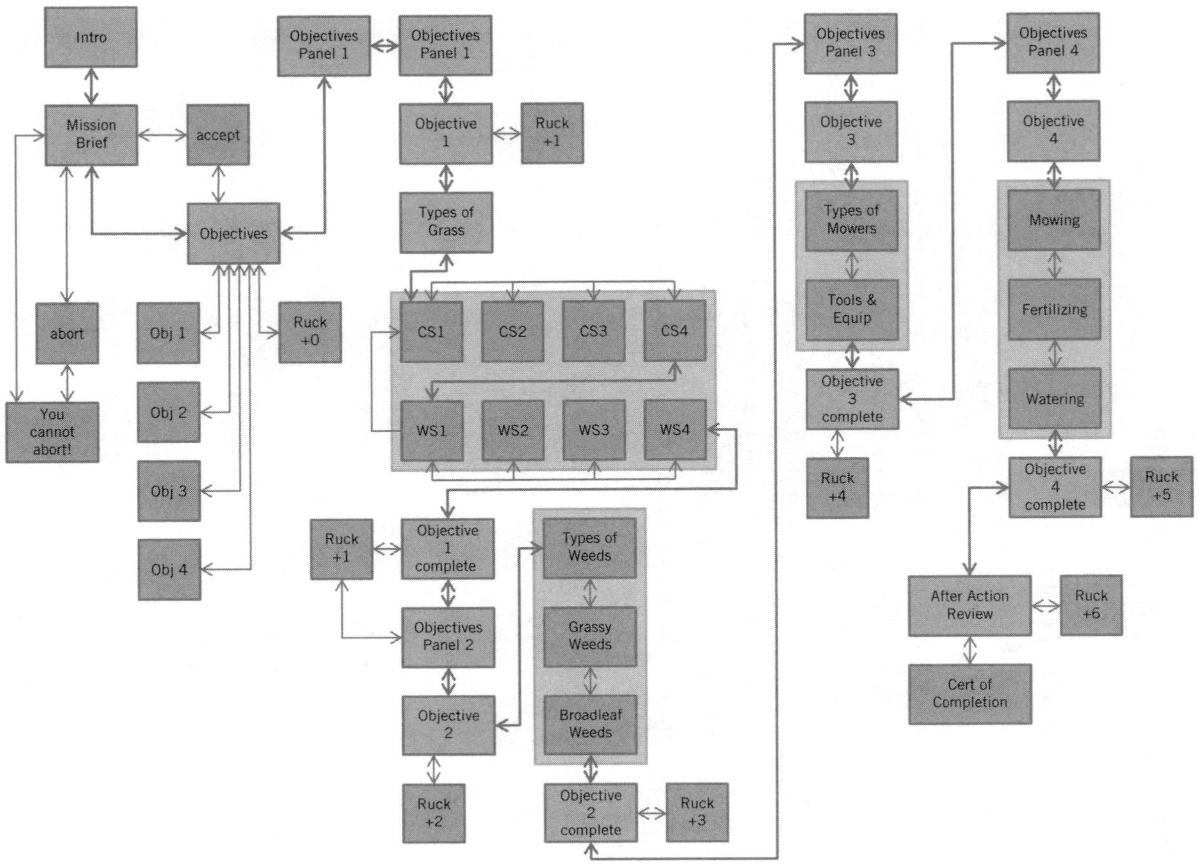

they both require deeper and more extensive thought during the instructional design process.

Storyboarding Simulations

Storyboarding for a simulation is an entirely different approach, not to go into the various types of simulations and their structures such as target acquisition simulations for the military or pilot training on a new plane simulations. Let's instead look at what simulations in the general workforce are instructionally designed for.

Fundamentally, simulations are set up and designed as the tell me, show me, let me practice model and typically involve video or screencasting media. There are countless variations to this model, depending on the subject, learner environment, audience, and so forth. Simulation games are similar to structural gamification where you add gamification elements to motivate learners through the simulation (content). I refer to these as *triptic* storyboards, or one main storyboard with three sub-storyboards all tied to the main instructional path based on the tell me, show me, let me practice model. Figure 14.3 is an example of a visual storyboard for a basic simulation with simple gamification.

Notice in the figure that each path in the simulation is categorized as Storyboard 1, 2, or 3. Because some simulation designs can be quite complex, breaking each of the paths into its own instructional design and storyboard helps with organizing content as well as allows you to focus on each path independently. The simple gamification in this example is the basic structure of the overall design and can easily be built upon in a modular concept or theme.

When designing the instruction for a simulation, think of ways that would make it challenging, more engaging, and fun. When designing learning games in general, the storyboarding process will help you visualize what the end product should look like. I can't emphasize the importance of their value enough, but I can say that, no matter what approach, template, or style you use to storyboard, you're doing it right. In the next section I'll discuss some techniques I've developed or picked up over time.

Figure 14.3 Simulation Storyboard

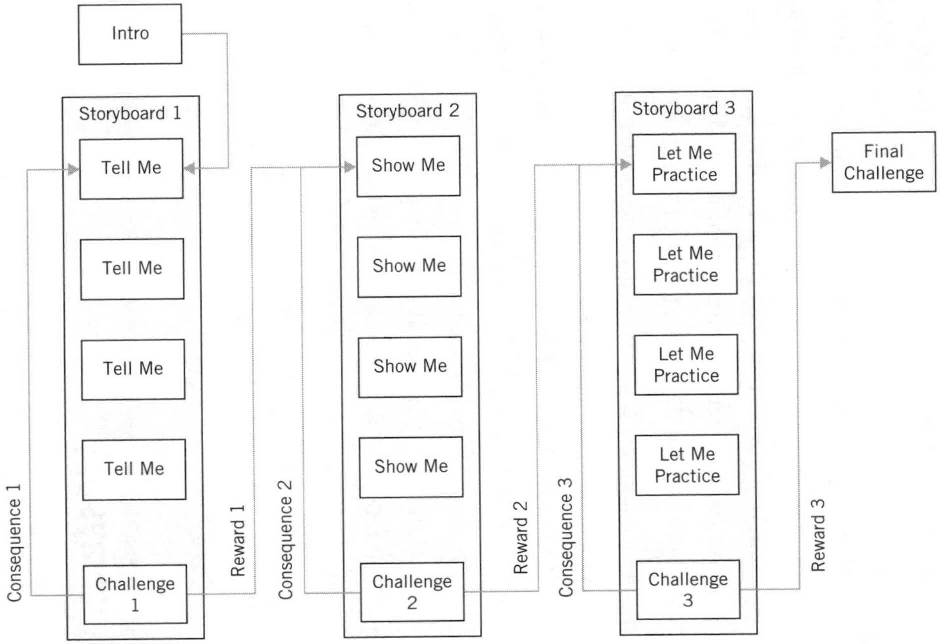

Storyboarding Techniques

Themes—Wrapping a theme around the instructional content aides in how and what the gamification elements are used. In the MISSION: Turfgrass course, the content was about domestic lawn care with a military-style reconnaissance theme wrapped around it. This allowed for a simple leveling-up idea of being promoted to the next rank. The theme also helped to form the idea of badges in the form of military gear to earn for a rucksack.

Storytelling—Stories are always fun to write. Writing a story is similar to wrapping a theme around the content, yet storytelling has to weave into the content. When writing a story for a learning game, start with the basic five-point story arc of setup/context, conflict, challenge, climax, and resolution/conclusion where the conflict part of the story leads into the challenge or game. Because a story is typically a sequential narrative, storyboarding this method is easy.

Production Notes—These apply if you're a one-person shop or if you pass the instructional design off to a developer or team of developers. Simple notes that specifically describe an action, event, or navigation not only help in the speed of development, but also for long-term updates and maintenance.

Use Tags to Describe Events—Using tags differentiates on-screen text, elements, audio, and other elements from actionable events for your users. For example, <onClick>. User advances to next screen when clicking button</onClick>. This tells the developer exactly what button and what action is to be applied to it.

Key Takeaways

Remember, storyboarding is a process by which you can pre-visualize your learning game prior to developing and potentially prevent unnecessary lost time figuring things out late in the game (no pun intended). A few quick takeaways:

- There is no right or wrong way to storyboard.
- Split your storyboards out into chunks for audio, video, production, etc.
- Storyboards are a set of reference documents used for updates and maintenance.
- Larger teams can visualize the overall outcome of the end product.

Case Studies

15

The Knowledge Guru

Sharon Boller

This case study provides an example of a quiz-type game effort used to teach concepts to a sales force. The quiz-type interactive learning experience has many game elements such as character, quests, and challenge.

Background

Bottom-Line Performance (BLP) is an Indianapolis-based learning design company with expertise in instructional design. The company was founded by Sharon Boller in 1995; today it's a team of twenty. The company touts itself as creating "the right learning solution" with "right" being different for each customer. BLP produces custom solutions that span classroom-based solutions, video, e-learning, gaming, and mobile.

Boller's personal passion is learning games; she's always been driven toward experiential activities as being a better learning tool than lecture-based or read/click activities. BLP was using game elements and game-based thinking in its solutions for a long time. The development of Knowledge Guru is a result of that passion.

The Challenge

Knowledge Guru is a quiz-style game that Boller conceived as a solution to a common problem she saw with BLP's clients. Many clients—particularly in sales-based organizations—wanted their employees to learn a lot of factual information: product features, industry background information, specifications, and other similar information.

Frequently, their method for helping people learn facts was to "sheep-dip" employees in presentation-style training experiences—either a PowerPoint-driven lecture or a "click next to continue" e-learning experience. Clients typically wanted to include a flood of information and, because of volume, they only covered this information once. The results were predictable: people didn't learn much of anything. Learners hated these experiences and Boller's company wanted no part in creating these kinds of experiences.

Knowledge Guru, a product with many game elements, was designed to eliminate these problems Boller saw happening over and over:

- Too little practice and rehearsal with the information;

- Too much information all at once;

- No fun factor to keep people engaged. People grew bored, which caused learners to mentally "check out" of the learning experience;

- No sense of accomplishment or mastery: learners had no way of gauging how much they were learning;

- Inability to "chunk" the time spent learning. Solutions were designed to be completed in a single sitting. This eliminated opportunities for spaced learning; and

- Lack of any metrics that the organization could use to assess employee mastery of facts.

Boller wanted a re-usable solution, one that clients could repurpose many times for many different games. The type of objectives that Boller felt Knowledge Guru should be able to address included ones like these:

- Define terms (ones used within an industry, ones associated with a specific product, etc.)
- Identify benefits and features
- Identify common objections
- List criteria, steps, common challenges, etc.
- Name components
- Recognize situations for which a product is a good fit
- Respond to customer questions

Why Game or Gamification?

Boller focused on a game format for four main reasons:

1. Games motivate in a way that "click next to continue" simply does not. Knowledge Guru uses a back story about a Guru atop a mountain. The visuals are fun and inviting. There are leaderboards and an achievement case to fill, mountain paths to climb, scrolls to deliver, and topics to master. (The fun appearance was actually a very common comment when BLP playtested the game with independent testers: "Oh, this looks fun!")

2. Feedback loops are powerful; they easily fit into a game format. With a game format, Boller knew she could provide continuous, immediate feedback on performance. With every question, learners received immediate feedback: they either answered the question right or they received information about their "misstep." With a misstep, they were able to immediately try again.

3. Spaced learning and repetition are powerful drivers to long-term memory. Boller felt a game could leverage these drivers. The three mountain paths players must ascend in the game are all about repetition. Each path contains a set of questions related to the mountain topic. The questions are all iterations of each other so that players respond to the content a minimum of three times to earn topic mastery. A "Grab Bag" game that unlocks after Knowledge Guru mastery status is attained offers a spaced learning opportunity as players work to empty the grab bag by re-answering all the questions in the database. Once a question is successfully answered, it is removed from the grab bag. At a minimum, though, players respond to the content three more times. Best of all, players could play in increments as small as five minutes—and this was actually better than if they attempted everything in one sitting.

4. The levels in games equate nicely to learners' need to scaffold (new info linked to previously learned info). Levels are a great way to help people chunk their learning experience, starting with basic stuff (terms and definitions) and expanding upward to concepts, rules, and application (such as customer scenarios where they applied information from earlier levels). With a Guru game, Boller could start people out with a level focused on defining terminology and progress them to a level where they applied what they learned to customer scenarios.

Within the walls of BLP, team members still debate whether Knowledge Guru is a bona fide game or a highly gamified learning experience. Learners definitely view it as a game—and they work hard to earn points and claim Knowledge Guru status. Boller's personal opinion is that to qualify as a full-fledged game, a game should involve some measure of strategy and chance in addition to a well-defined game goal. Guru does have a game goal (become a Knowledge Guru), but strategy is largely absent. Players who know the answers will gain points; players who miss a question lose points. Savvy players quickly realize that incorrect responses get them immediate feedback on what is the correct response so they can learn from incorrect answers.

Making the Case

BLP may have had a nice idea . . . but in a consulting world it's only a good one if they persuade their clients to buy into it and try it. ExactTarget was one of the early adopters of the game. The rest of this case study focuses on the game BLP produced for them—and the results ExactTarget achieved from the game. (Note: Since this chapter was written, ExactTarget has been purchased by Salesforce.com.)

ExactTarget's Scott Thomas, director of product enablement for the organization, was searching for a new tool in his product training toolbox. ExactTarget is a global marketing organization focused on digital marketing tools—email, mobile, and web. They continually launch new products and enhancements to existing products for their client base.

Thomas reached out to BLP one month before the scheduled launch of a new product, MobileConnect. Thomas had played one of BLP's free games—College Hoops Guru—and became intrigued by the possibility of hooking his employees on gameplay while learning about a product. Thomas wanted his department to help the company score a home run on the product launch; he saw Knowledge Guru as a way to do this.

Being able to show—rather than just tell—was critical to securing sponsorship of the game. Thomas's own play of a demo game was a pivotal part of his success in convincing stakeholders that the game could have value. He saw how the game worked and then communicated his experience to stakeholders. The other key was the game engine's ability to track what learners were doing and how they were performing. The metrics sold the game.

The Solution

The images and captions in the figures that follow provide a walk-through of the game experience. The web application was built using Adobe Cold Fusion with a back-end MySQL database that stores game and user data. Users log into the game via the Internet; the entire solution is hosted in the Cloud. There is also a native application available. A demo game called Nutrition Guru can be accessed and downloaded via the iOS App Store.

Players log into the system, as shown in Figure 15.1. First-time players complete a "sign up" form that captures their names, geographic regions, and departments, which is used for tracking progress and populating leaderboards.

When players enter the game for the first time, they see a narrative that explains how the game works, as shown in Figure 15.2. Ascend a mountain for each topic with a single ascent proving nothing! That's too easy. The player must ascend each mountain three times and carry the Guru a scroll of wisdom each time.

As shown in Figure 15.3, the game's "mountains" equal the instructional topics to cover. Each mountain has learning objectives associated with it. The leaderboard visible on the left tracks different kinds of achievements: high score by geographic area, daily high score, longest streak of correct responses, and so forth. If the player taps "Achievements" at the bottom of the screen, she can see specific achievements earned, such as a Topic Mastery award or a badge for hitting a specific score or for a streak of correct responses.

Figure 15.1 The Knowledge Guru Login Screen

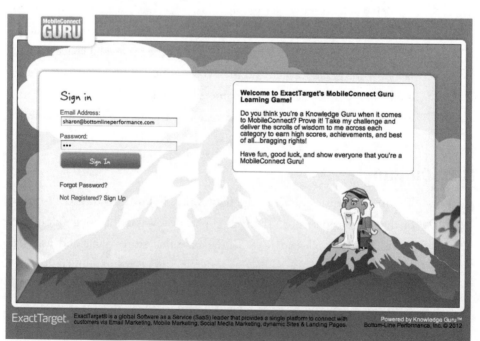

Figure 15.2 Narrative Screen Explaining How the Game Works

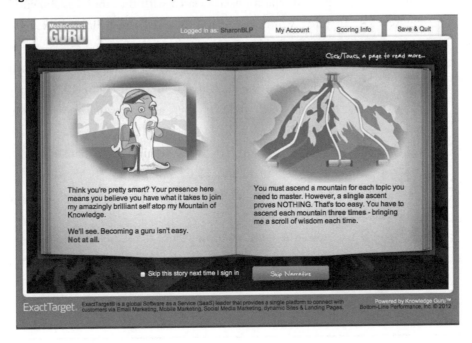

Figure 15.3 The Mountains in the Game Are Topics to Cover

Once players select a topic, they select a path. Each path contains a different iteration of the questions associated with that topic, as shown in Figure 15.4. In other words, everything is asked three different ways to ensure repetition and to develop understanding.

The players can see their scores as they answer each game question. If they answer correctly, their score goes up, as shown in Figure 15.5. If they answer incorrectly, their scores go down. There are consequences—just as in real life.

When players answer incorrectly, they receive immediate feedback and correction, as shown in Figure 15.6. When they click "continue," they are placed back on their "mountain path" exactly where they made the misstep.

Figure 15.7 shows the question again. Note the score has reset to zero because the player started with very few points. When the player makes a correct response, the score will go up.

Figure 15.4 Selecting a Path for Ascension Up the Mountain

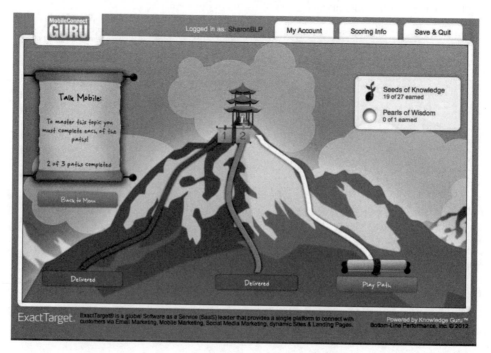

Figure 15.5 Players Can See Their Scores as They Answer Questions

Figure 15.6 Incorrect Answers Receive Immediate Feedback

Figure 15.7 Score Is Reset to Zero

The Guru game engine used to create and house the MobileConnect game has a detailed "back end," allowing specific tracking of designated information, as shown in Figure 15.8. This is one of several reports available. It enables a supervisor, a learning and development professional, a faculty member, or other vested stakeholder to see how players are performing. If needed, ad hoc support can be offered based on these results. An administrator can even drill down to see how a specific player is performing and determine what he has accomplished, where he has struggled, and how much time he has spent playing.

Once players complete the topic "levels" in the game, they unlock a new game called *Guru Grab Bag*. This game includes all the questions from all the topics. Players now are in a sudden death mode—miss a question and all points are lost and the game is over. Respond correctly and the player empties the question from the Grab Bag. This final game play ensures spaced learning, as players once again see the content they covered in their efforts to achieve topic mastery over all the game topics.

Figure 15.8 Detailed Data Is Provided for Each Learner

Qid	Question Stem	Objective	Correct Answers	Wrong Answers	Correct Response %
1	SMS = short message service. MTA = mail transfer agent. Which one is associated with text messaging?	T1	497	0	100.00
2	You just received a text message from a friend. How was the message transmitted?	T1	433	24	94.75
3	You are a mobile customer who has opted in to receive updates to your local bus route via text. Will these be delivered via SMS or MTA?	T1	436	12	97.32
4	FTEU means free to end user. Customers who opt in to FTEU programs don't incur fees from their wireless carrier when they send or receive messages. Does ExactTarget offer FTEUs?	T1	457	199	69.96
5	You opted into a FTEU program offered by a retailer so you can receive notifications via text free of charge. This program was generated by ExactTarget's MobileConnect application.	T1	413	45	90.17
6	ExactTarget does not offer FTEU programs.	T1	428	22	95.11
7	If you go mobile with your marketing efforts, two kinds of text messages will probably be part of your plans: MOs and MTs. Which statement is correct?	T1	444	219	66.97
8	If you are the marketer. will you send MOs or MTs to your customers?	T1	431	24	94.73
9	You are a local grocer who has a mobile marketing program in place. Your customers are submitting their email addresses to opt in to a newsletter via text messaging. What type of message are your customers sending?	T1	422	57	88.10
10	Short (5 or 6 digits) and long (8- to 10-digits) codes are numbers used to send text messages. Outside of the U.S., which type must be used if the marketer wants to run a global campaign through one code?	T1	432	20	95.58
11	Which set of numbers is an example of a long code, the type of code typically used to run global messaging campaigns?	T1	424	34	92.58
12	Which statement is true?	T1	421	65	86.63

ExactTarget deployed this solution as an optional activity that followed execution of webinars on the product they were rolling out. They put together an excellent marketing campaign that encouraged people to play, awarding prizes to daily high scores and to the overall winner. They also wrote a feature article on the overall winner, announcing him as the MobileConnect Guru.

Employee reaction to the game was outstanding. In Thomas's words, "I can't tell you how many people are coming to me wanting another game solution." Here's a sampling of the feedback Thomas received:

- "The repetition of the different paths helped me retain the information."

- "I'm a pretty competitive person so challenging myself to get one of the top scores added a layer of fun to learning about the MobileConnect product."

- "The game was a fun way to learn about MobileConnect. I enjoyed the scenario-type questions, which put it all into context."

The Benefits and Results

The immediate benefit of a game over a traditional training tool is its allure. People want to play games; they don't always want to attend a training session. ExactTarget did a terrific job marketing the game, and people wanted to play.

However, the "fun" factor doesn't necessarily translate to business results. And what really matters are the business results. ExactTarget achieved these:

- Average contract value is higher than for a previous mobile product.

- First call resolution is up.

- Of all the launches done in the previous two years to MobileConnect, the sales team has built the quickest pipeline for this product.

Lessons Learned

Here's what Boller advises to anyone creating a game:

"Playtest. Playtest. Playtest. Your first design will not be the best design, or even close to it. Think in terms of rapid iteration. Build a prototype quickly (you can do a paper prototype even for a game you intend to be online) and get people playing. Observe the play and debrief the experience. Then modify based on the feedback.

- Involve people who are your actual targets in some of your playtests. Their perspectives will be completely different from your own.

- As the game matures, shift playtesting to those who are not your friends. Your friends will say nice things. Other people will say honest things.

- Keep the instructional purpose FIRST and the game elements second. An instructional game does not have to be the most amazing game ever. It needs to be fun enough to accomplish your learning goals. You are probably not designing Angry Birds, World of Warcraft, or Settlers of Catan. You are designing a game to help people learn and remember what they learned.

- Be clear about what results you are seeking and design the game to fit the results you are targeting.

- Be able to sell the game to stakeholders. Have a compelling presentation on why games work. Stakeholders need data to confirm that a game isn't a waste of time.

- Make sure your target audience is receptive to a game solution. Don't assume they aren't because you wouldn't like to play a game, but don't assume they are because you love games. If they are lukewarm to the idea of games, test the waters. They may find they actually like playing games, but they don't like competitive games or games where they feel put on display. In these cases, you can opt for a cooperative game as opposed to a competitive game.

- Promotion is key. You cannot simply create the game and assume people will embrace it. It has to be thoughtfully positioned and its role clearly communicated to the target audience."

16

A Board Game: MPE

Robert Bell

This case study provides an example of a board game design, developed and used to teach a people management process within a food packaging business.

Background

Enspire Learning was founded in Austin, Texas, in 2001 with the mission to provide organizations with effective and engaging learning experiences. Today, Enspire Studios—Enspire's custom division—is a recognized leader in the creation of transformative learning experiences, trusted by the world's leading organizations to build custom learning solutions that address the unique needs of their audience.

ConAgra Foods, Inc., is one of North America's largest packaged food companies. Its portfolio includes consumer brands found in 97 percent of America's households, the largest private brand packaged food business in North America, and a strong commercial and foodservice business. Consumers can find recognized brands such as Banquet®, Chef Boyardee®, Egg Beaters®, Healthy Choice®, Hebrew National®, Hunt's®, Marie Callender's®, Orville Redenbacher's®, PAM®, Peter Pan®, Reddi-wip®, Slim Jim®, Snack Pack®, and many other ConAgra Foods brands, along with food sold by ConAgra Foods under private-brand labels, in grocery, convenience, mass merchandise, club stores, and drugstores.

The Challenge

ConAgra Foods sought to develop an intensive, one-day experiential learning program to introduce managers across all business functions to selected parts of the managing people essentials (MPE) integrated talent management process. This included the phases of the process, related job tools, and foundations for maintaining transparency and building trust between managers and employees. They turned to Enspire Studios as a vendor to design and develop this experience.

ConAgra specifically sought to create training around a phase of the process known as MPE: Succeed, which focused on high-level, strategic activities in talent management—namely the ways managers assess a talent pool against broad annual business goals and the development efforts they can employ to bring the talent pool in alignment with the company's strategy.

ConAgra's desired outcome for the training was to prepare business managers to successfully implement MPE: Succeed by:

- Practicing talent management decisions within relevant simulated scenarios;

- Experiencing the potential impacts of those decisions; and

- Conducting strategic conversations related to talent management decisions.

ConAgra expected participants to demonstrate two high-level behaviors as a result of this experience. Specifically, participants would be expected to:

- Utilize integrated talent management tools and processes and

- Assess employees' performance and potential.

This translates to an operational understanding among managers of a handful of concepts and processes, including:

- Critical positions

- Succession planning

- Talent flags

- Performance/potential matrix

Why a Game?

The solution that Enspire Studios developed for ConAgra Foods is called "Managing Talent for Results," a custom game based on a simulated talent management scenario. I classify this as a game rather than a pure simulation because game elements are core to its design. Specifically:

- Players have prescribed abilities to play with.

- There are clear game constraints that limit use of these abilities.

- Players must negotiate a series of risks to achieve rewards and work toward the game's overall goal, namely, to compete with other players on the basis of productivity and revenue.

- Managing Talent for Results is a one-day, sit-down board game experience supplemented by a web-based digital application used to compute player actions and generate their results—in other words, it contains no mobile elements. And it is distinct from a gamification solution insofar as it is not a set of game features applied outside of a game experience context; rather, it is a defined learning experience that contains intrinsic game elements.

Prior to Enspire Studios' selection as the vendor for this project, ConAgra had already started to explore the possibility of creating either a game or simulation for the MPE: Succeed workshop. ConAgra had previously used "off-the-shelf" leadership simulations, including Enspire products such as Business Challenge, and had found these kinds of interactive learning experiences to be highly effective with their audience of business managers. In this case, they wanted to give managers an opportunity to explore the processes and tools around MPE: Succeed in a simulated context, and they had this kind of custom experience in mind when they sought a vendor.

Still, after Enspire Studios was selected, there remained the question of whether we would be creating a game or a simulation. As the instructional designer for this project, I was somewhat agnostic on this question in the beginning. I had no preference beyond what would make the most engaging and instructionally effective learning experience for ConAgra's audience of business managers. Ultimately, the content and context of the proposed training workshop naturally lent themselves more to a game experience than a pure simulation in a few ways:

- ConAgra wanted to directly equate players' talent management decisions with monetary consequences for the company they were managing in this experience. In a game, this naturally becomes a reward system. In our *particular* game, players' choices ended up correlating to the amount of revenue they can earn for the fictional company they're managing.

- The content further suggested game elements more than they suggested purely simulated practice in a few ways. Namely, in addition to a rewards structure, there were obvious risks to making talent management decisions that were not aligned with best practices; for example, employees in this fictional company could become demoralized and quit based on player decisions, and this outcome would directly affect players' revenue results. In this way, a game-based risk and reward balance became part of the underlying model for this experience.

- The proposed experience was to be part of a recurring workshop on MPE: Succeed, with a sizeable group of managers participating in each workshop. This fact led us to the conclusion that participants should be split into teams to play this experience, allowing us to make use of face-to-face team dynamics to encourage strategic conversations among players. Further, given the risk and reward structure just described, our system of monetary rewards in the game allowed us to create competition among teams on the basis of revenue.

Making the Case

ConAgra Foods engaged Enspire Studios for this project with the express purpose of creating a game or simulation. We were incredibly fortunate to work with a forward-thinking client on this project; ConAgra had already correctly foreseen that a game or simulation would be the optimal learning experience given the selected content, which meant that we did not have to convince them of the efficacy of a game or simulation-based approach.

The Solution

Each team of players participating in Managing Talent for Results sits at a table on which a game board is placed. The board game is shown in Figure 16.1. This board represents the organizational chart for the fictional company they are running. Employee cards are placed on this board, representing the talent occupying given positions at any given point in gameplay.

Additionally, teams are provided with other paper-based game assets as well—shock cards, resource tokens, etc. In this way, Managing Talent for Results is primarily presented as a board game experience in that most of the gameplay is non-digital.

At the same time, the game employs digital elements. Specifically, each team has a laptop at its table in addition to the paper-based game elements. The team's talent management decisions for each round are entered into an input screen in a web-based application on the laptop, as shown in Figure 16.2.

Figure 16.1 Game Board for MPE Succeed

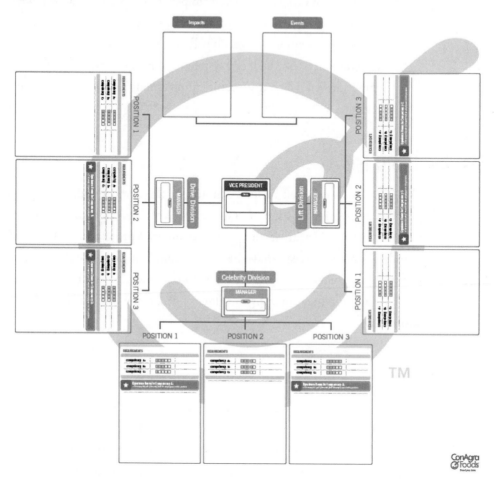

Outcomes from each round of decisions are computed and reported through a summary of changes screen for each team, as shown in Figure 16.3.

Finally, teams' comparative results are revealed to players on a results screen in the web application. The facilitator of Managing Talent for Results projects teams' comparative results at the front of the room at the end of each year of gameplay, as shown in Figure 16.4.

Figure 16.2 Input Screen for the Web Portion of the Game

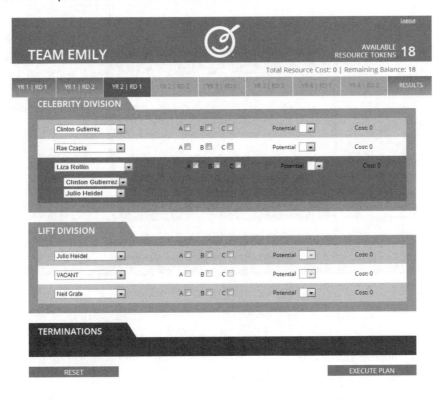

Figure 16.3 Summary of Changes Screen for MPE Succeed

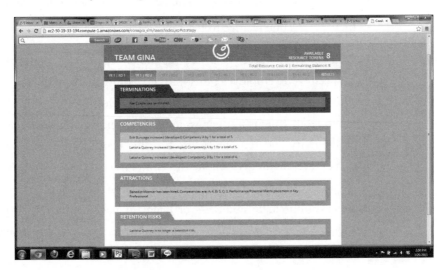

Figure 16.4 Results Screen

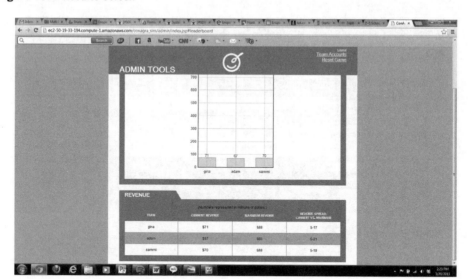

Managing Talent for Results is played over the course of four virtual "years" in the life of the fictional company, with two rounds of play comprising one full year in the game. In other words, there are eight total rounds in one full session of Managing Talent for Results.

Each team has the following high-level goals in the game:

- Increase total productivity at a higher rate than competing teams.

- Increase revenue relative to revenue targets in each round.

They accomplish these goals by aligning employees' performance levels—as specified on employee cards—to the requirements of the positions they occupy on the game board. The closer employees' performance levels are aligned to requirements in their assigned positions, the higher the team's overall productivity and revenue. More broadly, teams also want to make sure that they are aligning talent to the company's strategic goals, which appear as shocks throughout the game and change the state of play.

Teams have four main abilities—or talent management efforts—available to them, which allow them to align employees' performance levels to requirements and prepare for changes in the state of play:

- *Develop:* They may train current staff to develop their performance relative to position requirements.

- *Transfer:* They can transfer staff from their current positions to new positions.

- *Terminate:* They can release current employees from their positions.

- *Attract:* They can attract employees from an outside talent pool to meet position requirements.

Each team is provided with a limited number of resource tokens to invest in talent management efforts for each "year" of play. Allocating limited resources is a persistent challenge in the game. Additional challenge comes from the element of "retention risk"—the uncertainty of whether an employee will quit as a result of being overqualified and underdeveloped in a position or as the result of a termination within his or her division of the company. Finally, some positions are deemed "critical positions" within the company, and these provide an added challenge for players since the impact on productivity and revenue for critical positions is doubled and they must be filled according to a succession plan that the team must set in place before each round of play.

Players strategize their decisions using the game board and paper-based assets during each round of play, and they register their decisions in the web application at the end of each round. If they can overcome the challenges of play and succeed at the game's overall goals, they will best competing teams on the basis of productivity and revenue earned over the course of four "years."

The solution was primarily designed through iterative paper prototyping and playtesting. At a very early stage in the design process—as soon as we had established a core game design—we brought an initial prototype to ConAgra's Omaha headquarters to play with key stakeholders at the company. We continued to do this multiple times during the course of the design phase, as we created progressive prototype iterations. Each of these prototypes consisted of simple Word documents, spreadsheets, dice, poker chips, and other analog assets that allowed us to quickly express a core design and enable gameplay.

Playtesting these prototype iterations allowed us to demonstrate our design to the client during formative phases of design, which allowed them to have direct input into revisions of gameplay and content. Ultimately, this made the development process for Managing Talent for Results a highly collaborative one between vendor and client, with both contributing their respective strengths—namely serious game design expertise on the vendor side and subject-matter expertise on the client side.

Once the design of the paper prototype reached a stage at which the client was satisfied that it met the target instructional objectives and the vendor was assured that it sufficiently engaged participants in gameplay, it became clear that the game was too complex for the game's facilitator and players to manage on their own. At this point in development, I collaborated with our lead tech developer to translate the game's design into a logic flow that he used to create the game's Java application. At the same time, our graphic designers finalized the design of all paper-based assets in the game.

As previously mentioned, the final solution is deployed as part of ConAgra's MPE: Succeed workshop. It is intentionally designed to be an on-site, facilitated experience, meaning that it is not accessible to players outside of the workshop.

Managing Talent for Results is introduced to participants by the game facilitator in the morning of the first day of the MPE: Succeed workshop. At this point, the facilitator assigns positions to players in each team. Namely, each team has three managers and one vice president with the following responsibilities:

- *Managers:* Three players take on the role of manager of each of the three divisions in the fictional company. The managers are primarily responsible for analyzing and correcting gaps between performance and requirements for each of the three employees in their respective departments.

- *VP:* One player takes on the role of the group's vice president. The VP is responsible for leading the team through each game round and executing the team's talent management strategy.

The facilitator guides all participants on how to play the first round of the game, which takes the better part of the morning. After this round, though, teams are typically prepared to play subsequent rounds with minimal guidance. All told, the game's eight rounds are played over the course of a full day of the MPE: Succeed workshop.

In practice, gameplay is highly engaged and conversational among players within teams. There is a great deal of strategic discussion among teammates leading up to the execution of their talent management efforts at the end of each round. There is also a highly competitive atmosphere among teams as team results are presented to participants by the facilitator at the end of a "year" of play.

The Benefits

At the outset of the project, ConAgra intended for business managers to do the following things in the proposed learning experience:

- Practice talent management decisions within relevant simulated scenarios;

- Experience the potential impacts of those decisions; and

- Conduct strategic conversations related to talent management decisions.

Ultimately, we created an experience that enables participants to do all of these things, giving them the opportunity to construct understanding directly through a simulated experience. But the experience is not only valuable on its own; it also connects to learning within the broader workshop. As such, it is a ripe experience for instructors to build learning transfer on, ensuring that business managers carry key learning objectives from the workshop directly to their jobs.

The Results

We have three key pieces of evidence:

1. *Very high levels of engagement*—Initially the workshop was scheduled so that brief sections of didactic instruction followed each "year" of play. We eventually found that this frustrated participants, who did not want to pause gameplay, even for a moment. We ended up rearranging the workshop schedule to allow continuous play of the full game before participants start the didactic portion of the workshop. This speaks to the very high level of engagement we have seen pretty much without exception among participants.

2. *The model is closely aligned to the target*—Both our stakeholders at ConAgra and a clear majority of participants in the target audience agree that the game models the target objectives around talent management in a realistic and compelling fashion. It simplifies the experience without oversimplifying it.

3. *Optimal strategy in the game reflects optimal talent management behavior*—The team that achieved the highest result ever in a play session did so by aligning their talent to the highest designations in the performance/potential matrix—an optimal talent management behavior. This is an "aha" moment for players, which reflects the game's correlation to optimal talent management practice in the real world.

Lessons Learned

Design a serious game only if the content naturally lends itself to gameplay. I believe this experience is successful as a game experience because its core content contains risk and reward elements that naturally lend themselves to gameplay. If these elements had not been in place, we might have been better served creating a simulation or creating a more traditional learning program with gamification elements. I generally believe that the content should guide the form of the learning solution. It's riskier to decide on a serious game without thoughtfully investigating inherent game elements in the content.

Iterative prototyping and playtesting are essential to good game design as well as to a healthy collaboration between vendor and client. We were able to ensure that this experience satisfied both instructional expectations as well as provided satisfying gameplay through iterative prototyping and playtesting of paper-based game designs. Throughout the design phase, the input of playtest participants was critical to the improvement of our design. It also helped to forge collaboration in the vendor/client relationship in a valuable way, allowing the client insight and ownership of the design.

Serious games don't always have to be digital games. Digital games can be flashy and fun, but they can also be costly to develop and they have their limitations. In the case of this project, we determined early on that the experience of having participants gather around a table and play a board game not only made sense in the workshop environment, but it also encouraged the kinds of rich, strategic conversations that we wanted players to have. Where we used a digital game component, it was to do what digital games can do better than analog games, handle complexity. The lesson here is to be versatile when it comes to selecting the game medium that best serves the game's audience and its core purpose and to not discount the value of non-digital games.

17

Mobile Gamification: Mobile Cricket U

Robert Gadd

This case study provides an example of a mobile gamification platform implemented into a retail environment.

Background

OnPoint Digital is a provider of online and mobile learning solutions for enterprise customers. The eleven-year-old company develops end-to-end platforms that allow organizations to create, publish, distribute, and manage both formal and informal learning experiences for their employees, partners, and customers on virtually any computer or intelligent device with integrated social, collaborative, and game-enabled experiences. The OnPoint team supports more than one million licensed learners in more than thirty countries through direct relationships and partners/resellers across a variety of industries, including telecom, high tech, retail, transportation, pharmaceutical, medical, financial services, insurance, food service, and others.

Cricket Communications is the seventh-largest wireless communications provider in the United States. Founded in 1999 to make wireless phone service more affordable to more people, Cricket offers economical, pre-paid unlimited voice and data rate plans that do not require a contract. Today, Cricket Communications serves more than 5.8 million wireless customers in the United States, nearly double its subscriber total in 2006. Third-party agreements with Wal-Mart and Radio Shack allow it to serve customers in areas where it does not have stores. In 2011, Cricket introduced MUVE Music and became the first U.S. wireless carrier to offer customers unlimited music as part of a rate plan.

The Challenge

OnPoint Digital customer and strategic partner Cricket Communications was seeking improved and more innovative ways to reach the sales professionals working in its retail locations—through the introduction of mobile-enabled learning extensions to their existing Cricket University platform. Cricket University, a mature online learning portal, provides access to courseware and sales training materials detailing an ever-changing array of wireless products and services offered to Cricket customers.

As a wireless carrier and service provider, Cricket wanted to provide product training and information delivery to retail sales reps using the same mobile devices they sell to Cricket customers—fulfilling the promise of learning anywhere, any time.

The mLearning initiative, coined Mobile CU, launched in summer 2012 and was spearheaded by John Moxley, Cricket's director of leadership development, himself an avid mobile device and app enthusiast. Moxley has more than twenty years of experience implementing next-generation organization development and sales training programs across a variety of industries and is also heavily involved in the evaluation and use of popular content authoring tools and methods to produce mobile-friendly courseware to support untethered learning communities.

Cricket's enterprise-centric requirements for mobile learning drove John and his team of learning and development professionals to identify OnPoint Digital's CellCast Solution offering, an end-to-end platform for mobile content creation, management, and delivery already popular with other wireless carriers, high-tech original equipment manufacturers (OEMs), and retailers looking to support mobile workers with on-the-go training and business communications. The Mobile Cricket U offering leverages a set of highly customized native apps installed on a wireless handset or tablet that sync published assignments out to learners to enable any time, anywhere learning, as shown in Figure 17.1. The mobile solution set has also been integrated with the Cricket University learning management system (based on the Taleo Learn platform from Oracle) to ensure a common system of record for all employee training activities, whether delivered to PCs, laptops, tablets, or smart phones.

Figure 17.1 Custom User Experience with "My Games" Feature Enabled

Android Handsets   **Apple iPhones**

To make the learning experience more engaging and compelling, the Cricket team was one of OnPoint's first customers to implement a new CellCast gamification module used to associate flexible game mechanics and dynamics with either online or mobile learning experiences. Initial game-enabled learning was used for the introduction of Cricket's new high-speed long-term evolution (LTE) data network and designed to accelerate product knowledge delivery and retention with sales representatives across the Cricket coverage area.

The wireless industry is considered one of the most competitive and fast moving environments to support. Sales representatives are regularly inundated with new product and systems training. Accordingly, corporate training must rapidly educate and inform learners in innovative ways that are convenient to access for the sales representatives to provide a great customer experience.

The central learning objective was (and is) to deliver and measure the effectiveness of product, service, systems training, and professional development without requiring Cricket's sales professionals to leave the sales floor. Cricket also believed the introduction of game mechanics would improve representative engagement and knowledge retention, as well as reinforce key principles and behaviors. The CellCast platform provided the means and incentive for learners to quickly complete assignments, gain points, and advance their status in an ongoing competition.

Why Gamification?

The solution adds an integrated set of game mechanics to drive learning engagement via completion of formal assignments as well as participation in informal learning interactions. Cricket's training team can select varied game mechanics to accompany different learning programs and vary game points, lengths, rewards, and incentives for each learning audience. Cricket's learning and development team uses the CellCast Solution platform to define the specific "game profile," associating any collection of formal learning assignments (online courses, tests, instructor-led training sessions, or webinar participation) and informal learning interactions (reading documents, viewing

Figure 17.2 Game Profile Screen Used to Define Game Mechanics/Dynamics

videos, participating in forums, uploading user generated content) within the game. The game is then assigned to existing Cricket U groups, as shown on the assignment screen in Figure 17.2.

The primary motivation for introducing game mechanics to Mobile Cricket U is to drive learner engagement through a combination of achievement and competition. Learners complete assignments across a wide range of ever-changing products, pricing plans, and wireless innovations. The addition of mobile delivery methods helps to make learning motivational and the use of points, badges, and friendly competition provides the means to easily measure and reward progress.

Making the Case

Gaining buy-in from training leadership and the corporate marketing team was actually fairly easy to secure, as every business function at Cricket is keen on identifying ways to implement improved selling strategies, especially when the cost is low and leverages Cricket core technology—mobile devices.

The CellCast gamification module, when added as an optional module, is fully integrated into the Mobile Cricket U platform. The module provides instant access to an extended set of game mechanics, game interfaces, and leaderboards. It also provides detailed reporting tools learned and adopted by Cricket's training team in only a few days. This allowed Cricket's team to devise, plan, populate, and deploy their game-enabled programs with nominal effort and no programming while staying focused on building the actual learning assets that comprise the game-enabled learning experience. The CellCast gamification engine is a fully integrated module with the CellCast Solution platform, making it easy to associate game mechanics with any of the formal or informal learning experiences and interactions deployed in support of the Mobile Cricket U learning audience.

Exhibiting and promoting a strong, passionate "mobile mindset" is mission critical for every successful wireless carrier and Cricket is no exception, so business programs that can leverage mobile accessible technology to drive sales, increase productivity, or drive engagement are generally given fast and due consideration. It was important to demonstrate the technology for key stakeholder groups in a hands-on way, so they could directly experience the quality and convenience of the user experience.

That stated, the highly competitive wireless marketplace presents an array of ever-shifting financial challenges that can impact budgets and other capital expenditures. Special attention is given to programs and initiatives that drive top-line results without impacting bottom-line performance. The direct cost to add OnPoint's gamification feature set to the existing Mobile Cricket U platform was $5,000, and the effort required to bring the L&D team up to speed was under twelve staff hours of training and one-on-one technical support, making the entire effort both fast and cost-effective.

The initial success of game-enabled training drove interest in expanding the reach of the OnPoint platform to allow a larger number of internal Cricket employees to participate in gamified learning experiences through web-based delivery methods as well, through the addition of a customized portlet, as shown in Figure 17.3. The portlet is accessible from the main Cricket University learning portal; this expansion is currently under review and subject to budget approval.

Figure 17.3 Game Mechanics/Dynamics Accessed via Online Web Browser

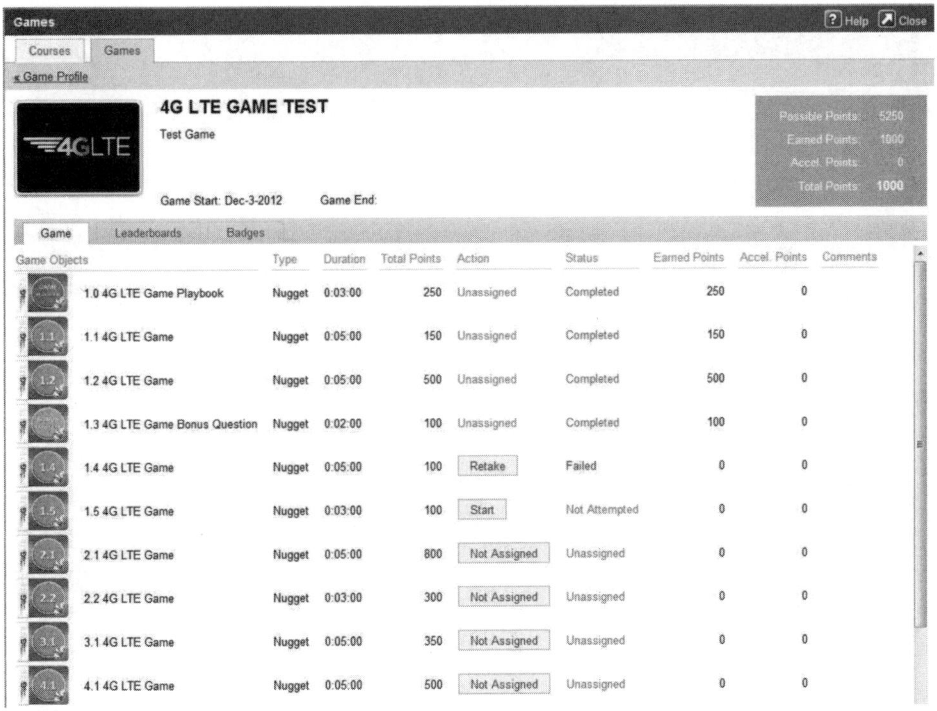
Games
Help
Close
Courses
Games
« Game Profile
4GLTE
4G LTE GAME TEST
Test Game
Game Start: Dec-3-2012
Game End:
Possible Points: 5250
Earned Points: 1000
Accel. Points: 0
Total Points: 1000
Game
Leaderboards
Badges
Game Objects
Type
Duration
Total Points
Action
Status
Earned Points
Accel. Points
Comments
1.0 4G LTE Game Playbook Nugget 0:03:00 250 Unassigned Completed 250 0
1.1 4G LTE Game Nugget 0:05:00 150 Unassigned Completed 150 0
1.2 4G LTE Game Nugget 0:05:00 500 Unassigned Completed 500 0
1.3 4G LTE Game Bonus Question Nugget 0:02:00 100 Unassigned Completed 100 0
1.4 4G LTE Game Nugget 0:05:00 100 Retake Failed 0 0
1.5 4G LTE Game Nugget 0:03:00 100 Start Not Attempted 0 0
2.1 4G LTE Game Nugget 0:05:00 800 Not Assigned Unassigned 0 0
2.2 4G LTE Game Nugget 0:03:00 300 Not Assigned Unassigned 0 0
3.1 4G LTE Game Nugget 0:05:00 350 Not Assigned Unassigned 0 0
4.1 4G LTE Game Nugget 0:05:00 500 Not Assigned Unassigned 0 0

The Solution

Game points are associated with the learning assignments and tests at the most basic level of play. The Cricket training team quickly established various achievement levels, earned points, and awarded badges that serve as the basis for new games and sponsored sales programs, as shown in Figure 17.4.

Points earned for completing certain formal learning assignments were "completion points," while finishing other formal learning assignments delivered "bonus points" calculated according to the score attained on an associated quiz or module-level assessment. Learners are also rewarded with "acceleration points" for completing assignments within a defined time period, thus incenting them to complete their learning tasks earlier to benefit the organization and customers by compressing the time to proficiency.

Earned points serve as the overall performance gauge for each game-enabled learning program. Progress for each individual learner is tracked

Figure 17.4 Managing Formal and Informal Learning Elements Within a Game Profile

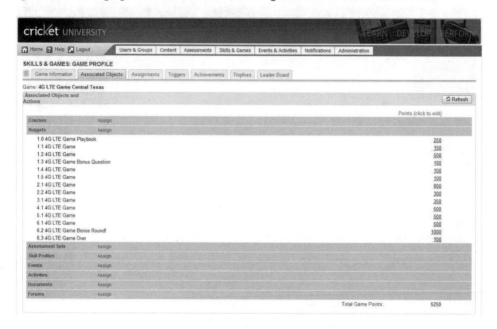

in the CellCast Solution game engine in a database and a dynamic listing of the top five learners is shown on an interactive leaderboard accessible within the Mobile Cricket U native app as well as via dashboards accessible to all managers/supervisors and learning administrators.

Points earned by every individual learner contribute to the overall score of his or her associated retail store (e.g., Store 213 in the Las Vegas region) displayed on a group-based leaderboard. At the end of the game period, all participating learners receive digital badges for completing their assignments and top point earners are awarded digital trophies promoting their attained status levels (Figure 17.5). Tangible prizes are also awarded to leading finishers placed in the top three positions for each competition based on the combination of completion, retention, and acceleration points earned during the game period. Typical prizes are gift cards and gift certificates.

Learners complete formal learning assignments such as watching videos, reading product literature, launching/completing mobile-friendly courses, passing short quizzes or longer module-level assessments, and by performing

Figure 17.5 Individual, Group, and Challenge-Based Leader Boards

Master Leader Board   **Group Leader Board**   **Challenge Leader Board**

similar activities that earn them points that contribute to their overall standing on the game's leaderboards. Achievement levels are defined based on an aggregate number of points attained or for completing specific formal learning assignments or informal learning interactions.

Digital badges are awarded for attaining each pre-defined level, and digital trophies are awarded at the end of the gameplay to each of the top point earners. The CellCast Solution platform ships with 150+ generic digital badges and trophies that can be associated with any defined game, but teams can design and deploy their own digital badges (Figure 17.6).

Individual progress is shown to all participants within a game via the various leaderboard options as well as via automated messages delivered when they attain specific achievement levels. These message streams serve as a "call to action" or reminder to all participants by encouraging them to stay involved and to complete their assignments (Figure 17.7).

All game mechanics were defined by Cricket inside the CellCast platform. Cricket worked with OnPoint's design team to enable the integrated gamification screens within the installed CellCast native apps and the customized mobile learning interfaces designed by Cricket.

Figure 17.6 Defined Trophies and Badges for Selected Game Profile

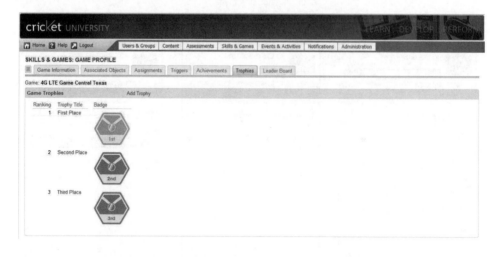

Figure 17.7 Game Selections, Game Details, and a Launched Assignment

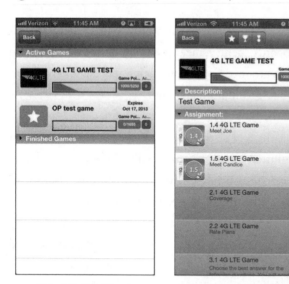

| **List of Active Games** | **Learning Assignments** | **Points Earned via Completions** |

Mobile Cricket U learners were invited to sign up for Mobile CU access through Cricket University announcements and emails. Approvals and registration information were sent upon completion of the sign-up form. All game mechanics, including a new tile/button on the top-level Mobile

Cricket U interface, automatically appeared to users when they next synced their handsets or tablets with the CellCast Solution server to check for new updates or materials. New content assignments and assessments were pushed to the app on the device in advance and ready for the learners to access at their convenience.

Mobile Cricket U learners were notified of the existence of the new game-enabled feature set through a series of electronic communications (email and system-generated text messages) sent to learners via their mobile devices. Games are made time-sensitive, and reminders are automatically triggered and sent to participants to make sure they stay engaged, are motivated to continue participating, and remain challenged.

The Benefits

Cricket's inaugural game-enabled learning program (in support of the 4G LTE product introduction) was conducted in late fall 2012 and the L&D team conducted a survey of participants to measure their new approach and offering. Survey questions measured reactions to the game-oriented learning approach, how easy it was to launch and understand the various game elements, and how effective the process was for sellers. When asked, "What was the MAIN motivation to complete the 4G LTE game," the following results were attained, as shown in the list below and Figure 17.8:

- "I want my store and market to win." (42.2 percent)
- "I wanted to be on the leaderboard." (18.18 percent)
- "I wanted to see what I remember from the training." (39.39 percent)
- "I wanted to please my manager." (0 percent)

More than 81.82 percent of surveyed learners from the Cricket sales channel agreed with the statement "I learned more about 4G LTE by playing the game" and 90.91 percent agreed with the statement "Playing the game was fun."

Figure 17.8 Post-Game Survey Results

4G LTE Post-Game Survey

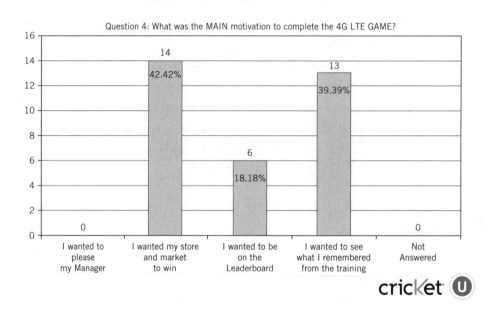

Lessons Learned

Overall, the Cricket team is very encouraged by the introduction of gamification into their Mobile Cricket U program and service offering and foresees a variety of ways they can leverage the extended feature set to drive learner engagement, increase sales readiness, and accelerate business performance. While the Cricket team values the fact that learning and gaming are now available to sellers via their omnipresent mobile devices, they now realize the value of having a gamified learning experience accessible to their broader learning audience via the existing Cricket University online web portal and steps are being taken to expand their license tool (Figure 17.9).

Cricket also anticipates game points and achievements earned in the learning environment might one day be translated into another "currency" as part of an external incentive/reward platform whereby learning points are combined with other selling incentives (e.g., devices sales, service activations) and then redeemable for tangible goods from prize catalogs like gift certificates, media, and electronics.

Figure 17.9 Online Cricket University Game Portal Interface (Planned)

Serious Game: Learning to Negotiate

Bryan Austin

This case study provides an online learning game designed to teach negotiation skills.

Background

Merchants® was developed by Gamelearn S.L., and is offered in the United States by Game On! Learning™. Game On! Learning is a training company that provides comprehensive game-based e-learning courses on key business skills required by corporate and government organizations. These courses create unmatched learner engagement and produce employees who will immediately and confidently apply their newly acquired business skills on the job. The revolutionary "serious games" offered by Game On! Learning™ developed by Gamelearn S.L. feature highly interactive, animated video game designs, fun competition versus colleagues, learner-individualized feedback, and real-world learning scenarios. (For more information please visit www.gameonlearning.com.)

An extraordinarily high degree of in-course skill practice helps ramp up employee performance, increase productivity, and move organizations more rapidly forward. The courses deliver lasting results in an unforgettable learning experience.

The Challenge

e-Learning has been utilized to deliver business skills training to corporate and government organizations since the 1990s. The potential is obvious: training is available wherever the employee is, whenever the employee needs it. The reality has largely been that, while e-learning is capable of reliably providing informational and knowledge-based training, it has shown little measurable ability to improve performance at the behavioral level.

Today, many organizations are struggling to persuade their employees to embrace e-learning at all, as most of the content delivered online is not considered engaging by learners.

In addition, traditional e-learning designed to teach skills provides little opportunity for the employee to practice and behaviorally embed those skills. This creates an unlikely scenario for training success, as the acquisition, mastery, and internalization of complex skills requires hours of practice in a safe environment, not minutes.

For example, in today's fast-paced and interconnected business world, employees at every level have to be skilled at developing collaborative, mutually beneficial relationships. Many employees also require the ability to communicate persuasively to increase revenue, lower costs, and negotiate agreements. Clearly, employees with the following skills will have great value to the organization:

- Apply strong persuasive communication skills to not only achieve business results but to also maintain long-term relationships.

- Uncover the interests of different parties and how they impact the communication strategy to reach agreements.

- Utilize tools and strategies to creatively generate negotiation and proposal alternatives to reach mutually beneficial agreements.

- Understand and employ tactics to avoid common traps in a conversation or negotiation.

The challenge is how to acquire and improve these skills by workforces that are often geographically dispersed. Most organizations no longer have the travel and training budgets to provide this training via instructor-delivered classes, and the performance effectiveness of most online training alternatives, as noted above, has been minimal.

Why a Game?

A comprehensive game-based simulation delivered in asynchronous online form has huge potential in meeting the challenge of improving persuasive communication and negotiation skills while providing the "anytime, anywhere" benefits of traditional e-learning.

The rationale for this strategy is evidenced by comparing the most prevalent skills-based learning strategy to a game simulation. Figure 18.1 illustrates this difference.

The diagram shows that most "skills-based" training still dedicates much more time to listening, reading, or watching than it does to "doing"—practicing the taught skills. A typical unit of informational instruction (via a trainer or e-learning) is followed by a test or brief role-play simulation, with perhaps a final test or grand mastery role play at the end.

Using the traditional training design approach, how effectively could the employees really have embedded and internalized the skills by the end of the training? How likely are they to apply their new skills after training, and how confident will they be in doing so?

Figure 18.1 Practicing Versus Listening

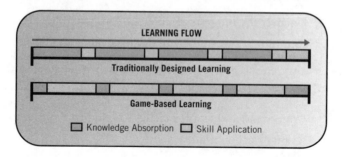

A game-based simulation, on the other hand, flips the traditional skill-building formula upside down. In a game-based simulation, the employee is given a packet of content to absorb (the premise and goal of the game, plus a scenario-based case study) and then spends 90 percent or more of the training by "doing" via the game. This is much more experiential for the employee, who must learn what works and what doesn't to succeed in the game.

If properly designed, a rapidly growing body of research shows this works much more effectively than the traditional design model for behavior-focused learning. The key (as it is for all training) is the design of the learning experience. Many of the design tenets for game-based learning are similar to the instructional design principles that have evolved over the last couple of decades—they are just applied via a learning model that is more aligned with the way we humans naturally develop our skills.

The Solution

The game-based simulation developed to address the challenge of more effectively teaching persuasive communication and negotiation skills to workforces around the world is a serious game called Merchants®, developed by European game developer Gamelearn® S.L. and distributed in the United States by Game On! Learning™.

Merchants is a highly interactive, game-based e-learning course that teaches the persuasive communication skills needed to achieve "win/win" results for employees and their internal and external customers. Key skills developed include communicating to build trust, resolving conflict, collaborative (rather than competitive) negotiation, and proposal presentation skills to reach agreement.

In this six-level interactive game-based simulation, learners assume the role of Carlo Vecchio, an aspiring Venetian merchant in the late 15th century, an era when Venice was the center of commerce in the Mediterranean and therefore the world, as shown in Figure 18.2.

Through an exciting competition with their colleagues, employees are challenged to grow their maritime trading company as well as to be the best negotiator and the top merchant in all of Venice.

The learning experience is managed by a sophisticated persuasive communication simulator. Under the guidance of Carlo's mentor at each level of the game, the employees negotiate their way through a series of

Figure 18.2 Main Character, Carlo Vecchio, Looking Out Over Venice

increasingly challenging situations, including customer conversations, acquiring business resources, and hiring and managing employees. The mentor is seen in Figure 18.4.

Learners continually practice and apply the skills taught at each level of the game through realistic scenarios, all the while receiving tips, tricks, and tools directly applicable to persuasive conversations with those inside and outside the organization. Up to 95 percent of learning time is dedicated to internalizing the optimal negotiating behaviors and practicing those skills through highly interactive animated video simulations, as shown in Figure 18.3.

The unique game design ensures an extremely high level of engagement and course completion.

Merchants is a completely online experience, and the game is recommended for groups of twenty to thirty per class (or cohort) within the organization. The approximate duration of the course is nine to twelve hours, completed by each cohort over a period of four to six weeks.

Merchants is currently available in English, French, Spanish, and Portuguese. Each learner specifies his or her language choice when starting the game, so cohorts can consist of colleagues from around the world.

Each employee progresses through the game asynchronously at his or her own pace, but performance is scored throughout the course, and each learner competes for high scores versus colleagues in that cohort. Each employee has a customized dashboard that summarizes his or her achievement through the learning process, as shown in Figure 18.5. They can also view their ranking versus their colleagues at the end of each level of the game. This healthy level of competition has been shown to increase learner engagement as well as course completion rates.

The level of detail and amount of personalized feedback provided through the game's negotiation simulator is much greater than could be replicated by a world-class trainer in a classroom session, as shown in Figure 18.6. After each negotiation, the learner receives a personalized feedback report detailing the strategies, proposals, and concession policy that he or she has utilized.

Figure 18.3 Choosing a Negotiation Strategy

Figure 18.4 Mentor Helping Carlo at Each Level of the Game

Figure 18.5 Progress Can Be Monitored Throughout the Game

Figure 18.6 Learners Receive Detailed Feedback

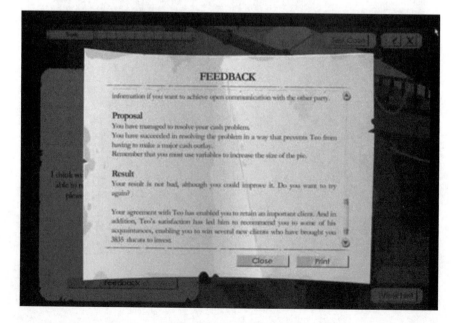

The Benefits

Since its release in late 2011, Merchants has begun to change the face of corporately focused business skills training. More than 250 corporations world-wide have now implemented the course and have reported the following benefits:

- The ability to deploy the training across organizational locations without incurring travel time and costs has resulted in huge cost savings.

- Because employees can play the game in English, Spanish, French, or Portuguese, its benefits can extend to a large portion of the organization's workforce.

- The level of competition and engagement created by Merchants has had a very positive impact on employee collaboration.

- Based on the challenging level of practice during the game, organizations report that employees emerge from the training with a much higher level of excitement and confidence about applying their new skills on the job.

- The implementation of Merchants has reflected very positively on the talent development organizations that brought the training in, and the "buzz" created by the game has increased the interest in this type of learning for behavior-based skill development.

The Results

The statistics below have been accumulated from learners in more than 250 organizations across five continents.

- Average course evaluation, to date: 9.4 out of 10
- Average assessment of educational value: 9.3 out of 10
- Percentage answering "Yes" to "I find it applicable to real life": 98 percent
- Percentage answering "Yes" to "I will recommend this course": 99 percent
- Percentage of learners who completed the course after starting it: 92 percent

The above results are aggregate averages from more than thirty thousand learners who have taken this course.

Beyond the feedback above, managers of those trained consistently report improved communication and negotiation skills post-training, as well as increased confidence in the skills which extends far after training.

A sampling of feedback from employees and their managers:

- "I really had a good time with Merchants. It's original, fun, challenging, outside of the ordinary. It hooks you!"

- "It is the best training product I have seen. Useful and, above all, educational."

- "This is the best online training I know of. It has had a positive impact on our business."

- "It's a very new and interesting program. The lessons from the mentor and the readings are very beneficial. You learn concepts to help you plan, and afterward negotiate in situations that reflect real negotiations that you have with clients."

- "Fun and effective! I had lots of fun and I learned so much!"

- "Very interesting cases. You learn very efficiently and effectively. Applicable to real life."

- "I found it very interesting, especially the lessons of the mentor. The main concepts are completely applicable to our day-to-day. I am already looking forward to the next course!"

Lessons Learned

The disadvantages of developing comprehensive behavioral game-based simulations are the time and cost of development. Merchant required nearly two years to create, at a development cost of nearly $1.5 million. Most of the development cost was applied to create the most sophisticated persuasive communication and negotiation simulator possible. This is certainly outside the reach of most corporate organizations. In the future, the time and cost for developing high-end comprehensive game-based simulations will almost certainly decrease.

Games like Merchants are available commercially on a seat-based license, so organizations interested in deploying the course can do so cost-effectively without having to develop their own games. This could become a trend in the learning and development industry. It is priced at about the same cost as a two-day instructor-delivered workshop.

Structural Gamification for On-Boarding Employees

Mohit Garg

This case is an example of structural gamification to on-board employees.

Background

MindTickle is a web-based learning platform that combines the power of social and game mechanics to make online training efficient and effective. MindTickle enables businesses, trainers, and individuals to transform their existing online content (PowerPoint, videos, documents) into an interactive learning experience to increase effectiveness and engagement. With over twenty-five thousand users from leading organizations such as SAP, Yahoo!, and InMobi, to name a few. MindTickle was awarded the "Best Use of Gamification in HR" award at the Gamification Summit in San Francisco in 2013. Founded in 2011, MindTickle is headquartered in San Francisco, California, with an office in India.

The Challenge

Engaging new hires and on-boarding them into the organization is both a challenge and an opportunity for organizations today. Research has shown that an employee's long-term commitment and longevity at an organization are influenced significantly by the experience during the first ninety days of employment. Hence organizations have an opportunity to enhance employee engagement and retention in a significant way by means of an efficient and effective on-boarding program. Even though most organizations realize the importance of a well-designed on-boarding program, one is rarely implemented due to several practical constraints. According to the MASIE Center, a think tank focused on the intersection of learning and technology, only 32 percent of people even start on-the-job e-learning courses.[1] While designing for an agile, easy to manage software application is a deterministic undertaking, designing an application that overcomes learner apathy and that motivates the users to exhibit intended behavior requires an in-depth understanding of user personas, their context, their motivation drivers, and designing user interaction and mechanics that build on this understanding to influence behavior.

Therefore, the primary learning objective of this project was to learn how social and game mechanics, when applied to new hire on-boarding, can help improve the user experience, user satisfaction, and desired outcomes such as adoption rates, retention rates, and completion rates.

Why Gamification?

MindTickle adopted a social-gamified-mobile approach to its solution for the following reasons:

- The gap in *user experience* for today's worker, between the applications and software used at work and during personal time, is widening at an unprecedented pace. Imagine the contrast for a person using Mint.com as a personal finance management tool versus using a popular ERP package at work. And when you benchmark against today's consumer space social and mobile applications, the contrast is even more pronounced.

- Today's organizations (and their CIOs) are far more open to the idea of providing access to enterprise applications outside the confines of their walled garden (popularly known as the intranet, which may soon become a thing of the past with evolution of *enterprise social networks* and knowledge management systems).

- Employees are insisting on access to their personal *tablet* devices and *smart phones;* therefore CIOs have no choice but to support mobile access for even productivity applications.

- Last, as digital natives start to dominate the workforce (or, as we like to call them, the gamer generation), traditional methods of motivating employees are going to become increasing ineffective. However, *game mechanics* that have proven to influence behavior in the consumer space hold promise in engaging these new age employees.

Making the Case

The MindTickle team created a data-driven approach document that built on evidence from credible research by experts and academics and the hard data from the MindTickle's experiments and user studies.

The proposed approach was grounded in measurable and actionable metrics, such that it aligned with the business objectives. The metrics that were identified in consultation with the stakeholders were as follows.

Metric 1: Employer Branding/Perception

Measurement: Administer a thirty-day survey with specific questions about the employer value proposition (EVP).[2] EVP, simply put, is defined as a set of associations and offerings provided by an organization in return for the skills, capabilities, and experiences an employee brings to the organization.

Metric 2: Reduction in Time and Training Required in Face-to-Face Classroom

Measurement: For the topics which learning content is administered in the pilot, the performance of the new hires who participate in the gamification pilot versus new hires who do not participate in the gamification pilot (past data or create a control group). You can potentially test this through a skill assessment test or survey or survey the managers on the state of readiness/awareness of the new hires.

Metric 3: Engagement Levels During the On-Boarding Process

Measurement: Can be done through MindTickle's analytics, which can provide detailed reports. The key metrics are

- Percent participation
- Percent completion
- Average scores
- Number of achievements/badges unlocked

In addition, the stakeholders were assured that the MindTickle system would collect feedback from the new hires in the form of surveys—to help assess the effectiveness of the proposed solution from both a qualitative and quantitative perspective.

The most important element to secure the sponsorship for the project was the alignment of the intended objectives and outcomes with business needs. Secondly, the decision-makers wanted an assurance about the measurability of the outcomes. Last, the stakeholders had concerns about the sustainability of the proposed solution in terms of operations costs, skills required to maintain such a solution, and long-term impact of gamification on the culture and alignment with existing business processes.

Therefore, MindTickle created an updated version of the proposal that outlined not only the near-term business case for the immediate year, but also highlighted the long-term economic and cultural benefits.

It was also extremely important for MindTickle to align with a champion within the client's HR team who was a firm believer in the approach and took ownership of assisting MindTickle with the implementation and getting the alignment with other departments such as IT, marketing, and recruiting.

The Solution

MindTickle designed and executed a two-part solution, described below.

Part 1: Pre-Joining Engagement with the New Hires Between Day of Offer and Day of Joining

In order to promote employer branding, retention, and engagement levels among the prospective new employees, MindTickle created a social and gamified application for engaging the new hires. It was created as an online quiz in the format of an online hot air balloon race based on general knowledge and trivia regarding the company, as shown in Figure 19.1. The design of application was around the following objectives:

- *User engagement:* The new hires were invited to participate and win medals by answering trivia questions regarding the company. There was a dynamic leaderboard and social updates showing progress of all participants. This competition resulted in a strong pull factor and new hires spent a lot of time learning about the company, its policies, vision, mission, products, and so forth so that they could score better. This application also resulted in a strong motivation to engage with the content and become more aware about the company.

- *Social interactions:* The application was designed in such a way that the users were incented to interact with one another by exchanging messages, viewing each other's profiles, holding discussions, and so forth in exchange for experience points (XPs) and social badges.

Figure 19.1 Screen Captures from Gamification

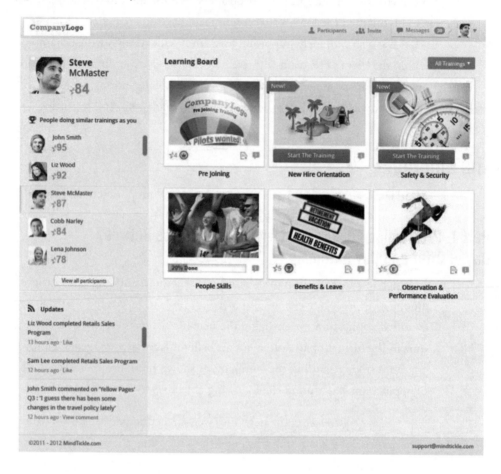

Part 2: Post-Joining Orientation of the New Hires

MindTickle designed a gamified learning platform that transformed the existing new hire orientation content (PowerPoint, videos, documents) into an interactive learning experience, shown in Figure 19.2.

The MindTickle team absorbed the new hire orientation material such as company's history videos, business overview presentations, policy documents, and employee handbook into its learning platform.

The new hires were provided the online link for this platform on the day of joining. The on-boarding content was presented in the theme of a board

Figure 19.2 Gamification of Course

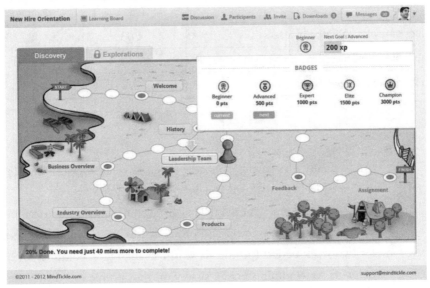

game wherein the new hires had to traverse a map and consume company content and take quizzes at each pit stop on the map.

The gamification rewarded the users with points, badges, and medals for demonstrating a grasp of content presented in the learning platform while the discussion board created a spirit of healthy competition.

The Results

The results for the overall effort were very impressive.

Pre-Joining Engagement Results

There were high engagement levels, participation, and completion rates as shown below:

- 248 new hire members were invited.

- Seventy-six percent of members registered to participate.

- Sixty-four percent of participants completed all rounds.

Table 19.1 Social Interaction Numbers

Social Interaction	Total	Average
Number of invites initiated by users	883	4.77
Number of instant messages exchanged	8340	45.08
Number of profile views	299	1.61

Additionally, the participants actively engaged in social interactions, as shown in Table 19.1, with a high level of engagement.

Almost 85 percent achieved the badge given for maximum social interactions and almost seventy thousand online social interactions were recorded over a two-week period (profile views, direct messages, comments, "likes"). Participants were administered a survey on the completion of the pre-joining engagement. Following are key results of the survey:

- Twenty-four percent indicated they learned new things about the company and were now even more excited to join.

- Thirty-four percent indicated they increased their knowledge and had fun.

- Twenty percent indicated they networked and got to know their fellow new hires.

The new employees were asked "How would you compare playing this game to other learning methods?" A select group of answers appears below:

- "Combines learning with fun. This makes things stay in mind without extra effort."

- "This game makes you remember stuff about the company we learned in a fun way . . . such ways are always more effective in terms of practice."

- "This is very interesting and I am able to remember many things."

- "This program is great and it's not only informational but also great fun playing it. Eager then ever to join !!!"

- "The idea behind this is really great. It's making us very active and curious to join u soon."

- "I can imagine life in the company now."

Post-Joining New Employee Orientation Results

In the post-joining of the new employee orientation, these results were indicated:

- 243 new hire members were invited.

- Ninety-two percent of the members registered to participate.

- Seventy-five percent of participants completed all rounds.

- Forty-nine percent indicated "awesome" on the question, "How would you rate your post-joining on-boarding experience on the basis of content/learning?" Fifty percent rated it as "good." One percent rated it as "average."

When asked, "What aspects of the post-joining on-boarding experience did you like the most?" Forty-one percent indicated that the game format was appealing. Twenty-nine percent indicated the content was interesting, and 30 percent indicated they learned new things.

When the new hires were asked, "How would you compare playing this game to other learning methods?" they indicated the following:

- "Combines learning with fun. This makes things stay in mind without extra effort."

- "This game makes you remember stuff about the company we learned in a fun way . . . such ways are always more effect in terms of practice."

- "This is very interesting and I am able to remember many things."

- "Way better."

- "Awesome."

- "I can learn while I play."

- "Excellent and effective."

- "It's engaging."
- "It is more informative."
- "Fun and learning is more interesting!!"
- "The UI very intuitive, it's a fun way to learn!!!"
- "This is truly unique."

Summary

The quantitative results and the qualitative survey feedback demonstrate that the application of interactive learning techniques such as online social interaction and game mechanics can help create learner engagement, especially in a new hire on-boarding scenario. Such an approach can not only enhance employer branding, but also help increase employee engagement and learning effectiveness, resulting in reduced cost and higher productivity.

Lessons Learned

The following design factors that were duly incorporated in the design of MindTickle's online new hire on-boarding platform were instrumental in achieving the successful results:

- *Setting user expectations:* The messaging and communication sent to the participants was crafted appropriately to set user expectations in terms of time commitment required, expected benefits, and how to play the game.

- *Content design:* The platform presented the learning content and the exercises/challenges in an engaging format keeping in mind that the user not bail out of it due to fatigue and/or attention deficit.

- *Accessibility:* The platform design ensured that users had an intuitive and easy-to-remember way of accessing the online game. The fact that it was accessible over mobile devices such as the iPad or Android tablets ensured seamless access, even when the users were away from their work desks.

- *User experience:* To create a consistent and smooth-flowing user experience, significant time and attention were paid to how to minimize potential issues that users are likely to encounter. Undergoing several iterations of user-experience study and user-interaction refinements was vital for ensuring that the user experience was intuitive and seamless.

Medical Simulation

Kevin R. Glover

This case study provides an example of a physical simulation incorporated into a training program.

Background

B. Braun Medical Inc. (B. Braun), a leader in infusion therapy and pain management, develops, manufactures, and markets innovative medical products and services to the health care industry. The company is committed to eliminating preventable treatment errors and enhancing patient, clinician, and environmental safety. Guided by its "Sharing Expertise"® philosophy,

B. Braun continuously exchanges knowledge with customers, partners, and clinicians to address the critical issues of improving care and lowering costs.

The B. Braun group of companies includes B. Braun, Aesculap® and CAPS®. B. Braun's U.S. headquarters is located in Bethlehem, Pennsylvania, with its global headquarters based in Melsungen, Germany. It employs more than forty-four thousand employees in more than fifty countries throughout the world.

The Challenge

The Introcan Safety® IV Catheter (Figure 20.1) is designed to minimize accidental needle sticks. It is B. Braun Medical's most profitable product.

In 2007 Introcan Safety IV Catheter sales represented 6.6 percent of B. Braun's total revenue in the U.S. market and almost 20 percent of B. Braun's profit. Historically, the Introcan Safety IV Catheter had been a successful product for B. Braun Medical since its launch in 1999, but between 2003 and 2007 the annual growth of the brand had dropped to 1.5 percent. In 2007, only five out of every twenty customers who evaluated the product decided to convert to the product (25 percent) and post-conversion customer retention of the product was an abysmal 40 percent. Only two of every five customers who converted to the product continued to use the product four to six months post-conversion. When one considers the direct expenses and lost opportunity costs of failed Introcan Safety conversions, like the one at the General Hospital Health System described below, our need to invest in a different customer training approach was obvious.

Approximately 4,384 General Hospital nurses were trained between August 2004 and December 2004 by B. Braun Medical representatives—our customer facing staff. Our direct expense for conducting 138 total days of training at this eight-hospital system was $187,200, a sound business decision considering the account's potential to generate $1,100,000 in annual sales revenue, or approximately $715,000 in annual profit. Ultimately, the General Hospital was lost shortly after the product conversion due to a variety of factors, including those listed below.

Figure 20.1 The Introcan Safety® IV Catheter

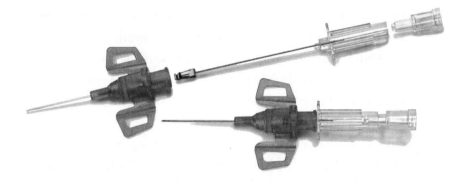

- General Hospital nurses thought that the Introcan Safety IV Catheter was too dull, resulting in an increase in patient complaints.

- They thought that the Introcan Safety IV Catheter was too hard to thread.

- They preferred the insertion technique associated with the competitive catheter being replaced by the Introcan Safety IV Catheter.

- They thought there was more blood exposure with the Introcan Safety IV Catheter.

- They forgot to advance the Introcan Safety IV Catheter and needle together 1/8-inch, parallel with the patient's skin, which resulted in a failed procedure.

The nursing complaints at the General Hospital were consistent with the feedback we received from other "lost" accounts between 2003 and 2007. Why couldn't we overcome these nursing perceptions of what we knew to be a clinically superior product?

The customer environment in which our sales representatives and clinical educators (customer facing staff) taught nurses how to use the Introcan Safety IV Catheter during product evaluations and conversions was thought to be one of the reasons.

A typical hospital nurse is responsible for seven or eight patients on any given shift. He or she must perform a variety of tasks involving monitoring each patient's status throughout the shift. The tasks include periodic wound assessment, dressing changes, checking fluid input and output, administration of medications, assessing medication side-effects, checking respiratory rates, and many other critical procedures. Additionally, nurses are confronted with continuous distractions during the course of the shift, including taking calls from the hospital lab with results that need to be acted on, physicians calling with new patient orders, and trying to contact physicians to obtain new patient orders.

When B. Braun customer facing staff arrives on the nursing unit to conduct Introcan Safety IV Catheter training, they are (at best) considered to be another distraction that needs to be juggled amidst the chaos. At worst the Introcan Safety IV Catheter training means something personally important to the nurse will be sacrificed, perhaps taking a break.

Human beings have very limited working memory capacity. We can only accept and hold a limited amount of sensory input. This sensory input is stored for about a half a second, at which point it is either processed, because we pay attention to the stimuli, or the sensory input is lost to accommodate new stimuli.[1]

Our Introcan Safety IV Catheter nursing trainings were ineffective because our customer facing staff were failing to overcome the nurses' surrounding environmental sensory input with a product that did not arouse their curiosity or interest. In addition, Introcan Safety was just another IV catheter. Nurses use IV catheters every day. They felt no personal relevance in the training, and without some connection to intrinsic personal or professional "wins" nurses were not attending to our educational efforts. Finally, and most importantly, nurses were usually passive observers during this training, inactively watching demonstrations of the Introcan Safety IV Catheter procedure—often using just the paper lids of the product's packaging material to represent the patient's skin for pseudo insertions. Training without "doing" resulted in minimal retention of instruction.

We required a training intervention that would arouse nursing curiosity and interest so nursing customers would attend to Introcan Safety training. We required a learning intervention that helped nurses "connect" to the product, professionally or personally, so that they would be motivated to learn how to use Introcan Safety correctly. Last, we wanted a training intervention that required nurses to exert a high level of effort during training because research demonstrated that learner effort correlated with a higher probability that nursing attention would be captured.[2]

Given that learner effort via deliberate practice also plays a vital role in the acquisition of expert skills performance, our training intervention also needed to require nurses to use Introcan Safety IV catheters repeatedly during training sessions. Reznek and his colleagues at Stanford University's School of Medicine estimated that the learning curve for IV catheterization is approximately ten procedures.[3]

We predicted that a learning intervention that aroused nursing curiosity, connected personal pertinence to the training, and included nurses as active participants in their learning would result in greater customer retention of the Introcan Safety IV Catheter post-conversion, which would lead to increased revenue and profitability for B. Braun Medical.

However, we also knew that we could not solve these clinician educational issues without first addressing re-educating our customer facing staff, who were responsible for training these clinical customers. Our customer facing staff had lost their focus and desire to sell Introcan Safety. They were not confidently setting appropriate expectations for successful clinical product use or confidently conducting product in-service education because they lacked deep peripheral IV catheter procedural expertise. Beyond superficial product features and benefits, they also lacked deep Introcan Safety IV Catheter product expertise and knowledge of competitive catheters beyond basic information.

Why a Simulation?

Our obstacle to achieving success with Introcan Safety was self-inflicted. Our sales representatives, sales managers, and clinical education employees did not believe in the product and did not believe in themselves. They didn't feel they possessed the clinical expertise to be credible, and that lack of confidence was evident to customers. This condition resulted in our customer facing team agreeing to virtually every customer request related to the product and customer trial and/or conversion education, which lead to inefficient and ineffective utilization of company resources on poorly qualified customers.

Our new customer facing staff training curriculum had to be redesigned to achieve two primary objectives. We had to transform our employees into a team that would be perceived as clinical consultants or trusted advisors, as opposed to product vendors. We had to create a new Introcan Safety selling methodology. Training also had to convince our customer facing team to use this new methodology so that we collectively engaged in a business-oriented approach to customer qualification and provided effective customer education. Our new nursing customer education protocol would require six to ten deliberate Introcan Safety peripheral IV insertion practice procedures on an Advanced Four-Vein Venipuncture Task Training Aid (Figure 20.2).

Our mission was to create a customer facing team of IV catheter clinical experts. This meant that, after training, all of our employees had to believe they were the clinical experts regarding Introcan Safety IV Catheters so they could confidently set customer expectations regarding required product conversion training. To achieve this result, the sales training and marketing department embarked on an eighteen-month journey to develop and deliver a comprehensive training program. We also undertook a concurrent project to develop a new selling and customer education process because research indicates that the most effective simulations are embedded within a larger curriculum.

We felt that IV catheter clinical expertise wasn't enough to rejuvenate the brand if our customer facing team continued to chase the wrong targets and conduct ineffective customer training. We needed to create a customer facing team of better business people and better instructors, which meant that, after training, all selling and clinical education employees needed to fundamentally believe that not all sales opportunities are profitable opportunities. They had to understand that their "harder" short-term decisions almost always lead to better long-term results and that responding "no" is sometimes the most reasonable and responsible response to a customer's request. Most important, they needed to believe that the most significant identifiable factor leading to clinical competency with any new skill is deliberate

---

Figure 20.2 Advanced Four-Vein Venipuncture Task Training Aid and the SIMULATION Adult
Injection Training Arm

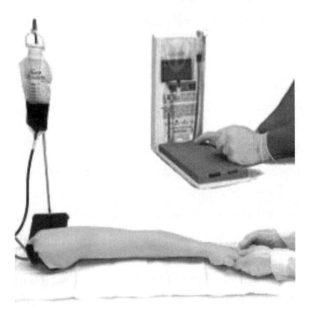

and sustained practice. The goal of the new customer facing team education
process was that our entire field force would ultimately "own" the following
key understandings:

- Customer facing employees are able to identify the most appropriate customer accounts for selling Introcan Safety, which results in
  the best total return on organizational investment.

- Customer facing employees will only invest their time and company
  resources with those clinical customers who are willing to make the
  personal and professional sacrifices required (deliberate and sustained practice) to successfully evaluate and/or convert to Introcan
  Safety.

We knew that we would encounter significant resistance in our efforts
to re-educate a sales and clinical education team on a product that most
had been selling or teaching about since 1999, so we conducted a learning
styles survey prior to our curricular build. Our hope was that a training

program that was aligned with the learning preferences of our customer facing team would mitigate some of the anticipated resistance. In December 2006, we conducted this survey with the 120 customer facing employees who would require Introcan Safety training. Of this target audience 85 percent had more than five years of experience with B. Braun Medical (and had sold or provided Introcan Safety product instruction for at least five years); 45 percent of the group were between thirty and forty-two years old and 46 percent were older than forty-three. Males represented 61 percent of the group and females 39 percent.

We received ninety-six learning styles survey responses (80 percent) that showed us that 89 percent felt live workshops were the most effective training format. However, the same survey indicated that 62 percent of our field force felt videos to be an effective training medium and 52 percent felt the same about print. In the same survey, the cognitive channel preferences of our customer facing employees were 41 percent kinesthetic, 41 percent visual/auditory, and 18 percent verbal/readers. We found it interesting that 62 percent of our field force felt training videos to be effective, even though we had never produced training videos. This, coupled with the fact that 41 percent of our field staff were inclined toward visual/auditory learning, inspired us to include a series of videos and animations as a part of the new Introcan Safety IV Catheter curriculum to support both print-based and live classroom activities. These findings suggested that we develop a blended curricular approach with an emphasis on simulation-based, experiential training programs.

Making the Case

An anemic annual Introcan Safety brand growth of 1.5 percent between 2003 and 2007, plus weak product evaluation to conversion results of 25 percent (five out of every twenty customers who evaluated the product decided to convert to the product), in addition to an abysmal post-conversion customer product retention rate of 40 percent (only two of every five converted customers continued to use the product four to six months post-conversion) caused so much organizational discomfort that sales and marketing leadership was open to a dramatic learning intervention.

The Solution

The final blended training program contained almost fifty hours of learner engagement, which was delivered sequentially over a thirteen-month time period, between January 2007 and February 2008, and included the following training deliverables:

- Print-based self-study modules (supplemented with animations and videos)

- A clinical venipuncture certification program (didactic lecture plus hands-on simulation)

- Simulation-based IV mastery learning including the following technology:
  - The SIMULUTION® Adult Injection Training Arm (2007–2010)
  - Limbs and Things Advanced Venipuncture Arm (2010–Present)
  - Advanced Four-Vein Venipuncture Training Aid (2007–Present)
  - Laerdal Virtual IV Haptic Simulator (2010–Present)

- Consultative selling and presentation skills training (role-play simulation)

- Teach backs (high-stakes role-play simulation), which included:
  - Sales management pull through, coaching, and feedback
  - Peer-to-peer tutoring in simulated customer environments

Our goal was to support intrapersonal, interpersonal, logical mathematical, verbal linguistic, visual spatial, and body kinesthetic learning styles with sequential instruction that would enable field force learners to move beyond fundamental knowledge to a depth of understanding that would result in a customer facing staff that would become trusted clinical advisors to their clinical customers, in addition to the ability to make sound business decisions that benefited both our customers and B. Braun Medical.

All customer facing employees were required to participate in all coursework and summative assessments were administered throughout the program to validate that field force learners were fluent in the required knowledge and procedural skills. In addition, authentic performance assessments were used throughout the curriculum, which required participants to use their collective product knowledge, clinical knowledge, clinical skills, customer and market knowledge, and competitive knowledge to wisely and innovatively address unique challenges in real-world simulated environments. As with any simulation-based training, it is important that the simulation be embedded within a larger curriculum, and that is the approach that was taken. A description of the blended course work is summarized below.

Print-Based Self-Study Modules Supplemented with Animations/Videos

Customer facing staff were required to absorb the clinical, product, competition, market, and selling information in five self-study learning modules (over five hundred pages of content with support videos and animations) and to prepare for and practice teaching lessons on ten need-to-know key topics to their peers. The instructional materials are shown in Figures 20.3, 20.4, and 20.5 below.

Each section of the learning modules began with a list of learning objectives and ended with a formative self-assessment quiz (multiple choice, fill in the blank, and short answer), which helped field force learners measure their retention of important fundamental knowledge. After completing each learning module, customer facing employees took an online summative assessment and were required to achieve a passing grade of 80 percent or better. The self-study teach back module utilized a sequentially organized write-to-learn workbook with periodic live feedback coaching sessions. Teach backs were authentic live performances conducted at our national sales meeting in February 2008.

Clinical Venipuncture Certification Program (Didactic Lecture Plus Hands-On Simulation)

Our customer facing team participated in a one-day IV venipuncture certification course conducted by an approved provider of continuing education in nursing by the Pennsylvania State Nurses Association. During the course of this program our field sales team learned how to:

Figure 20.3 Introcan Safety IV Catheter Print-Based Self-Study Learning Module

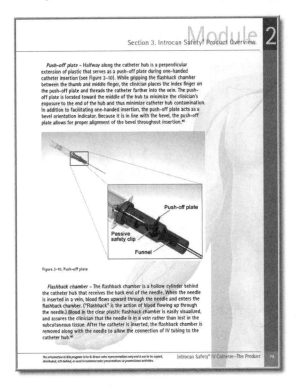

Figure 20.4 Introcan Safety IV Catheter In-Service Education Video

Figure 20.5 Introcan Safety IV Catheter In-Service Education Animation

- Identify the specific layers of the vein wall.
- Identify and locate superficial veins of the upper extremities and outline the criteria for appropriate vein selection.
- Identify various complications of IV therapy and how these complications are treated.
- Describe the legal implications of IV therapy.
- Properly insert an intravenous catheter.
- Document an intravenous venipuncture procedure.

Field force personnel were evaluated during this coursework using both multiple-choice tests and a performance assessment in which they needed to locate an appropriate vein, using a simulated arm, and demonstrate a complete IV venipuncture procedure, including inserting an IV catheter and documenting the procedure. A performance assessment was used to grade the venipuncture procedure.

Simulation-Based IV Mastery Learning

Our customer facing team spent two days in a live training session. This training session was application-oriented and focused on selling products and consultatively solving customer clinical problems. Emphasis was placed on fluent verbalization of selling the clinical benefits of Introcan Safety and all competitive IV catheters and effectively demonstrating each product's insertion procedure after repeated deliberate practice using the Advanced Four-Vein Venipuncture Task Training Aid (which was the simulation tool we would now be requiring our nursing customers to practice with during our training sessions) and the SIMULUTION Adult Injection Training Arm (Figure 20.2).

In 2009 the SIMULUTION Adult Injection Training Arm was replaced by the Limbs and Things Advanced Venipuncture Arm (Figure 20.6), which increased the fidelity of the IV insertion simulation by adding blood pressure variability in the vasculature and a human factors component—a real patient at the end of the prosthetic simulator. The pressurized fluid system with this simulation tool allowed for realistic blood flashback and the ability to simulate tourniquet application with pressure and release of pressure for tourniquet removal. We also added the Laerdal Haptic (tactile feedback) Virtual IV trainer (Figure 20.7). Practicing IV insertions with the Laerdal VIV had customer facing employees select the appropriate IV site (based on the patient case presented), prepare the site using the proper tools, and select the appropriate gauge catheter.

Customer facing staff then conducted the procedure with the simulated-catheter in a haptic device, which allowed the learner to feel the patient's skin, veins, and venous puncture. Field force students view the procedure on a computer monitor that displays visual results of the actions performed using the haptic device. For example, a flashback of blood is visible when the simulated needle successfully enters the patient's vein. A case review, included after each simulated patient case, reports scoring of the learner's procedural performance. In our course, customer facing employees need to practice with the IV until they achieve a score of 90 to 100 percent (passing with a successful stick and no critical errors). A critical error is any mistake in the process that prohibits a successful IV start, such as missing or blowing a vein.

Customer facing staff end this portion of the course with a knowledge and simulation-skills summative assessment. The Limbs and Things Advanced Venipuncture Arm is attached to a live person, which provides the learners with the sense (and stress) that they are performing the venipuncture procedure on a real patient. Each field force employee receives a doctor's order and plays the role of a clinician placing the IV, including entering the room, assessing the patient, choosing the appropriate IV site, selecting the correct IV supplies, conducting the venipuncture procedure, dressing and securing the IV, talking with the patient, disposing of waste supplies appropriately, exiting the room, and documenting the procedure in the patient's chart. The class facilitator and one observer assess each learner utilizing a thirty-step IV performance skills checklist. No feedback is provided during the actual procedure. All feedback and a performance review are given at the completion of the simulated IV procedure.

Consultative Selling and Presentation Skills Training (Role-Play Simulation)

An additional two and a half days were focused on improving fundamental consultative selling and presentation skills—the way our sales team dressed, the way they talked (their tone of voice and speech patterns), the quality of and kinds of questions they asked, and the way they walked and presented themselves (nonverbal cues and body language). This consultative selling and presentation skills training was designed to help our customer facing team identify the specific customer-centric benefits of the Introcan Safety IV Catheter, which would motivate them to action.

Customer case studies were provided so that field force employees could focus on key points directly related to specific customer needs. The proper use of visual aids to enhance presentations was stressed. This live classroom session was designed to help field force staff observe and experience what exceptional customer engagement and Introcan Safety presentations looked like. The session required customer facing employees to perform and apply the learned skills in a simulated hospital environment. The best of these presentations are videotaped and the best practices are shared with peers who were not present during the simulated performance (Figure 20.8).

Figure 20.6 Limbs and Things Advanced Venipuncture Arm with Adjustable Venous Pressure "Attached" to a Live Patient, Providing Students with the Sense (and Stress) That They Are Performing the Venipuncture Procedure on a Real Patient

Figure 20.7 The Laerdal Haptic (Tactile Feedback) Virtual IV Trainer

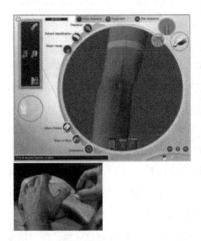
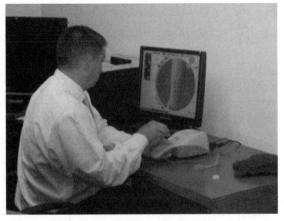

Figure 20.8 Introcan Safety IV Catheter Simulated Presentations Are Videotaped and Those Demonstrating Best Practices Are Shared with Field Force Peers Who Were Not Present During the Simulated Performance

Teach Backs (High-Stakes Role-Play Simulation)

The cumulative learning event that closes out the coursework is a high-stakes role-play simulation called a "teach back." The expectation in a teach back is that the student becomes the teacher who conducts a randomized ten-minute lesson on one of ten key product topics to a randomized classroom of peers, subordinates, and/or superiors.

As our customer facing employees prepared for their teach back assignments they restudied and reflected upon what they had collectively learned in their self-study modules, IV certification training, simulation-based product, consultative selling, and presentation skills practice sessions. As the learners prepared, they engaged in two one-on-one calls with their region manager or zone vice president, who helped provide direction and guidance. Region managers and zone VPs utilized a teach back coaching facilitation guide that ensured that stated expectations and speaking points were consistent across a variably talented management team. During these calls sales managers asked their customer facing staff a series of questions designed to help them construct the flow of their presentations, starting with the fundamental information related to a given topic. After field force employees answered these fundamental questions, the region manager asked increasingly difficult follow-up questions to push the employees to deeper levels of understanding.

We concluded our sequence of instruction when this component of the curriculum was first launched during a four-hour live teach back training session at our national sales meeting in February 2008. The field force was separated into round table groups of six or seven participants and one region manager or zone vice president facilitator.

There was a high degree of anxiety before this training session because customer facing employees, region managers, and zone VP facilitators were not told their assigned presentation topics and peer groups prior to the training session. The blind presentation topics and groups created a high-stakes performance environment that extrinsically motivated all participants to prepare to the best of their ability. Outside of the comfort of their typical working groups, no manager-facilitator or customer facing employee wanted to look foolish or unprepared. We deliberately assigned more competent managers with less competent field force personnel and less competent managers with more competent field force personnel to push weaker individuals to higher levels of performance.

The Results

After we re-trained our customer facing employees with this new blended, simulation-based, mastery learning curriculum, we initiated the new nursing customer education protocol in February 2008. This new product conversion education protocol required that nurses learning how to use the Introcan Safety IV Catheter practice using the product six to ten times on the Advanced Four-Vein Venipuncture Training Aid (Figure 20.2). The results of the simulation-based, mastery learning intervention with our customer facing team, combined with our simulation-based, deliberate practice approach with task trainers for nursing customer education, lead to outstanding and sustainable business results.

Our Introcan Safety IV Catheter sales growth at the end of 2008 was 10.5 percent, compared to an average growth rate of only 1.5 percent each year between 2003 and 2007. Customer trial to conversion decisions improved from 25 percent in 2007 to 95 percent in 2008 and post-conversion retention rates increased from 40 to 85 percent. This meant that for every twenty customers who decide to evaluate the Introcan Safety IV Catheter nineteen switch to the product and sixteen of these stayed as customers.

Had we not designed and executed a comprehensive blended training program in 2007 that included a heavy emphasis on hands-on simulation-based training, our annual Introcan Safety IV Catheter growth rate would have remained at 1.5 percent, resulting in a lost opportunity cost to the company of $5,473,900 in revenue and $3,723,063 in profit in 2008.

As mentioned earlier, we have continued to enhance our Introcan Safety sales training curriculum by adding higher fidelity simulation-based training equipment since 2008, but the fundamental coursework, field force employee and nursing customer expectations have remained the same. Introcan Safety IV Catheter annual sales growth has averaged more than 6 percent since 2008 and customer trial to product conversions and retention rates have stayed steady at 95 percent and 85 percent, respectively. Best of all, in a flat IV catheter market Introcan Safety IV Catheter market share has grown from 12 percent in 2007 to 19 percent in 2012.

Lessons Learned

Here is what we learned from implementing a peripheral IV catheter simulated deliberate practice component in training our customer facing employees and our nursing customers:

- Deliberate practice using the Introcan Safety IV Catheter with the Advanced Four-Vein Venipuncture Task Training Aid increased the confidence of our nursing staff customers so they could successfully use the product.

- Simulation of the IV insertion required active effort and aroused curiosity and interest during our training so nursing customers better attended to Introcan Safety training.

- Immersion in simulation-based IV procedures provided our customer facing staff with the clinical knowledge, practical skills, ability, and confidence to become trusted clinical advisors to the hospital staff.

- The results of this simulation-based, mastery learning intervention with our customer facing team, combined with our simulation-based, deliberate practice approach with task trainers for nursing customer education, has lead to outstanding and sustainable business results.

21

Financial Game-Based Learning

Andrew Hughes

This case study provides an example of an online game created to help home-owners and others learn about the financial implications of owning a home.

Background

Designing Digitally, Inc., is an award-winning full-service provider of interactive and engaging e-learning programs, 3-D training simulations, virtual worlds, and web design services. Designing Digitally has been developing creative, end-to-end, digital design solutions for many different types of clients for over a decade.

The New Hampshire Housing Finance Authority (NHHFA) is a self-supporting public benefit corporation. Although established by statute as a public instrumentality, the Authority is not a state agency and receives no operating funds from the state government. The Authority administers a broad range of programs designed to assist low- and moderate-income persons and families with obtaining decent, safe, and affordable housing. NHHFA contracted Designing Digitally to develop a program that would guide potential homeowners and others to achieving financial freedom by managing their money and improving their credit.

The Challenge

NHHFA knew that homeowners needed a push in the right direction to keep them focused on their financial goals. With a developed training program of nearly ten learner hours, the challenge was to not only provide the homeowners with engaging information but to keep them coming back. The key learning objectives NHHFA wanted to accomplish were to help the homeowners and others to:

- Become financially literate
- Develop a savings and spending plan
- Build financial assets
- Improve credit ratings

Why a Game?

NHHFA wanted to provide a learn-by-doing approach in a fun way. The idea and overall approach was to look at life from the perspective of a typical American in debt.

By having the homeowners play a game related to financial elements that occur in life, they could see how unforeseen circumstances can impact their financial goals and expectations.

Making the Case

The NHHFA was looking for a way to provide an engaging learning experience for the homeowners that would teach them about finance. They decided to provide the vendor with the flexibility to recommend an innovative learning experience that would be engaging and educational. The NHHFA wanted an approach that was unique and that surpassed what other housing authorities have done in this educational area.

Since the project was grant-funded, the NHHFA knew that any solution that provided education to potential first-time homeowners in a manner that encouraged engagement would have a positive impact. The idea was to educate first-time homeowners so they would be financially prepared to own a home and would not end up defaulting on the loan.

The Solution

The program provides this guidance in three ways. Its educational component consists of two training modules that teach about managing a budget and managing one's credit. It also provides a set of activities that step the person through the actual processes. Its coaching component consists of guidance and assistance from a coach.

The Education

The Financial Freedom Island Cruise is an online board game consisting of the Household Budgeting and Credit Counseling modules, as shown in Figure 21.1. The seven Household Budgeting and four Credit Counseling lessons are represented by islands. To cross each island, the player answers questions and studies the content. As learners answer questions, they earn game dollars they can use later to purchase a house and car.

As learners progress through the game, they move from one location to the next. Figure 21.2 shows progression on the game board and Figure 21.3 shows a sample question.

The Activities

Outside of the game, the learners complete one or two activities for each lesson. These activities are designed to help them reach their goals. For instance, they conduct family meetings, track expenses, obtain copies of their credit reports, and track their credit scores as they improve their credit records. Figure 21.4 shows a calculator that users can work with to determine savings goals.

Figure 21.1 Using an Island Theme for the Game

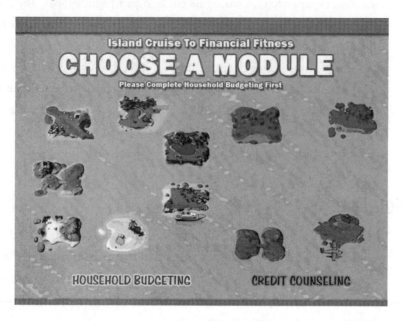

Figure 21.2 Progressing on the Game Board

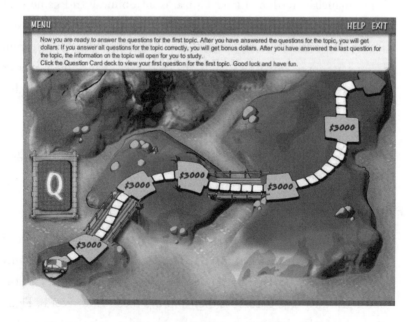

Figure 21.3 Sample Game Question

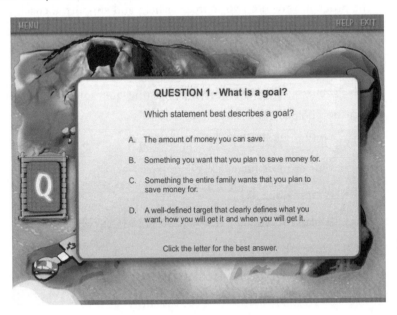

Figure 21.4 Calculator to Help Determine Savings Goals

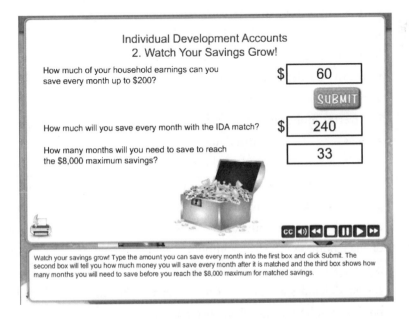

Coaching

The program provides two sources of help and support: a coach and a discussion board. When a person signs up, he or she is assigned a coach. The coach answers questions and provides guidance via the message center. As learners work on the lessons and activities, they can also communicate with their coaches and other students by posting questions and answers on the discussion board.

When they are finished, learners have

- One or more financial savings goals
- A family budget
- A plan for reducing debt and reaching their goals
- Three credit reports
- A series of credit scores and a plan to improve them
- Strategies for protecting their identity

The first-time homeowners or soon to be homeowners begin the game by working through a mock scenario of paying off their debt and saving their money to purchase a house and car at the end of the program. The learners start by answering some preliminary financial questions. If answered correctly, the learner is rewarded. From there, the learner views the information for the financial topic and is given a bonus question. If this is answered correctly, the learner receives a bit of extra money for scenarios such as having a yard sale or inheriting money from an uncle. If the question is answered incorrectly, money is deducted from their savings for an unexpected expense such as new tires or medical bills.

When learners complete the program, they can purchase a house and car, depending on how much money they've accumulated throughout the game. Learners then have the ability to enhance their homes and yards using a three-dimensional simulation. The simulation lets them customize aspects of their homes with their additional savings. Successful learners can add a garage, patio, and even a backyard pool. To help learners succeed, the website also includes a number of tools, such as an expense tracker, discussion board, periodic savings calculators, and more.

For website administrators, there are reporting features within the site to detail learner progression and learning capacity. This provides an important method of observing progress and helping learners if problems or issues arise.

The solution is deployed for a web browser and is built with a custom system to meet the needs of NHHFA. The website is available to anyone who is interested in learning more about homeownership but is geared specifically toward individuals within New Hampshire.

The Benefits

New Hampshire Housing Finance Authority has an engaging financial training program that allows their potential and current homeowners the ability to learn at their own pace and from their own homes. With a sense of security, the learners can safely input their financial information and have the option of their coach reviewing their budgets and family financial goals. Coaches encourage their students by providing them with resources and important information throughout the program.

Homeowners and others are having a good time learning about financial planning and homeownership. Here are some of the comments.

- "That game REALLY IS A BLAST!!! I never imagined myself laughing while working on financial stuff! I bought a headset today and I'm glad I did or else I would have missed out on all of the funny sound effects of the game!"

- "I am really having fun with this. In fact I have reviewed the Savings and Spending lesson again. Ready to do the Credit Counseling lessons again."

- "I'm thrilled with this program and feel even more motivated and capable of managing my finances than ever before!"

- "My family has long dreamed of owning our own home. We are enjoying the Island Lessons and are learning so much! We are taking the advice and, more importantly, taking concrete steps toward our goal of homeownership."

The Results

- More than four hundred students registered in the first year.
- More than one hundred students are using Savings & Spending plan budgeting tools.
- Of those tracking credits scores, 55 percent improved their FICO score in the first six months.
- Currently eighteen agencies throughout the country are using Find Financial Freedom to supplement their financial education programs.

Lessons Learned

Be creative!

Take the time to ensure you have a strong design document.

Take into consideration the possibility that a third-party LMS might not have the features for tracking the analytical data you want from a game. So be prepared to build a customized system for collecting the necessary data.

You can see the game in action by visiting https://www.findfinancialfreedom.org/features.

22

Sales Training Game: An Avaya Case

Anders Gronstedt

This case study outlines sales leadership training created to certify sales reps on various skills in realistic scenarios using a game approach.

Background

Avaya, a Fortune 500 global leader in business communications, was faced with the challenge of improving sales performance by better uncovering customers' business issues and problems and becoming a trusted advisor. The sales leadership decided to certify sales reps on various skills in realistic simulated scenarios. The skills range from strategic account planning to sales call preparation, and from presentation skills to product knowledge. The responsibility to assess these Level 1 sales skills fell to Rhonda Duesterberg, senior manager of Global Sales L&D, who partnered with game and simulation leader Gronstedt Group.

Why a Game-Based Simulation?

"Our solution was a series of spy-themed learning and assessment games," says Duesterberg. Points, high-scoring lists, badges, levels, cut-scenes, and storytelling are used to certify and reinforce sales skills. The solution had to be a realistic simulation that engaged and motivated busy sales reps, giving the feeling of accomplishment offered by games.

The Solution

Each game opens with a fast-paced video trailer. The "mission" is presented with a dramatic video by a "commander" who introduces the challenge and the main protagonist, as shown in Figure 22.1.

In one of the challenges, Avaya reps journey through the story of how Cindy develops a value proposition for a global financial service client while she's being pursued by an evil competitor. The story is told through live-action video with skilled actors, produced by a professional video crew. Each decision point offers a teachable moment in which the player has to make the call. The sales rep playing the game becomes part of the unfolding story line instead of just a passive audience member. Figure 22.2 shows one of the scenes from the mysterious game.

The learners are presented with several articles, company annual reports, and announcements about the client. They must identify the best person to meet with as well as essential data points about the company and the industry. For each successfully completed activity, players earn the instant gratification of a badge, which is displayed in the learning environment. Correct decisions earn players experience points by the hundreds at unpredictable intervals. The uncertainty of receiving random large bonus points makes learning more engaging and memorable. Top performers are featured on a leaderboard for everyone at Avaya to see. After all, what's the point of being a high-scorer if you can't rub it into the face of your colleagues?

Figure 22.1 The Main Protagonist Provides a Mission to the Learner

Figure 22.2 You Have to Be on Your Toes at All Times in This Learning Game

Cut-scenes drive the storyline forward; these live-action videos break up the gameplay to advance the plot and provide additional information. Some assignments feature a timer ticking down, raising the stress level and motivating action; players earn bonus points if they complete the assignment in time. The entire user interface has the look and feel of a game. Such game aesthetics are important in motivating the sales reps to engage in the experience.

Once the player has prepared for the sales call, it's time to help Cindy conduct a sales call with the client. The player watches a "surveillance video" and feeds questions through an earpiece to Cindy, as shown in Figure 22.3.

What's a game without any techno toys? By selecting questions to ask and statements to make and watching the client respond in video, players prove their skills. As they advance through the game, they "level up." Sales skills are built and reinforced as a player progresses through each level, providing a feeling of mastery and accomplishment. The capstone level of the "Customer Value" game introduces an ultimate challenge: Based on skills learned in previous levels, players have to put together a value proposition to win the game. Leveling up to increasingly more difficult levels keeps players in a state of "flow," where they are completely focused and engaged. "Flow" is a gaming concept describing the delicate balance between difficulty and player skill levels where players are neither frustrated nor bored.

Each game stays true to the spy theme, while employing different game mechanics. The "Communication Skills" game features a sales presentation by Cindy. Players are challenged to stop the video when they observe a problem with gesturing, pausing, eye contacts, etc. The "Mobile Communications" game features "machinima" video of avatars in the virtual world of AvayaLive Engage, instead of live action video with actors, as shown in Figure 22.4.

What this animated format lacks in realism, it makes up for in flexibility to update content; unlike live actors, avatars don't age or change hairstyle, making it easier to modify the video sequences over time as products and content change. Some of the installments end with a real-life assignment that reps need to submit to their sales managers for review, such as a video of a sales presentation or a completed account plan.

Figure 22.3 Helping Cindy Conduct a Sales Call with the Client Through "Surveillance Video"

Figure 22.4 AvayaLive Engage Is Used as Part of the Overall Game Because of the Flexibility to Update Content

Benefits and Results

Avaya has developed an entire suite of the popular sales games.

"These challenges reinforce previous training and provide our reps with an opportunity to apply and demonstrate those skills in realistic simulated scenarios with fun-filled game mechanics," explains Michelle Bigham, program manager at Avaya, who manages the development of the programs. This new generation of game-based sales simulations make learning fun *and* effective, which is not as oxymoronic as it might sound. Professor Brian Sutton-Smith put it best: "The opposite of play isn't work. It's depression."

In the process of gamifying sales training and certification, Avaya is challenging traditional academic notions of "courses," "classes," "curriculums," and "exams," and replacing them with gaming vernacular of experience points, badges, levels, quests, goals, achievement rewards, time pressure, and cut-scenes to make sales learning engaging and inspiring. Gamification promises to revolutionize sales learning and certification at Avaya, which would be an epic win.

Lessons Learned

- Using live-action video dramatization in games adds realism and engagement, but "machinima" shot in a 3-D virtual world is easier to update:

- Don't just give a predictable pattern of single points for every completed activity; offering unpredictable bonus points makes the gameplay more engaging.

- Don't take yourself too seriously; everyone loves humor.

- Don't just develop a one-off game; develop an entire franchise.

Glossary

ADDIE—A model for developing instruction with five phases, each represented by the first letter in the acronym: Analysis, Design, Development, Implementation, and Evaluation.

Affinity Diagram—A brainstorming tool used to organize ideas and data. The affinity process works by people individually placing ideas on sticky notes, and then in a group setting the "like" ideas are bunched together to show connections and most popular items.

Allegory—A technique where characters, events, or elements within the game represent or symbolize ideas or concepts. An allegory can be used when an analogous representation of an event or experience is more effective than the actual event in terms of training. Sometimes an allegory can be easier to apply an interesting story to or, in the case of therapeutic games, easier for the player to deal with issues indirectly. This is particularly effective when a process can be re-created using simple game mechanics.

Alpha—Stage in development when key functionality is implemented, assets are 40 to 50 percent final (the rest are placeholders), it runs on the correct hardware in debug mode, and there is enough working that you can get a feel for the game, gamification, or simulation. Features might undergo major adjustments at this point, based on testing results and other feedback.

Affective Domain—Deals with attitudes, interest, values, beliefs, and emotions.

Alternate Reality Game (ARG)—A game where the gameplay integrates real life and online activities through a storyline that seeks to engage learners in an experience that seems real.

America's Army—A massively multi-player online role-play game where a player assumes a role of a soldier in the U.S. Army and then goes through missions as that soldier. Missions include acting as a medic or an infantry solider. The game is one of the recruitment tools of the Army.

Anthropomorphic—Having human-like characteristics or form. Something that is not human but has taken on human-like characteristics and/or form. The personification of an object. In this case, the characteristics of a computer-animated character that interacts with the learner in a human-like interface.

Artificial Intelligence (AI)—The logic that gives the illusion of intelligent decisions by computer-controlled characters in the game.

Augmented Reality Games—Games where there is a technology overlay on reality that contributes to play. An example is the yellow first down line superimposed on the football field. Often smart phones are used with augmented reality games.

Avatar—Virtual character a person assumes as he or she moves about within a game. The virtual character you play in a game or assume in a virtual world is an avatar.

Behavior Rules—Rules that govern the social contract between two or more players, in other words, the rules related to being a good sport about the game. These rules are game etiquette. Also known as Implicit Rules.

Beta—The stage in development when the code and asset are complete. Art, design, and engineering only focus on fixing bugs that are listed in the bug database.

No new assets are generated; no new features are coded; and no changes are made to existing features and functionality unless it is identified as a bug.

Bloom's Taxonomy—An educational taxonomy to define different domains of learning. Bloom's taxonomy defines learning in three categories: Cognitive (mental), Affective (emotional), and Psychomotor (physical).

Branching Storyline Simulation—A story where the story *branches* or changes direction at various points based on participant decisions or input.

Collision Detection—Detecting whether two objects in your game are intersecting. This could be the player touching an enemy or the player moving into a wall or a weapon hitting an enemy. Detecting collisions is very resource-intensive. It is frequently handled by the game engine.

Conceptual Knowledge—Knowledge about ideas, events, or objects that have a common attribute or a set of common attributes.

Construct—A fabricated addition to a simulation that does not exist in the real world. Constructs are used in order to make the players' experience more interesting, give them better information, or enhance training effectiveness by accentuating certain aspects of an interaction. Constructs can also be used to limit or empower the player. Game mechanics like the ability to slow or reverse time is an example of a construct. Things like points and levels are also a type of construct.

Content Gamification—Application of game elements and game thinking to alter content to make it more game-like. For example, adding story elements to a compliance course or starting a course with a challenge instead of a list of objectives are both methods of content gamification.

Declarative Knowledge—Knowledge that can only be learned through memorization. Also known as verbal knowledge or factual knowledge.

Design Document—A document that is contains a written and visual description of all the elements of a game, gamification, or simulation. The document is meant to drive the development of the ILE.

Distributed Practice—A method whereby the learner distributes time dedicated to learning content or information over a series of small time periods rather than doing it all at once, which is known as mass practice or cramming.

Easter Egg—A message, graphic, sound effect, or unusual change in program behavior that occurs in response to some undocumented set of commands, mouse clicks, keystrokes, button presses, or other stimuli intended as a joke, an amusing entertainment piece, or to display program credits.

Enabling Learning Objective—A component of or support for a terminal learning objective. Typically described as a set of knowledge, skills, and attitudes that a learner must obtain.

Equipment/Software Simulation—Creates a representation of a mechanical or software system, like a flight simulator, which accurately represents the operations of an airplane. Software simulations are used to teach a new software system. The demand for accuracy on equipment/software simulations is very high, as the simulations must operate exactly as the equipment or software does.

Experience API—A component of the training and learning architecture (TLA). The purpose of the xAPI is to store and provide access to learning experiences. It is designed to deal with data and information that was difficult to track with SCORM, such as mobile learning and content that is accessed outside of a web browser.

Extrinsic Motivation—Behavior undertaken in order to obtain some reward or avoid punishment.

Feedback—A method of providing insight to the player on his or her decisions. Feedback may be *intrinsic*, integrated into the story of the game, or *extrinsic*, delivered as a report or evaluation outside the game storyline.

Feedback Loop—Created when information is given to a player about his or her performance or the game state and the player responds to the feedback by altering strategy.

First-Person Shooter—A game that involves moving around an environment encountering obstacles from a first-person perspective and using weapons to dispatch enemies.

First-Person Thinker—A game that involves moving around an environment encountering obstacles from a first-person perspective, but not using violence to overcome the obstacles or solve problems.

Flowchart—A common tool for mapping out the complex event flow of a game or simulation.

Flow State—A state of mind wherein a game player forgets his or her normal cares and the passage of time. The gamer derives intense satisfaction from performing the activity required by the game and becomes engrossed within the game itself. The game becomes a sort of reality and the gamer reacts just as he or she would in an actual situation. The concept was developed by Mihaly Csikszentmihalyi.

Future State Simulation—A simulation that creates an environment that doesn't exist yet, but is expected to, in order to allow learners to practice behaviors and gain familiarity with the new environment.

Game—A system in which players engage in an abstract challenge, defined by rules, interactivity, and feedback that results in a quantifiable outcome, often eliciting an emotional reaction.

Game Design Document—Provides an outline and guidance to a team involved with a gamification project.

GameFest—The process of getting individuals into the same room and having them play different games for a short period of time and then moving on to the next game. The idea is to expose people to a large variety of both online and physical games to give them all a common frame of reference when having discussions about games, gamification, and simulations. Works well to bring low game literacy individuals up-to-speed quickly.

Game Loop—Central component of the game program. How many times per second the game checks for user input, moves players, checks for collisions, redraws the screen, plays sounds, etc. One of the tasks that is handled by the game engine.

Game Mechanic—Refers to a rule or set of rules that enable or restrict player action by creating a cause-and-effect relationship.

Gamification—Using game-based mechanics, aesthetics, and game thinking to engage people, motivate action, promote learning, and solve problems. See Structural Gamification and Content Gamification.

Geometric Progression—A risk of branching storyline simulation, where constant story branching creates an unmanageable number of scenarios.

Goal-Based Scenario—Includes a goal or a set of goals that need to be achieved; the point of going through the story is to achieve the goal.

Graphical User Interface (GUI)—The visual elements on the screen through which a learner interacts with content. They can be icons, maps, arrows, menus, or other elements that guide the interaction.

Halo—A video game in the first-person shooter (FPS) genre available for the Xbox consoles. Subsequent versions include Halo 2. The game revolves around a character named Master Chief, a human super-soldier equipped with armor who battles aliens.

Heads-Up Display—A method of conveying knowledge to the learner on a computer or game screen with information "overlaid" on top of the game environment. The learner doesn't need to look away from the game environment to gain information.

Hero's Journey—Common story structure wherein the hero is forced out of a comfortable, albeit boring, lifestyle and undergoes a transformation through mental and physical trials and tribulations.

Illusion of Complexity—Technique of designing a simulation so it appears to have more branching options and choices than it actually does.

Implicit Rules—Govern the social contract between two or more players, that is, the rules related to being a good sport about the game or game etiquette. Also known as Behavior Rules.

"In Order to" Chain—A process whereby you work your way backward from your goal and determine what must take place "in order to" achieve that goal.

Instructional Objectives—Performance objectives for the game. It is critical that instructional objectives be granular enough to allow for the diagnosing of instructional problems. At a minimum, objectives should address (1) behavior to be measured, (2) conditions under which the behavior will be measured, and (3) a minimum level of achievement needed to demonstrate mastery of the objectives.

Interactive Learning Experience (ILE)—Umbrella term used to describe three interactive types of learning: games, gamification, and simulations.

Intrinsic Motivation—When a person undertakes an activity for its own sake, for the enjoyment it provides, the learning it permits, or the feeling of accomplishment it evokes.

Laws and Rules—Give the player a framework to work within inside a game, gamification, or simulation. A *law* is something like gravity that is fundamental to the game or simulation world. A *rule* is something like speeding that we hold the player accountable for following.

Learner's Advocate—A member of the production team who serves as a spokesperson for the best interest of the learners.

Level Design—Design of a level within a game, gamification, or simulation. Usually results in a series of documents, such as storyboards, flowcharts, and instructional objectives or each level that a learner will experience.

Low Game Literacy—Extremely low or non-existent video game experience, or knowledge. The person may never have played a video game before.

Knowledge, Skills, Attitudes (KSAs)—The supporting elements that comprise a learning objective: information that is pertinent to a specific subject, skills to perform a task in an optimized way, and attitudes related to a specific subject.

Leaderboard—List of the players who have the high score in a game or a game-like activity.

Massively Multiplayer Online Role Play Game (MMORPG)—Player assumes a role and identity not typically related to his or her real-world self and attempts to earn points to move to a higher level within the game. Once a role is assumed, the player embarks on adventures or quests with a team, guild, or clan, seeks treasure, battles monsters, or accomplishes other specific goals and objectives that are an inherent part of the world.

Meta-Analysis—A study of studies when researchers take the results from many separate studies and compare the results to find commonalities among them.

Metrics—Specific measures of performance that define success or failure in a task. Represent the end-state final outcome of a task. Defining metrics at the beginning of a design process makes is easier to define the activities that a game or simulation must include.

Mimicry—Pattern of play related to simulation or role play.

Mind Mapping—A brainstorming process whereby thoughts and related thoughts are visually displayed on a board for examination and to visually create connections among items. Typically, the mind map is drawn around a single idea, concept, or word in the center.

Multi-User Dungeon (MUD)—A real-time virtual world described entirely in text. MUDs were one of the first virtual environments in which people could interact online. The term "dungeon" was used because these text-based games were an extension of the board games in the genre of Dungeon and Dragons. The characters, rooms where chats took place, topics, and environment were similar to the Dungeon and Dragons games. They were also referred to as multi-user dialogue or multi-user dimension.

Non-Player Character (NPC)—A computer controlled character that can interact with the human players in the game. Typically provide instruction, give hints, or otherwise communicate pre-scripted dialogue within the game.

One-Page Design Document—A depiction of the major elements of a game, gamification, or simulation. The idea is to capture the concepts in a concise treatment for showing and communicating to others. Can be used in conjunction with a full-blown design document.

Operant Conditioning—The use of consequences or rewards to modify the occurrence and form of behavior.

Operational Rules—Describe how a game is played.

Paper Prototype—A paper version of a game, gamification, or simulation created for the purposes of testing the concepts, ideas, and playability.

Performance Objective—What a participant will be able to do as a result of completing an experience.

Persona—Representations of people in archetypal forms.

Playtest—The process of testing a game, gamification, or simulation by playing it.

Predictable Unexpected—A storytelling technique in which the reader/learner is engaged by a jolt or twist in the story that is unexpected, but not unrealistic or implausible within the story's context.

Pre-Production—The planning phase that lays the foundation upon which the entire game, gamification, or simulation is dependent. Results in documentation that will serve the team throughout the lifecycle of the production.

Procedural Knowledge—Knowledge of step-by-step instructions for performing a particular task in a particular order to reach a specific outcome.

Process Simulation—See Systems Dynamics Simulation.

Producer—Person responsible for overseeing the development of a video game. In instructional design circles, called a project manager.

Pro-Social Behavior—Behavior that is not aggressive and contributes positively to a social situation, such as helping others.

Psychomotor Domain—The intersection of physical skills and cognitive skills.

Release Candidate—The stage in the process when all bugs have been addressed and the build is ready to be shipped. The code is tested against the QA test plan, and any crash bugs or other critical issues are fixed as necessary.

Rule-Based Knowledge—Expresses the relationships between concepts. Rules indicate cause-and-effect and if/then relationships.

Scaffolding—The design of instruction that encourages learners to move from one level of knowledge to the next with increasing difficulty and the need to apply more skill to master the new level.

Scrum—A development process based on the agile software development model where multiple small teams work intensively and interdependently for short, quick bursts and then reconvene to reassess progress and create new priorities. Led by a scrum master.

Serious Game—A game designed for a purpose other than pure entertainment.

Shazam Session—Process where a game, gamification, or simulation idea is developed, designed, and playtested within one week. It is a good technique for getting the idea off of the ground.

Simulation—A self-contained immersive environment in which learners interact within the environment in an attempt to learn or practice skills or knowledge. Typically, only one person can navigate the on-screen avatar and interactions are only between the computer and the learner. One of the most common types is a Branching Story Simulation.

Situated Learning—Learning that occurs in an environment that matches the setting where the knowledge would be utilized in the real world.

Sprite—A game graphic frequently consisting of a grid of several images that show a game character in different positions. The animation of the character is created by displaying the individual images in rapid succession.

Storyboard—Method of mapping the flow or progress of a game, gamification, or simulation.

Structural Gamification—The application of game elements to propel a learner through content with no alteration or changes to the content. Only the structure around the content is gamified. The primary focus is to motivate the learners to go through the content and to engage them in the process of learning through rewards.

Systems Dynamics Simulation—Models how complex systems operate over time by using complex mathematical formulas to define how the system works. Allow "What if?" scenarios by allowing participants to change certain variables and observe how they impact the rest of the system. Also known as Process Simulations.

Teaching Game—Game designed to teach the learner new knowledge, skills, attitudes, or psychomotor skills. The emphasis is for the learner to learn new information.

Terminal Learning Objective—The highest level of learning objectives that usually contains a behavior a learner must perform to a certain standard under specific conditions.

Testing Game—A game design to test knowledge , skills, attitude, or psychomotor skill. The emphasis is for the learners to recall knowledge or information they already possess.

Three-Dimensional Game—A game that uses three-dimensional (3-D) graphics and allows movement in all three dimensions.

Two-Dimensional Game—A game in which the graphics and movement are limited to two dimensions. Platform games are a good example for 2-D games.

User Interface (UI)—What the player interacts with in order to control software or observes to gather information.

Uncanny Valley—A design principle that states that as an avatar is made more humanlike in appearance and motion the emotional response of players to it will become increasingly positive until a point is reached at which the response suddenly becomes strongly repulsive because the avatar or character is almost human.

Variable Interval—Reinforcement for a behavior provided after a variable amount of time has elapsed.

Variable Ratio—Reinforcement for a behavior provided in unpredictable intervals.

Walkthrough—A step-by-step rehearsal of what learners see and experience as they interact with a game, gamification, or simulation. The idea of a walkthrough is to test learners' experience to expose any problems or gaps.

World of Warcraft (WoW)—One of the most popular massively multiplayer online role play games. Players assume one of many roles and do battle against each other or travel on quests.

Notes

Chapter 1

1. See the official Nike Fuelband website for more information. www.nike.com/us/en_us/c/nikeplus-fuelband.
2. Moore, A.E. (2012). Wireless asthma inhaler teaches proper use. CNET, News, Health Tech. http://news.cnet.com/8301-27083_3-57395380-247/wireless-asthma-inhaler-teaches-proper-use/
3. Moore, A.E. (2012).
4. See the official Google Glass website for more information. www.google.com/glass/start/

Chapter 2

1. Pope, A. (1711). Essay on criticism. Text retrieved from www.poetryfoundation.org/learning/essay/237826
2. Sitzmann, T. (2011). A meta-analytic examination of the instructional effectiveness of computer-based simulation games. *Personnel Psychology, 64*(2), 489–528 and Sitzman, T., & Ely, K. (2010). *A meta-analytic examination of the effectiveness of computer-based simulation games.* Binghamton, NY: ADL Research Lab.

3. Employee engagement: What is your employee engagement ratio? (2010). Gallup Consulting. www.gallup.com/strategicconsulting/121535/Employee-Engagement-Overview-Brochure.aspx

4. Employee engagement: What is your employee engagement ratio? (2010). Gallup Consulting. www.gallup.com/strategicconsulting/121535/Employee-Engagement-Overview-Brochure.aspx

5. Deloitte augments their leadership development program. Badgeville Case Study. Information courtesy of Badgeville and Deloitte.

6. Deloitte augments their leadership development program. Badgeville Case Study. Information courtesy of Badgeville and Deloitte.

7. Rosenberg, R.S., Baughman, S.L., & Bailenson, J.N. (2013). Virtual superheroes: Using superpowers in virtual reality to encourage pro-social behavior. *PLOS One., 8*(1), 1–9.

8. Liau, A.K., Khoo, A., Bushman, B.J., Huesmann, L.R., Douglas, A.S., Gentile, A. Anderson, C.A., Yukawa, S., Ihori, N., Saleem, M., Ming, L-K., & Shibuya, A. (2009, March 25). The effects of pro-social video games on pro-social behaviors: International evidence from correlational, longitudinal, and experimental studies. *Personnel Soc Psychol Bulletin, 35*, p. 752.

9. Peng, W., Lee, M., & Heeter. (2010). The effects of a serious game on role-taking and willingness to help. *Journal of Communication, 60*, 723–742.

10. Peng, W., Lee, M., & Heeter. (2010).

11. Hahn, S.H. (2012). Transfer of training from simulations in civilian and military workforces: Perspectives from the current body of literature. Advanced Distributed Learning, www.adlnet.org.

Chapter 3

1. Kapp, K.M. (2012). *The gamification of learning and instruction: Game-based methods and strategies for training and education.* San Francisco: Pfeiffer.

2. See the official Minecraft website for more information. https://minecraft.net/

3. See the official Assassin's Creed website for more information. http://assassinscreed.ubi.com/ac3/en-us/gameinfo/info/index.aspx

4. Bloom, B.S. (1953). Thought processes in lectures and discussions. *Journal of General Education, 7.*

5. Krathwohl, D.R. (2002, Autumn). A revision of Bloom's taxonomy: An overview. *Theory into Practice, 41*(4), The Ohio State University.

6. Kapp, K.M. (2012). *The gamification of learning and instruction: Game-based methods and strategies for training and education.* San Francisco: Pfeiffer.

7. Simpson, B.J. (1966). The classification of educational objectives: Psychomotor domain. *Journal of Home Economics, 10*(4), 110–144.

8. Malone, T. (1981). Toward a theory of intrinsically motivating instruction. *Cognitive Science, 4,* 333–369.

9. Kapp, K.M. (2012). *The gamification of learning and instruction: Game-based methods and strategies for training and education.* San Francisco: Pfeiffer.

10. See the official FoldIt! website for more information. http://fold.it/portal/

11. See the official Rails for Zombies website for more information. http://railsforzombies.org/

Chapter 6

1. Kim, A.J. (2011). Gamification workshop: Designing the player journey. SlideShare.net. www.slideshare.net/amyjokim/gamification-101-design-the-player-journey

Chapter 7

1. Clark, R.C. (2013). Why games don't teach. *Learning Solutions* magazine. www.learningsolutionsmag.com/articles/1106/
2. Dondlinger, M.J. (2007). Educational video game design: A review of the literature. *Journal of Applied Educational Technology, 4*(1), 21–31.
3. Graafland, M., Schraagen, J.M., & Schijven, M.P. (2012). Systematic review of serious games for medical education and surgical skills training. *British Journal of Surgery, 99*, 1322–1330.
4. Blunt, R. (n.d.). Does game-based learning work? Results from three recent studies. Unpublished manuscript. Advanced Distributed Learning. http://patrickdunn.squarespace.com/storage/blunt_game_studies.pdf
5. Wilson, K.A., Bedwell, W.L, Lazzara, E.H., Salas, E., Burke, C.S., Estock, J.L., Orvis, K.L., & Conkey, C. (2009, April). Relationships between game attributes and learning outcomes. *Simulation & Gaming, 40*(1), 217–266.
6. Connolly, T., Boyle, E., MacArthur, E., Hainey, T., & Boyle, J. (2012). A systematic literature review of empirical evidence on computer games and serious games. *Computers & Education, 59*.
7. Gibbs, G. (1981). Twenty terrible reasons for lecturing. SCED Occasional Paper No. 8, Birmingham. www.brookes.ac.uk/services/ocsld/resources/20reasons.html and Bligh, D. (1972). *What's the use of lectures?* New York: Penguin.
8. Bloom, B.S. (1953). Thought processes in lectures and discussions. *Journal of General Education, 7*.
9. Isaacs, G. (1994). Lecturing practices and note-taking purposes. *Studies in Higher Education, 19*(2).
10. Sitzmann, T. (2011). A meta-analytic examination of the instructional effectiveness of computer-based simulation games. *Personnel Psychology, 64*(2), 489–528 and Sitzman, T., & Ely, K. (2010). *A meta-analytic examination of the effectiveness of computer-based simulation games.* Binghamton, NY: ADL Research Lab.
11. Dominguez, A., Saenz-de-Navattete, J., de-Marcos, L., Fernadez-Sanz, L., Pages, C., & Matrinez-Herraiz, J. (2012). Gamifying learning experiences: Practical implications and outcomes. *Computers & Education, 63*, 391.
12. Kapp, K.M. (2012). *The gamification of learning and instruction: Game-based methods and strategies for training and education.* San Francisco: Pfeiffer.
13. Hahn, S.H. (2012). Transfer of training from simulations in civilian and military workforces: Perspectives from the current body of literature. Advanced Distributed Learning. www.adlnet.org.
14. Hahn, S.H. (2012).

Chapter 9

1. Co-author Rich Mesch is an ardent collector of Captain Marvel comics and memorabilia, and founded the first Captain Marvel fan website way back in 1995.

2. Captain Marvel. (n.d.). Retrieved March 31, 2013, from http://en.wikipedia.org/wiki/
    Captain_Marvel_(DC_Comics)
3. Special thanks to Joseph Powell for this one-page design document.

Chapter 11

1. Lepper, M.R. (1988). Motivational considerations in the study of instruction. *Cognition and
    Instruction, 5*(4), 289–309.
2. Lepper, M.R. (1988).
3. Eisenberger, R., Rhoades, L., & Cameron, J. (1999). Does pay for performance increase or decrease
    perceived self-determination and intrinsic motivation? *Journal of Personality and Social Psychology,
    77*(5), 1026–1040.
4. Eisenberger, R., Rhoades, L., & Cameron, J. (1999).
5. Lepper, M.R. (1988).
6. Lepper, M.R. (1988).
7. Beswick, D. (2007, February 15). Management implications of the interaction between intrinsic
    motivation and extrinsic rewards. www.beswick.info/psychres/management.htm.
8. Ryan, R.M., & Deci, E.L. (2000). Intrinsic and extrinsic motivations: Classic definitions and new
    directions. *Contemporary Educational Psychology, 25*, 54–67 and Ryan, R.M., & Deci, E.L. (2000).
    Self-determination theory and the facilitation of intrinsic motivation, social development, and well-
    being. *American Psychologist, 55*, 68–78.
9. American Society for Training and Development (ASTD). (n.d.). The world's largest association
    dedicated to the training and development profession. See www.astd.org for more information or to
    join.
10. Harter, S. (1981). A new self-report scale of intrinsic versus extrinsic orientation in the classroom:
    Motivational and informational components. *Developmental Psychology, 17*, 300–312.
11. Lepper, M.R., Iyengar, S.S., & Corpus, J.H. (2005). Intrinsic and extrinsic motivational orientations
    in the classroom: Age differences and academic correlates. *Journal of Educational Psychology. 97*(2),
    184–196.
12. Lepper, M.R., Iyengar, S.S., & Corpus, J.H. (2005).
13. Many of the designer notes in this section are from L. Blair, Congratulations! Selecting the right in-
    game achievements. In K.M. Kapp (2012), *The gamification of learning and instruction: Game-based
    methods and strategies for training and education.* San Francisco: Pfeiffer.
14. Carey, B. (2007). This is your life (and how you tell it). *The New York Times.* Melanie Green.
    www.unc.edu/~mcgreen/research.html.
15. Jones, B., Valdez, G., Norakowski, J., & Rasmussen, C. (1994). Designing learning and technology
    for educational reform. North Central Regional Educational Laboratory. www.ncrtec.org/capacity/
    profile/profwww.htm and Schlechty, P.C. (1997). *Inventing better schools: An action plan for educa-
    tional reform.* San Francisco: Jossey-Bass.
16. Clark, R.C., & Mayer, R. (2011). *e-Learning and the science of instruction: Proven guidelines for con-
    sumers and designers of multimedia learning.* San Francisco: Pfeiffer.
17. Baylor, A.L., & Kim, Y. (2005). Simulating instructional roles through pedagogical agents.
    International Journal of Artificial Intelligence in Education, 15(1), 95–115.

18. Sitzmann, T. (2011). A meta-analytic examination of the instructional effectiveness of computer-based simulation games. *Personnel Psychology, 64*(2), 489–528 and Sitzman, T., & Ely, K. (2010). *A meta-analytic examination of the effectiveness of computer-based simulation games.* Binghamton, NY: ADL Research Lab.

Chapter 14

1. Finch, C. (2011). *The art of Walt Disney* (rev. ed.). New York. Abrams.

Chapter 19

1. Tauber, T. (2013, March) The dirty little secret of online learning: Students are bored and dropping out. http://qz.com/65408/the-dirty-little-secret-of-online-learning-students-are-bored-and-dropping-out/
2. Employee value proposition. (n.d.). Wikipedia http://en.wikipedia.org/wiki/Employee_value_proposition

Chapter 20

1. Driscoll. M.P. (2005). *Psychology of learning for instruction* (3rd ed.). New York: Pearson Education.
2. Ericsson, K.A., Krampe, R.T., & Tesch-Romer, C. (1993). The role of deliberate practice in the acquisition of expert performance. *Psychology Review, 100*(3), 363–406.
3. Reznek, M.A., Rawn, C.L., & Krummel, T.M. (2002, November). Evaluation of the educational effectiveness of a virtual reality intravenous insertion simulator. *Academic Emergency Medicine, 9*(11), 1319–1325.

Index

Page references followed by *fig* indicate an illustrated figure; followed by *t* indicate a table.

About the American Society for Training & Development

The American Society for Training & Development (ASTD) is the world's largest professional association dedicated to the training and development field. In more than 100 countries, ASTD's members work in organizations of all sizes, in the private and public sectors, as independent consultants, and as suppliers. Members connect locally in 130 U.S. chapters and with 30 international partners.

ASTD started in 1943 and in recent years has widened the profession's focus to align learning and performance to organizational results and is a sought-after voice on critical public policy issues. For more information, visit www.astd.org.